MEDIA AND COMMUNICATIONS -
TECHNOLOGIES, POLICIES AND CHALLENGES

MEDIA ANTHOLOGY

A CRITICAL READER – VISUALISING MASS MEDIA FROM A MACRO PERSPECTIVE

MEDIA AND COMMUNICATIONS - TECHNOLOGIES, POLICIES AND CHALLENGES

Additional books in this series can be found on Nova's website under the Series tab.

Additional e-books in this series can be found on Nova's website under the eBooks tab.

MEDIA AND COMMUNICATIONS -
TECHNOLOGIES, POLICIES AND CHALLENGES

MEDIA ANTHOLOGY

A CRITICAL READER – VISUALISING MASS MEDIA FROM A MACRO PERSPECTIVE

THEOPHILUS KOFI GOKAH
EDITOR

nova publishers
New York

Library of Congress Cataloging-in-Publication Data
Names: Kofi Gokah, Theophilus, editor.
Title: Media anthology : a critical reader : visualising mass media from a macro perspective / editor, Theophilus Kofi Gokah.
Description: Hauppauge, New York : Nova Science Publisher's Inc., 2016. |
Series: Media and communications | Includes bibliographical references and index. | Description based on print version record and CIP data provided by publisher; resource not viewed.
Identifiers: LCCN 2016018867 (print) | LCCN 2016008515 (ebook) | ISBN 9781634849630 () | ISBN 9781634849319 (hardcover)
Subjects: LCSH: Mass media--Technological innovations--Social aspects. | Social media.
Classification: LCC P96.T42 (print) | LCC P96.T42 M44 2016 (ebook) | DDC 302.23--dc23
LC record available at https://lccn.loc.gov/2016018867

Published by Nova Science Publishers, Inc. † New York

CONTENTS

PREFACE

"Communication is ancient and newly emergent, interdisciplinary in heritage, the home of scholars and professionals, a science and an art, or humanity, and concerned with technology."

Brent D. Ruben, Communication Scholar.

The Communication discipline is both one of the oldest and one of the newest academic disciplines. Its roots date back to ancient Greece, when rhetoric--the study of discovering and using "the available means of persuasion"--was an important part of the citizenry's education. By the beginning of the 20th century, its ambit grew to include oral interpretation, interpersonal communication, small group communication, and mass communication. The scholars realised the importance of other forms of human communication, apart from public speaking to warrant in-depth and systematic study. Today the discipline encompasses intercultural communication, gender communication, organizational communication, performance studies, educational communication, family communication, health communication, political communication, and the study of communication in other specific contexts.

The postmodern epoch has witnessed an unprecedented creation, distribution, and dissemination of data (be it infotainment or edutainment) altering the concept, modes and meaning of communication. The emerging social and other new media, transformed by technological innovations and convergence, hurled the human civilisation into 'life-style' changing ways in which we communicate and consume data. This has led to the evolution of a multi-disciplinary approach to the strategies inherent in the communication processes. Further, there is a growing recognition of the significance of the dynamic and interactive relationship between communication and information dissemination in a global context.

Today, Media and Communication Studies is concerned with understanding how the media works; for whom it works; how media act as public agenda setters at the behest of gatekeepers, arbiters of cultural values, and sites of education as a key framing and priming agent. The aim is to understand how and to what effect media, as society's principal storyteller, filter virtually every aspect of our world, shaping both what we learn and how we learn. It also aims to facilitate empowerment of the student community through development of skills to use the media effectively and optimally to communicate their own ideas. Media, as well as, Communication studies programs have roots in the departments of theatre, film or speech, and with more interest in "qualitative," interpretive theory, critical or cultural approaches to communication study. In contrast, many mass communication programs historically lean toward empirical analysis and quantitative research -- from statistical content analysis of media messages to survey research, public opinion polling, and experimental research.

Why this Book?

Information literacy is an integral aspect as well as a critical weave of our social and academic fabric. In fact, I would say it is a significant parameter that determines the quality of our lives and the future of mankind. Therefore, it is of little surprise that 'Research' is a subject diligently taught at most universities around the world.

However, I find it alarming when a student thinks that "Googling" and 'researching' are synonyms, since there is a marked difference between information floating around in the digital public domain and scientific peer-reviewed research papers.

To begin with, one is free and the other is not. 'Disinterested' third parties scrutinizing studies for scientific merit undertake the scientific peer review process. They contribute to the body of validated facts and tested theories. Studies that fail the benchmarking never make it to the pages of quality journals and books.

On the other hand, most of the data or information publicly available may consist of personal opinions, platitudes or common knowledge bereft of scientific validity and moorings.

Undertaking research in today's world is easier than it used to be. Most schools subscribe to electronic databases that students can access online.

However, students are in urgent need of being ordained in the ways of undertaking research electronically and shunning the 'copy and paste' culture.

The idea for this book first evolved early spring of 2013 when some of our knowledge facilitators, felt strongly while asserting themselves by rejecting the excuse, that today's students do not understand the importance of 'in-text citations' and refusing to let them off with just a reference page to support their study. These individual students' papers, initially few and varied, triggered a penchant to view and review the ever evolving media landscape through critical eyes. Further, the publication of such student-faculty deliberations became a necessity, as it would chart growing maturity of insight. This book, a natural corollary to Media and Communication Research and Analysis Wing (MCRAW) International Conference 2015, is the School of Media and Communication (SOMC), Manipal University Dubai Campus' first step to map the ever evolving media dominated landscape through the eyes of future media professional and scholars.

Building a healthy Research Culture is paramount and yet its benefits may not be so obvious in the near future or to some section of society. To them I would like to quote Albert Einstein: "If we knew what it was we were doing, it would not be called research, would it?" I am firmly convinced that the nascent steps taken by our students through Media and Communication Research and Analysis Wing (MCRAW) International Conference Publication will effectively contribute in our understanding of the ever-increasing role and impact of media in society.

This Book would have not been possible without the extended support of our valuable patrons who share with us the vision and intension behind 'Media Anthology: A Critical Reader.'

Special Thanks

Dr S. V. Kota Reddy, Academic President, Manipal University Dubai

Mr. N. C. Krishnakumar, Head of Facilities, Manipal University Dubai

Megna Kalvani, Assistant Professor, School of Media and Communication, Manipal University Dubai

Prof. Rashid Narain Shukul, Ph.D., School of Media and Communication
Manipal University Dubai

INTRODUCTION

The preface in this book makes it clear who the intended readership of this anthology is aimed at. It is intended to look at [mass] media and communication theory and practice from a broad perspective. Its ethos is designed to serve as a reference material and a textbook for students, faculty, researchers and professionals with interest in the subject. We are mindful of the fact that there will always be cross-disciplinary works in understanding issues of mass media and communication in contemporary society. Different perspectives, after all, provide intellectually helpful ways of understanding how issues in a seemingly complex and growing field can be engaged for purposes of scholarship. Tying up theory with practice make visualizing mass media and communication easy to perceive and appreciate as a field of practice; in other words, it gives authentic meaning to its analytical and aesthetic understanding.

Alistair's (1999) imagery of a 'giant melting pot' in reference to the media provokes deeper analysis of the role of [mass] media and communication in contemporary society. Alistair argues that 'computers, for example, are turning into television, telephone lines into publishing machines, texts into hypertext.' This allusion suggests a possible convergence of mass media and communication. No doubt media convergence is a subject of on-going discussion (Winseck, 1999; Menon, 2005; Dong-Hee, 2006; Saltzis and Dickinson, 2008; Jungwoo and Sohn, 2015). It has since been used to describe relationship between computing, media and communication technology (Lind, 2004). Whilst this relationship in itself may be complex, the emergence of social media and an expanding worldwide web makes this convergence more feasible, if not complex.

The emergence of new forms of communicating has the potential for adaptation of existing or previous forms of communication (Heesvelde, 2000). In Cho and Shin's (2014) opinion for example, Social Media has not just enlarged social relations and communication but also broadened the means of how we communicate with each other. This challenges traditional [Mass] Media in terms of the speed in which messages are passed to (target) recipients; some news sources have been traced to these 'new' channels of communication, notably, twitter. It is important to state that the emergence of new media does not diminish news value or worthiness of traditional mass media (Zhou and May, 2007). If anything, they provide a 'synergy effect' in content produced from various media platforms aimed at accomplishing the goal of "dissemination." What communication professionals choose to emphasise and how content is articulated, through whatever medium, is dependent on many factors and from different social points (Gitlin, 1980).

We understand from Gerth and Siegert's (2012) knowledge about neutrality of media professional and communicators, however, media convergence or its near convergence has created ethical and sometimes an unhealthy contest for scoops and brand parody (Jean, 2011). This position keeps media and communication ethics in sharp focus and scrutiny (Beckett, 2003). This pressure is however not always noticeable among the wider swathe of communicators such as those found on social media platforms (Johson and Fahmy, 2010) because it does not always translate into retribution. Having said that, it is worth noting that occasional legal and administrative challenges can arise from abuse or misuse of social media; in Arab countries, for example, misuse of social media can lead to dire consequences.

The survival of [mass] media is not only dependent on creative content but on what Berman (2011) calls 'creative intelligence' where users are tracked for their opinion, preferences and taste; all these help shape content. As media continues to evolve, both its consumers and publics will also evolve as their taste and preferences change. Media organizations will, in deed, need new and better strategies to respond to these changes.

Similarly, the battle for attention will also become a subject of attention. When that happens media publics and consumers will equally be faced with choices of media channels and platforms. It will become an issue of traditional vs. new media; digital vs. analogue and so on. This enthusiasm is also more likely to create a steady increase in demand for different kinds of media experiences. Its stimulus could enhance communication experience in traditional or folk media and visual communication by revitalizing interest in the images and imageries they portray.

We understand the role of [Mass] Media communication as providing information, education and communication, I.E and C (Gokah, 2009: 3 – 7). This role however comes with an added responsibility of ensuring that information or advice in the public domain is accurate and adequate (Griffiths and Mathias, 1994). The essential truth about the way media education and information works is about people's information experience (Bruce et al., 2014). Diversifying information experiences is significant in achieving this experience. As society seek, rely and use different media platforms in communicating and disseminating information and sharing knowledge in the best possible way available to them, they are in effect articulating and epitomizing that experience; an act which hither-to was unable to be provided by traditional media. Opinion differs on this point, for instance, Hobbs' (1998) has argued that 'the debate about whether [Mass] Media merely reflect or more powerfully shape social values, norms and behaviour seems to have become extinct in popular culture since the late 1980's.' Hobbs may be right to some extent because it is the same [mass] media that is used in oppressive countries in battles over images and ideas, as protagonists seek to shape audiences' views by managing available information through the media (Galloway, 2005). Notwithstanding, current debates on the Internet and the worldwide web, social media and web 2.0 prove other wise. To illustrate this point further, we are witnesses to the role social media has played in exposing oppression and servitude (Smith, 2002), rallying mass support (Sturges, 2004; Morady, 2010), and bringing to global attention human rights violations (Papademas, 2011). If anything, the seeming 'death' of popular culture referred to by Hobbs has resuscitated and strengthened popular culture in different forms especially in societies where descent, for example, is heavily suppressed.

Against the backdrop of [Mass] Media influence, we cannot underestimate the importance of media and communication. In fact, media and communication seat at the junction of all disciplines for the simple reason that it is the 'mouthpiece' through which others channel their information to the public. If the Media and Communication practitioners gets it wrong, society will in-turn get it wrong. What is being emphasized here is that, media and communication ought to be seen as a 'companion field' of study other than a lesser discipline when compared to, say, physical sciences.

When public officers in their interaction with the media scream of being misquoted or taken out of context, as it were, they are only alluding to one simple fact, and that is, media and communicators need to be properly trained and well resourced to practice their trade properly (Mateas, 2005; Hewat, 1997). In that case, it makes logical sense to see training as a strategy for development (Dirani, 2011), which will require adequate investment (Buckley and Caple, 2007). After all, formal training is a vital component in individuals and organisational development (Noe et al., 2006; Keep, 1989 and Prais, 1995).

Traditional [Mass] Media may be struggling to keep up the digital pace but we are seeing television churning out 3-D images (Waterman and Han, 2010) and on-line versions of news and features (Soo-Guan, *et al.*, 2012; Swatman, et al., 2006). In some developing countries film, cinema and visual documentaries remain a viable and useful method in community education (Gokah, 2009: 267 – 282). All these may account for reasons why society is yet to write its requiem for traditional mass media.

It is against this background, that Media Anthology discusses various themes on [mass] media and communication. For instance, in chapter one, *Professor Rajesh Sampath* examines Postcolonial Ontology of the Media in Developing Countries. He bases his paper on the ideas of French philosopher Jean Baudrillard's concepts of 'hyperreality' and his thoughts on the media. This writer will argue that a certain temporal paroxysm is at work in media production and narrative in a developing context, such as India, with regards to what the nation believes itself to be, what it was and what it will be. This paroxysm will lead to new categories and ideas that transcend Baudrillard's assumptions and assertions.

In Chapter two, *Dr. Fran Apprich* leads a discussion on the importance of using Autonomous Sensory Meridian Response (ASMR) as a healthy way of relaxation from information overloads and distraction that pertains among a generation of Social Media users.

Saheel Iqbal, *Lajwanti Kishnani* and *Vipul Parmarthi* take on the subject of Indian Education System as Portrayed in the Novel of Chetan Bhagat *Five Point someone* in chapter three. These authors question the orthodoxy in Indian Education System that identifies knowledge of students in terms of grades and CGPA students score which incidentally the media applauds.

In chapter four, *Dr. Meena Pillai* argues about selfie and commodification of women as being the virality of the male gaze. Selfie she argues is not an 'innocent' picture of one's own self; so what is it? Pillai will lead readers to understand that the object we see in a selfie is one that is poising itself in ambivalent spaces between technologies of the self and technologies of power.

In the fifth chapter, *Revathy Rajan* takes a cursory look at crime solving procedures between Indian and western television crime shows.

Chapter six focuses on celebrity endorsements on youth buying behaviour. Writing from his particular perspective *Kanika Mathur* argues that many firms use celebrities as endorsers to sell their products. Celebrity endorsements, he argues, is used as a decoy to get young consumers to spend on target products.

In Chapter seven, *Seidon Alexis* looks behind musical turntables in a desert. His research paper investigates the Electronic Dance Music (EDM) culture, from bedroom producers and club DJs to the various dance music festivals and fans in Dubai.

In chapter eight, *Hansabe Luximan* contributes to Gender roles and Environmentalism as represented in animation films. In Social Science discourse, gender and environmentalism is pitched in different ways – as political actors or social actors. Whilst the former is perceived in the literature as violent, the later is seen as likely to suffer silent repression – ridicule and stigmatisation with an aim of silencing them. From religious-cultural perspective, Muslim women in particular, have been identified as an untapped potential for mosques to build upon Islam's existing environmental ethic and develop an environmental agenda. Whether, this reflects in the animation imageries that Hansabe examines should be a matter of interest.

In chapter nine, *Sayema Wasi* discusses the subject of cultural appropriation and the misrepresentation of people of colour in mainstream Hollywood movies. Wasi's discussion reinforces the uneasiness the surrounds cultural misappropriation and representation. The choice of medium to label certain social or population group as 'insignificant others' is the focus in this paper.

In Chapter ten, *Disha Dadlani* discusses Bollywood in Dubai. Bollywood is the equivalent of Hollywood in America. In India, Bollywood is seen as a mega industry in terms of size and impact on the economy. Disha examines the reasons underpinning cosmopolitan Dubai being a viable market for Bollywood films.

Lippy Ramchandani explores the literature on 'trolling celebrities' in the eleventh chapter. This presentation does not only seek to deconstruct ambiguities associated with "trolling" but also to conjecture a working definition for what constitutes trolling and who a troll is.

Chapter twelve is based on the rebirth of vampire stories in the 21St Century. Its author, *Suha Sabith*, contends that 'the 21st century has seen an explosion of vampires in different media like literature, film, television and music.' Suha thus takes a microscopic interest in this "newly unearthed vampire" and would like to know what is in the future for these fascinating creatures in terms of visual representations and popularity?

Chapter thirteen of this anthology is dedicated to *Sabir Haque and Biju's* work on reasons behind the phenomenon of Retweeting. Their research on what drives tweeple (people who use twitter) to re-tweet is grey and offers readers an understanding of the phenomenon and its effect.

Finally, in Chapter fourteen, *Professor Abderrahmane Azzi* takes on the subject of ethical theory of social media. Drawing on Kant's Categorical Imperative and Draz's Positive Obligation, he examines ways by which ethical theory can inform the use of social media in modern society. Abderrahmane's discussion is relevant in contemporary society dominated by social media. His work adds to existing and on-going discourses on the need for social media users to exercise decorum in speech and content on such platforms.

In: Media Anthology
Editor: Theophilus Kofi Gokah
ISBN: 978-1-63484-931-9

Chapter 1

TOWARDS A NON-POSTCOLONIAL ONTOLOGY OF THE MEDIA IN DEVELOPING COUNTRIES

***Rajesh Sampath**, PhD**
Heller School for Social Policy and Management
Brandeis University, Waltham, MA, US

ABSTRACT

This paper explores the ideas of French philosopher Jean Baudrillard, particularly his conceptual innovations on the media, both traditional television/cinema and the Internet/cyberspace. The paper appropriates his ideas and critically reconstructs them to explore different problems and issues that arise when examining the functions and production of the media in developing country contexts. The main thesis of the paper is that media production in decolonized, developing countries presupposes a complex temporal horizon, which can be contrasted with some of the basic assumptions of postcolonial studies. The paper initiates an inquiry into the conditions of developing a non-postcolonial ontology for the purpose of constructing a complex theory of world-historical time. It concludes with the possibility of how this theory would be able to treat the problem of identity and non-identity of developing country contexts in an age of media and globalization.

---

* rsampath@brandeis.edu.

This paper will explore the ideas of the French philosopher Jean Baudrillard, particularly his concepts of 'hyperreality' and his thoughts on the media. Baudrillard spoke of information in media not representing facts or events but information being an event itself [1]. He also said media blurs the line between content and form/message/transmission [2]. This occurs when the mechanism to deliver content becomes the content and 'information devours itself' [3]. He also spoke of the ironic notion that although media has to amalgamate information, facts, events, content from different sources to produce its narrative or image, the final product itself forbids any kind of response [4]. External resistance to media content is already pre-inscribed within the content and in fact a product of it. All of these ideas point to the need for a change in our philosophical understanding of reality whereby technology, such as the media (both traditional T.V./Cinema and today's Internet), transforms the conditions by which we are able to know anything at all. It also changes the conditions of experience, and the relations between experience and knowledge, the experience of knowledge and the knowledge of experience [5]. What this suggests from a phenomenological point of view as problematic is the common-sense notion that the viewing subject is an external entity 'outside' the media content they are viewing while the content itself is contained 'inside' the media for which the viewer cannot control. Yet this entire distinction of 'outside-subject and inside-content' becomes questionable.

The contribution of this paper will see to what extent Baudrillard's ideas have to be extended, adapted, transformed, and mutated to understand how media functions in certain developing contexts. It is not beyond the bounds of reason to imagine that contemporary developing country contexts generate experiences that require a deconstruction of Baudrillard's categories and formulations and the venturing of new ideas and concepts. This paper will argue that a certain temporal paroxysm is at work in media production and narrative in a developing context with regard to what a developing nation or region believes itself to be, what it was and what it will be. The paper's aim is to explore all dimensions of this paroxysm, which will require new categories and ideas that transcend Baudrillard's assumptions and assertions.

INTELLECTUAL HISTORICAL CONTEXT

Many developing countries constantly pivot between the repression of trauma from a previously colonized state and a continuous post-colonial imagination of whether they can truly be independent of that trauma but often times in response to it. There is 'repetition and difference' in a manner that resists any easy three-moment dialectical synthesis [6]. They are caught in a vertigo where the past resurfaces in the present but points to a future, albeit a transformed past, or the future appears as repetition but always in response to a present trying to break free from history. History always seems to be produced outside a linear alignment of past, present and future. Four points seem to intersect but in a non-circular and non-linear way when we try to understand time in this context. The fundamental nature of this investigation is peering into the idea of historical time at work in many developing country contexts. Even the temporal assumptions of the 'postcolonial' itself have to be questioned. The nature of time and trauma manifests differently and in different contexts. This usually occurs unconsciously and is not visible in the content of the current media outlets that is produced, particularly in popular films and even news reporting. The content seems neutral, value-free, sanguine and harmless, just more fantasies as products of a globalized world. But not far beneath the surface lurks a presence waiting to be described. Baudrillard's ideas give us the initial impulses to unlock that presence and to bring it to light.

In 2000, Baudrillard published *Ecran total*, which was then translated in English as *Screened Out* in 2002 [7]. A chapter that goes by the same name as the title of the book of essays stands out for our purposes [8]. In that text Baudrillard attacks the very notion of 'interactivity' across media forms ('video, interactive screens, multimedia, Internet, virtual reality') and constitutes it as a 'threat' [9]. Baudrillard has always been deeply disturbed by the encroachment of the information technology age in which the 'hypperreal'- or when constructed virtual objects become more real than physical reality takes over [10]. The issue is not just loss of control by the human subject, which we believe is responsible for the production of media content, which is then consumed or manipulated by other human subjects. The real question is to assess the possibility and limits of building an analytics to understand how distinctions between the human subject and media object, production and consumption, etc. begin to dissolve, thus unveiling a far more complex reality than traditionally understood. But now he turns his attention to media specifically. Baudrillard is renowned for blending poststructuralist philosophical critiques and psychoanalytic analysis with a political-economic analysis of the nature of hegemony and domination in the age of information [11].

The question for our paper is how to mutate and transform Baudrillard's concepts, ideas and arguments to investigate our question of historical time and developing countries in light of their production and use of the media. In particular, Baudrillard's essay focuses on the Internet, virtual reality and computer simulation as a form of media but also focuses on traditional media such as television. We must keep in mind that a poststructuralist analysis does not begin from an essentialized subjectivity that may be internal to a psychological or biological understanding of the physical mind. There is little here by way of a traditional empirical analysis that presupposes experience as an external event that occurs to an internal mind or subjectivity [12]. Rather, the 'experience' that is produced inside, outside, in between and beyond the media is remarkably diverse ways given the phenomenalization of techniques that proliferate in the contemporary production of media, particularly in globalized contexts. Indeed, this analysis looks at structures, processes and dynamics in pluralistic and non-binary terms on how subjectivity is constituted in 'real and virtual' terms. Here, literal and symbolic language plays a constitutive but not dominant role since anything called 'reality' is irreducible to any one category—say Marxist materialism or Freudian psychoanalysis. Poststructuralism is concerned with a critique of hegemony and domination but is not wedded to any single type of critique [13].

Yet, poststructuralist thought grew out of a Western context, most notably France from the 1960s to 1980s [14]. For the most part, it responded to Western history, social theory, linguistics, literary criticism, phenomenology, structuralism, psychoanalysis and philosophy, and from that context began to explore issues in globalization. Post-colonialism in many respects drew from the influence of major Western thinkers [15]. Yet, a critical evaluation of postcolonial studies and its roots in postmodern and poststructuralist thought is not the route this essay will take. Rather, we want to appropriate Baudrillard's ideas while developing our own philosophical-historical sense of historical time for developing world contexts. The project is eminently philosophically and unapologetically metaphysical against the poststructuralist suspicion against metaphysics and metaphysical subjectivity. In contrast, from our perspective, physical nation-states and cultures, along with the virtual realities they produce and are produced by, constitute meta-subjects that are ripe for analysis. The historical temporalization of these meta-subjects is the object of investigation. We do not characterize the work in traditional postcolonial terms if postcolonial studies typically rely on other intentionally non-metaphysical branches of the humanities, such as literary criticism, or the social sciences, most notably history, anthropology and sociology. To philosophize with Baudrillard and against him is the aim. This will require inventing new philosophical categories of analysis.

Main Text

It is one thing to believe that with the ubiquitous intrusion of the media in every aspect of life, and the twenty-four hour cycle that it dominates, there is very little resistance in Western societies and Eastern/Global South societies with advanced, industrialized developed economies to media onslaught. Media marks the supreme tyranny of our age from which there is no escape from its reach. There is no palpable way to challenge the thinking that is created for individuals before they are allowed to form their own thoughts. There is no escaping the media (or information in general) that bombards one through the course of the day, regardless of the technology available - video, Internet, mobile phone, and all interrelations therein. This is assumed and no one questions it. However, we need to alter our assumptions about the ubiquity and omnipresence of the media. That means questioning the *a priori* conditions of space and time within which we understand the very ontology of this 'thing' called global media. Inversely, media generates a sense of time and space that interconnects subjects globally while forcing us to imagine what our historical subjectivity even means, i.e., what it means for human subjects to imagine themselves occurring in the historical present and in the flow of history [16]. This is particularly acute when we think of developing world contexts with regard to a hypothesized notion of world-historical time that accounts for the interrelations of developed and developing countries given the legacy of colonialism. The question is how media is a function of this world-historical temporality and how it produces it at the same time.

In order to develop our hypothesis, let us first unpack some assumptions underpinning Baudrillard's central thesis on the nature of the media:

> That nowhere—in art, morality, or politics—is there now any possibility of moral judgement. With the abolition of distance—of the 'pathos of distance'—everything becomes undecidable. And this is true even in the physical realm ... when an event and the broadcasting of the event in real time are too close together, this renders the event undecidable and virtual, stripping it of its historical dimension and removing it from memory. Whether it is virtual technologies, which

> create undecidability, or our undecidable world which gives rise to these technologies is itself undecidable [17].

There is a lot to unpack in this passage. We can stay with the passage and think from within our comfortable, developed context, and from the standpoint of this author within a Western context. However, that is not a challenge. We want to digest these gems of reflection from within a non-postcolonial, developing context, and imagine how to expand or adapt the categories offered here. By non-postcolonial, we do not presuppose any intuitive temporalization of what 'post-' stands for: namely after the empirical, chronological period of colonialism, which began *circa* 1500 and ended with the decolonization of many countries in the Global South throughout the twentieth century (while Latin America decolonized in the nineteenth century). The repercussions are massive because the power imbalances between media's influence in a developed context compared to a developing country context has yet to be explored with regard to the problem of world historical temporality: that is in how developed and developing countries share an experience of a single continuum compounded by the problem of globalization, or how they differ in their own experiences of what it means to be in a world-historical time structure common to all humanity in a linear, chronological frame. We need to overcome the fundamental metaphysical problem of the one and many, which descend from Plato's philosophy, but applied to the problem of world historical time [18]. In other words, we need to think how these categories of Baudrillard would alter if we tried to imagine them from within a non-postcolonial, developing country context and a new temporal horizon [19].

We could be at a complete loss to understand the relation between (a) Being in history for developed and developing countries alike (and hence the fragmentary eclipse *and* reconstitution of that distinction given the complexity of globalization) and (b) Vertiginous possibilities in Baudrillard's passage about the nature of media. What we need are categories of the production and consumption of historical time within a developing world media context in relation *to* but also resistant *of* the Western production of historical time in its media content: the latter's narrative constantly has to re-inscribe the non-West/Global South as a colonial by-product, which threatens the stability of how the West continues to struggle with its own sense of historical time. There is a certain war within this sensibility that constantly pushes to engulf the Western notion of historical time into a radical indiscernibility, even chaos.

Let us bifurcate Baudrillard's passage into its elemental parts. Baudrillard raises the issue of 'art, morality, and politics.' We are not concerned with whether he is discussing this in the Western context only, which is quite possibly the case. Rather, we seek to extract his statements and transfer them to a different context we are trying to analyze, outside the fields of semiotic theory and postcolonial studies [20]. The point is to take these statements and apply them from within a non-postcolonial, developing world context while trying to imagine a new type of temporalization.

Returning to Baudrillard's passage, he states: "That nowhere—in art, morality, or politics—is there now any possibility of moral judgement." Obviously, for Baudrillard, in Western culture, there was a time in which and through those entities ('art, morality, politics') moral judgements became possible, but no longer. However, we can try to deconstruct this as strictly a Western, nihilistic reaction to its own postmodern relativism. But what about developing country contexts in the non-West or Global South, which could not experience that empirical historical time trajectory because it is already past and unrepeatable? That is a legitimate question if we are not to reproduce old assumptions about theoretical categories, like Baudrillard's, as trans-universal. To assume that all humanity lives in a time-continuum in which different parts can coexist within it and experience that continuum in different ways while maintaining the belief in a singular continuum runs into certain contradictions: *either* we believe that one civilization experiences world history at the expense of another by conquering that other and that is experienced from a single and only time-frame for world history; *or* we have to admit, embarrassingly so, that such a single-time frame is impossible because the conquered no doubt not only made the conqueror's world-historical trajectory possible, but that their current decolonized 'freedom' today somehow comes 'after' in that world-historical trajectory. Hence the problem of historical time arises when thinking about Western colonial developed history vs. decolonized, non-Western, developing history. And for this investigation the entire theoretical critique of the media and technology age, like the one expressed in Baudrillard's reflections, further complicates matters.

One can say there never was a self-same, homogeneous possibility for 'art, morality, and politics' to develop the conditions for 'moral judgements' as they did in specific and singular ways in the West, beginning with the eighteenth century Enlightenment. To re-imagine those historical moments in which the individual was freed from all strictures of tradition, caste, hierarchy, and intergenerational fatalism is difficult precisely because the conditions for that unique epochal shift may never be discovered [21]. In that time, constitutional monarchies, which were legitimated through divine justification based on medieval Christian heritage, were literally decapitated by decoupling the possibility of moral judgement from purely religious and specious metaphysical grounds: the possibility of judgements were transferred to the realm of politics and public reason, which themselves experienced continued experimentation and reinvention with no possible grounds to verify the methodological certainty of arriving at a final truth. Individual freedom became a goal in itself but not determined by any metaphysical essence [22] Modern politics and science were born at the same time in the late eighteenth century, in which each tried to legitimate the other (but anarchically experimental in nature) in the absence of a tyrannical, religious metaphysical hegemony that governed every sphere of knowledge. The Western peoples decided, fatefully, that human existence was one big experiment and with no remorse for that decision even unto this day.

However, in decolonized, developing contexts that either tried to create their own 'secular, liberal, constitutional democracies' or those whose democracies were foisted upon them during decolonization, something else seems to have occurred. The simultaneity of mid-twentieth century technological media such as TV, and then a few decades later the Internet, and a newly found 'freedom' in decolonization meant that 'art, morality, and politics' as the ground of secular public reason could not take root in the non-West as it did in late eighteenth century Europe and colonial America: in the latter, democratic revolutions, a nascent industrial revolution and secular public reason came into being at a singular moment. Therefore, the *temporality of decolonization* in relation to the birth of democracies in a twentieth century technological age cannot replicate what Baudrillard says occurred in his reflection: the latter is the disappearance of the possibility of moral judgements in secular art, politics and morality, judgements which used to occur in a pre-technological media age in the West. And this has nothing to do with the claim about some fundamental inability to create a secular, constitutional, legal, and liberal democracy that respects individual political and group civil rights first and foremost in pluralistic, ethnic, cultural, and religious societies in the non-West. This suspicion against the possibility of secular, liberal, constitutional democracy in non-Western contexts descend from appropriations of Huntington's *The Clash of Civilizations* and its variations in Zakaria's 'illiberal democracies' [23]. Or to qualify our statement, how 'art, morality, and politics' occurs in the age of the media and virtual space in developing country contexts without 'moral judgement' has to be rethought without using Western historical narrative as a norm or criteria of analysis. Baudrillard's formulations seem woefully empty as we try to encounter this historical complexity: the latter is an eclipse of the distinction between 'developed and developing countries,' which itself is built into Western self-conception of world historical time.

Baudrillard is talking about the death of moral judgements in art, morality and politics in the postmodern age of media in the West. But what does that say about geographically defined non-Western contexts in a globalized age where moral judgements never took root in art, morality and politics in the same way to begin with, particularly given the legacy of amoral colonialism whose sole responsibility lies with the West? Elites who control governments in developing countries, which do not tackle widespread poverty and inequality, i.e., by promoting 'development,' are part of this legacy. What constitute 'elites' in Western democracies are not single individuals *per se* given the size of most Western economies. Rather, elitism is a confluence of changeable interrelations of groups and individuals that cut across the public and private sectors that constantly fight to increase power and profits while working within the legal constraints of a democratic system that truly enforces a separation of powers, namely the executive branch, the judiciary and the legislature. In the West, the law transcends the single individual and in the age of technological media, that is all the more the case; but what about other parts of non-West and Global South?

If we take for example, the secular, liberal, constitutional democracy that formed in India as a response to independence from British colonialism, how can we explain the profound amorality and immorality of the caste system (enshrined within the religion/culture called Hinduism, which is now being nationalized through the current right-wing party in power)? And one of the best weapons used to propagate and reinvent caste politics, which then conceals profound social and economic inequalities, is the power of the media [24]. These days that includes the Internet, social media and World Wide Web. How do we understand the illusion of freedom presented in the media, and through the prospects of social media and the Internet, which then conceals the hidden reality of trenchant inequality, marginalization and exclusion of major segments of the population? [25]. To answer these questions, we need to proceed through and against Baudrillard's remaining formulations in the passage we just quoted.

CONCLUSION

In order to expand our ideas in the interstices of Baudrillard's passage we must take some precautions before moving further. Phrases such as the 'pathos of distance' and the 'undecidable' [26] become problematic in a globalized context, particularly when seen from a developing world perspective. Globalization seems to collapse the 'physical,' but in fact, it is silently producing new differences, whether physical or non-physical, with regard to how the 'producers and consumers distinction' constantly reinvents itself. In general, distinctions of an 'inside' and 'outside' become blurred, whether we speak of an inside or outside reality from the standpoint of a human subject, or the reality that lies inside or outside the vehicle/medium/machine known as the media. A whole other ontology is at work. The question is how these Baudrillaridian formulations about the 'abolition of distance' and the 'pathos of distance' gets reconfigured on the issue of the 'undecidable' with regard to developing country contexts. The problem is that the distinction between 'developed' and 'developing' contexts gets caught up in this question too with regard to the problem of a multi-faceted and multidimensional world historical time.

Baudrillard questions the distinction between physical events and virtual events and how it problematizes a simple idea of historical memoralization, which itself presupposes an external, linear, physical sense of time. He speaks of the undeciability of the virtual event and its historicization [27] This raises more questions than answers. What do we really know about events in real time, the nature of the event, and its de-historicization? For today's developing context is both a de-decolonization and avoidance of re-colonization and a perpetual striving to overcome the baggage of the past and an ironic clinging to it. The result is real, tangible physical socio-economic inequalities that only get exacerbated, namely poverty and social exclusion since they are built into the very structure of society. The impoverished masses only have recourse for enjoyment, namely the media - both virtual and cinematic theater - as they are pushed to the brink of exasperation. This creates a gap in which the production of fantasy from misery creates a momentary escape from the reality of impoverishment, which descends from colonialism and is exacerbated by neocolonial globalization. And the latter itself is propelled in the age of media technology.

This leads Baudrillard to link the idea of 'virtual technologies' with the very 'undecidability' that constitutes an ontological complexity of the world itself. He states: "whether it is virtual technologies which create undecidability or our undecidable world which gives rise to these technologies is itself undecidable" [28]. The interrelations between virtual technology and undecidability both in, out of and outside developing world contexts makes the Baudrillardian distinction about whether virtual technology produces undecidability or vice-versa more complex than it would appear. As Heidegger wrote decades ago when exploring how technology constitutes a new epoch in the history of Being in the West, we need to raise the question of technology and the polyphonic nature of media in developing contexts and the age of neocapitalist globalization. The difference between Heidegger's text and a future text would have to show how the apparent circle of the technology producing the undecidable and vice-versa explodes into a fourfold structure. Given the movements and counter-movements of a pre-colonial indigenous past in non-Western/Global South contexts, the colonial superimposition of world-historical time upon developing contexts, the epochal tensions between decolonization (born in the twentieth century age of media and technology) and the early twenty-first century resistance to neocolonial pressures: all of these four constantly negotiate between Western influences of media technology in developing world contexts and the creative mutation of new signs and sensibilities that transcend the Western context. The former is what Baudrillard's theoretical critique does not fully develop.

We must overcome Baudrillard's distinction between technologies that create undecidability *or* undecidability that gives rise to technologies in order to think within this fourfold. Technology's mad rush to get to the post-human state takes on a new twist in the developing world context since previous distinctions of unfree, colonized human beings and newly freed decolonized human beings becomes problematized [29]. If the technological produces the ontological undecidability of what it means to be human and 'post-human' in the age of the virtual, then the technological-undecidable nexus becomes even more complex when we think of the interchange and fluid permeability of identities and non-identities that move between these poles: we speak of the pre-colonial, colonial, decolonial and neocolonial age of globalization in which a multidimensional notion of world-historical time becomes the horizon for understanding the experience and complex subjectivities of developing world contexts. It is the aim of a future project to develop this concept of world-historical time in a way that surpasses the definitions offered by Baudrillard on the age of media technology and the virtual itself.

References

[1] Jean Baudrillard, *Screened Out*, trans. Chris Turner (London: Verso Press, 2002), p. 177.

[2] Ibid.

[3] Jean Baudrillard, *Simulacra and Simulation*, p. 80-83, from the original French, *Simulacres et simulation* (Paris: Gallilée, 1981).

[4] Jean Baudrillard, "Requiem for the Media," from *The Critique of the Political Economy of the Sign*, trans. Charles Levin (St. Louis: Telos Press, 1981), pp. 164-184. Reprinted in *Video Culture: A Critical Investigation*, ed. John Hanhardt (Rochester: Visual Studies Workshop Press, 1986), p. 280. The *Critique of the Political Economy of the Sign* was originally published in French in 1972.

[5] See Albert Borgmann, "Information and Reality at the Turn of the Century" in Robert. C. Sharff and Vaal Dusek, eds., *The Philosophy of Technology: An Anthology* (London: Blackwell Publishing, 2003), pp. 571-577. Of course one of the earliest and arguably the most significant examination of technology in light of the history of metaphysics is Martin Heidegger's "Question Concerning Technology" in David Farell Krell, ed., *Basic Writings* (New York: Harper Collins Publications, 1977).

[6] The phrase of 'repetition and difference' is an allusion to the ideas of the poststructuralist philosopher Gilles Deleuze, particularly his two main philosophical works, *The Logic of Sense* (1969) and *Difference and Repetition* (1968). Deleuze made his own unique contributions to the study of the media, particularly in his volumes on *Cinema 1: The Movement-Image* (1983) and *Cinema 2: The Time-Image* (1985). In a future work, we hope to read these texts and apply to them an analysis of the media in developing world contexts.

[7] Baudrillard, *Screened Out*.

[8] The chapter was originally published as an essay in 1996. That was the year Google was born.

[9] Baudrillard, p. 176.

[10] The Swiss linguist Ferdinand Saussure first theorized that the 'sign' is the unity of the signifier (oral or written representation) of the signified (the mental image or object). See his *Cours de linguistique général* published posthumously in 1916. Saussure wrote at the turn of the twentieth century and would not have built his linguistic model on the basis of the age of the Internet and virtual reality. This is where Baudrillard's innovations come in.

[11] See Mark Poster's innovative appropriation of Baudrillard in *The Mode of Information: Poststructuralism and Social Context* (Chicago: University of Chicago Press, 1990). As you can see the title is a play on Marx's famous 'mode of production.' Poster was a brilliant modern

European intellectual historian of twentieth century France who then branched out on his on in his theoretical studies on the nature of our information society and age. For example, in his introduction to an anthology of Baudrillard's essays, he states: "Like the poststructuralists, Baudrillard rejects traditional assumptions about referentiality. As Lyotard put it, the metanarratives of the past have collapsed, creating a new theoretical situation in which the concept can no longer pretend to control or grasp its object. In Baudrillard's terms, 'hyperreality' is the new linguistic condition of society, rendering impotent theories that still rely on materialist society, rendering impotent theories that still rely on materialist reductionism or rationalist referentiality. In these respects, Baudrillard's work is important to the reconstitution of critical theory, and, more generally, appeals to those who would attempt to grasp the strange mixture of fantasy and desire that is unique to late-twentieth century and early twenty-first-century culture." Mark Poster, ed., *Jean Baudrillard: Selected Essays*, 2nd edition (Stanford: Stanford University Press, 2001), p. 2. This essay is dedicated to his memory.

[12] That topic is really a matter for the natural sciences, such as cognitive science, neuroscience and neuropsychology. Analytic philosophers then try to make problematic and uncovering new logical complexities beneath the work of natural scientists that the latter do not tend to see. For leading works in the philosophy of mind, see David Chalmers, *Philosophy of Mind: Classical and Contemporary Readings* (2002), Jaegwon Kim, *Philosophy of Mind* (2010), and John Heil, *Philosophy of Mind: A Contemporary Introduction* (2012).

[13] Exemplars of the poststructuralist approach are Foucault, Deleuze, Derrida, Serres, Lyotard and Baudrillard. See Vincent Descombes, *Modern French Philosophy* (Cambridge: Cambridge University Press, 1980).

[14] See Descombes, *Modern French Philosophy*. For a critique of this tradition from the standpoint of intellectual history, see Martin Jay, *Downcast Eyes: The Denigration of Vision in Twentieth Century Thought* (Berkeley: University of California Press, 1994). Also see David Harvey's Marxian-related critique in *The Condition of Postmodernity: An Inquiry into the Origins of Cultural Change* (Malden: Blackwell Publishers, 1990).

[15] For example the works of Gyatri Spivak on postcolonial studies were influenced to a great extent by Derridean deconstruction.

[16] As Dilthey once formulated as the hermeneutic circle- 'man is the subject and object of history' or what makes and is made by history. Thus for the very thing that is made by history to turn around and try to reflect back on that history as to how we arrived to the present state seems to constitute a circle. For the historical reflection is made by history itself. History makes history (i.e., subjects become historical while looking back on history) and therefore the reflection of history at the same time. This is to say that historical reflection not only occurs within history happening, or history has a historicity, but also history happening becomes an object of historical reflection. Further complications can ensue when trapped within the circle, and yet the circle itself is shattered when we enter into developing world contexts, which we will seek to explain. See Wilhelm Dilthey, *Hermeneutics and the Study of* History, Rudolf A. Makkreel and Frithjof Rodi, eds. (Princeton, New Jersey: Princeton University Press, 1996) and Wilhelm Dilthey, *Introduction to the Human Sciences*, Rudolf A. Makkreel and Frithjof Rodi, eds. (Princeton, New Jersey: Princeton University Press, 1989).

[17] Baudrillard, *Screened Out*, p. 176.

[18] This is in reference to Plato's most difficult work- *Parmenides*.

[19] In that regard Baudrillard's assumption about how the media changes our experience of space and time and complicates our place in history still derive from a Western conception of world historical time that is based on a universal, single, linear time-frame. And what explodes this conception is the contemporary paradoxes of media and the cyberspace age that Baudrillard deftly describes. However, our project does not derive from the same assumptions when seen from a developing world context.

[20] We leave it up to Baudrillard specialists and enthusiasts to try to decipher the hidden intentions and meaning of his texts to determine if in fact he intended to speak from a globalized context that transcends the West and non-West distinction, or Global North and South, developed and developing world contexts. The point is that he did not try to venture concept of world-historical time that arises from and erases the difference between developed and developing world contexts and their temporal horizons of interpenetration.

[21] It would behoove researchers in the philosophy of history to return to original works on the nature of epochal shifts and historical time, such as Hans Blumenberg's *The Legitimacy of the Modern Age* (1966) and

Reinhart Kosselleck's *Futures Past: the Semantics of Historical Time* (1979), which examined for the most part Western history. But the idea is to deconstruct those texts while problematizing the whole Western/Non-Western, developed and developing distinctions by trying to reconceive a more complex, multidimensional, non-linear, and non-circular sense of world historical time. This is something yet to be achieved in a grand, metaphysical sense within development studies, which tends to rely on economists' strictly empirical assumptions of time and change.

[22] This of course points to the legacy of Kant's transcendental philosophical critique of metaphysics applied to the problem of human freedom.

[23] See Samuel Huntington, *The Clash of Civilizations* (Touchstone: New York, 1996), and Fareed Zakaria's The Rise of Illiberal Democracy in *Foreign Affairs*, November/December 1997 Issue.

[24] See for example Dipanker Gupta's *Mistaken Modernity: India Between Worlds* (New Delhi: Harper Collins Publishers, 2000).

[25] The eminent sociologist Manuel Castells tries to answer this question in his pioneering works. See for example the three volumes- *The Rise of the Network Society: The Information Age: Economy, Society, and Culture, Vol. 1* (Oxford: Wiley-Blackwell, 1996); *The Power of Identity: The Information Age: Economy, Society, and Culture, Vol. 2* (Oxford: Wiley-Blackwell, 1997); and *End of Millennium: The Information Age: Economy, Society, and Culture, Vol. 3* (Oxford: Wiley-Blackwell, 1998).

[26] Baudrillard, *Screened Out*, p. 176.

[27] Ibid.

[28] Ibid.

[29] Over fifty years ago, in his classic *The Wretched of the Earth*, Frantz Fanon raised path-breaking questions that revolutionized our understanding of the process of decolonization as an inherently 'violent' process. He asked not how colonial subjects went from unfree to free human beings but how they must create a new humanity given that colonialization essentially destroyed a previous humanity. See *The Wretched of the Earth*, trans. Richard Philcox (New York: Grove Press, 2004).

In: Media Anthology
Editor: Theophilus Kofi Gokah
ISBN: 978-1-63484-931-9

Chapter 2

The Impact of ASMR on Social Media Generation

Fran Apprich*, PhD
Dean, School of Communication and Media Studies,
Health and Environment,
Canadian University Dubai, UAE

Abstract

Using ASMR (Autonomous sensory meridian response) footage as a release of anxiety of the social media pressure is among the most common activities of today's social media generation. Any ASMR Web site has facilitated to experience a sense of peace and calm so alien to nowadays-constant flow of information and accessibility. The ASMR community interacts via social media sites, including social networking sites such as Facebook, MySpace, and Twitter; video sites such as YouTube; and blogs. Such sites offer today's youth a portal for relaxation and have grown exponentially in recent years. For this reason, it is important that researchers, journalists, educators, parents and youngsters become aware of the nature of social media sites and their impact. Researchers and journalists are in a unique position to help families understand the constant flow of information and how to maintain a healthy lifestyle where relaxation rather than distraction and content

* franziska@cud.ac.ae.

consumption can be practiced. The emergence of ASMR is the anti-movement to the overload of information and distraction.

Introduction

ASMR is often described as a 'tingling sensation' and its impact on the social media generation is not simply another influence that can be overlooked. The interaction between social media generation and ASMR defines the need of relaxation within our current society; dismissed by most academics as sexualized whispering; ASMR defines the nature of our society and the need for a space without an overload of information and interactivity [1].

In this paper I will argue that an analysis of ASMR, understood as a relaxing extension of social media forum palette, can bring us closer to an examination of the social media impact of social media generation nowadays. Social media established itself as a platform, which, from the outset, stimulated and manipulated its audience by making them perceive, receive, interact and buy into a certain product, service or celebrity. The audience is encouraged to interact and strive for a better image of themselves, whether physically or mentally. Not only adults are put under this ever-rising pressure but also children and vulnerable teenagers. This impact can be perceived when children wear suggestive outfits, expect opportunities without hard work/effort and behave like spoiled divas.

Discourse

If one watched social media content, a virtual illusion of celebrity status and perfection is provided and perceived by the social media generation. Therefore, the paradox of social media trends towards ASMR, which offers relaxation through calm, eye and ear contact whispering (without the overwhelming emotionally manipulating impact of music). Social media content is often accompanied by music and interactive links which are initially employed to intensify the emotional impressions of the on-screen visuals.

It is important to remember that the introduction of social media has economic as well as artistic consequences since viewers have to equip themselves with technology that would allow them full perception of the content (visually, sonically, content wise and linkage).

Academic critics reinforce the sense of social media content as being realistic but in reality the relationship is more like plastic surgery, extending and manipulating the physical appearance of the portrayed. The Dove advert and self-esteem campaign of the distortion of media content was a ground breaking advertisement showing the media generation that not everything perceived on social media truly exists. Things can be altered – made prettier than they are and the strife for perfection but still the social media generation, regardless, strive for perfection and a fast life, with fast food, fast pleasures, immediate gratification, fast content and short attention span. Youngsters are getting plastic surgery, living their own celebrity life-style that they exhibit on their social networks, with overspent credit cards, wearing shoes they cannot afford. It is not only that they share this lifestyle among each other but put pressure on each other. Nowadays, even an infant is getting entertained during Friday Brunch Dubai by IPads and online gaming. It is also important to reflect on the metaphor of birth of social media, in relation to other art forms, it is in fact still in its infancy. Dangers will only be captured later and harmful patterns noticed when it is already too late to revert.

We explore the complexity of ASMR on social media through the analysis of a number of specific critical texts wherein ASMR's unique expressive potential may be observed. I use the terminology of ASMR 'on,' rather than 'in' or 'with' social media since I believe it to be important to reflect on the psychological reality of the process. Critics are familiar with the basic principles of social media but very little analysis has been given to the psychological reality of the content, which utilizes content during projection and obviously raises valid questions that should be incorporated within any critical examination for the ASMR experience.

ASMR content spreads three-dimensionally (same as sound as it embodies sound and stimulates through both visuals but most commonly sound) [2]. The recording of a sound seeks to recreate the sound source's three-dimensional character. This created an intimate calming environment and a certain illusion of the presence of the other. Whereas the photographic recording of an object converts the represented object into a two-dimensional still or moving image on the screen - the object is robbed of one dimension, which is then represented by the convention of perspective, which has dominated the European pictorial tradition since the Renaissance. Whereas sound in a film/content environment uses its own grammar, it does not display some elements of the image such as perspective, framing and focus.

When contacted, one critic (name confidential), associated with ASMR rejected the idea to collaborate on my research on ASMR and mentioned that numerous journalists had contacted him before and that he had nothing to do with ASMR. Such statement surprised me as ASMR represents one of the most popular social media trends of our time and has a proven track record of relaxation against anxiety. Another professor from an IVY league University first connected with me but then ignored my e-mails. Was this a sign? Had ASMR such a bad reputation?

It is important to reflect on the ASMR YouTube comments – it shows ASMR fans and people who do not understand it – do not know its purpose. ASMR is still in its infancy and it is important that we explore it as much as we can and identify its benefits.

ASMR and its online popularity raise crucial questions about relaxation and the need for it. We must ask ourselves weather ASMR is the answer to our stressful lives and acts as a counterpart. Whereas many attempts have been made to analyse psychology, surprisingly few psychologists, media critics or musicians have paid attention to the rise of ASMR's expressive forms and meanings. Early psychologists recognized mediation and its unique potential on the human brain…but somehow ASMR remains less explored. When talking to the neurologists (who I thought had all answers) they mentioned the secret of the brain and the very complexity of it and that was still very much unexplored. So should we not somehow explore more?

I believe that this liberation of ASMR and its use can bring us closer to a state of peace and calm – and what better research is there to concentrate on? The introduction of ASMR as a respected and scientifically proven outlet for the social media generation requires ambassadors to stand with it, explore it and celebrate it. The fact that ASMR was temporary motivated only by sexualized primitive content to gain subscribers should not overshadow its great character and usefulness [3].

I undertook a scientific research with a Neurological Center in Dubai. My scientific research sought to explore the relationship between ASMR sound (only the sound of a person chewing gum) with the research participants. I argue that that ASMR has it unique expressive form and that effective use of ASMR sound will lead us to a state of calm. I first thought of using the ASMR sound of whispering but to leave the sexualized notion behind, I wanted to simply concentrate on the sound of somebody chewing gum [4].

The research participants were placed onto a bed and covered with a blanket. The lights were dimmed, eyes closed and the sound of chewing gum played. At first the neurology team was very sceptical of the research. Nevertheless, they became more open to it and when they started to experience the tingling effect themselves they were so excited and asked more people to participate in the research [5]. People with anxiety problems, sleep problems, depression all were exploring ASMR and interviews were held. People with anxiety problems became calm; people with sleep disorder fell asleep, people with depression felt lighter [6].

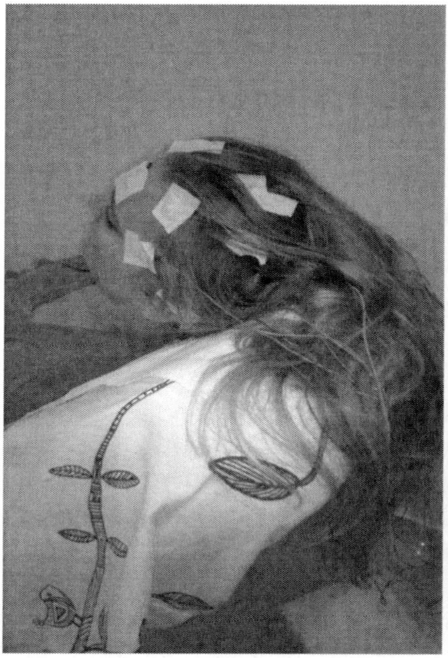

Figure 1. Neurology Center: ASMR research EEG measuring.

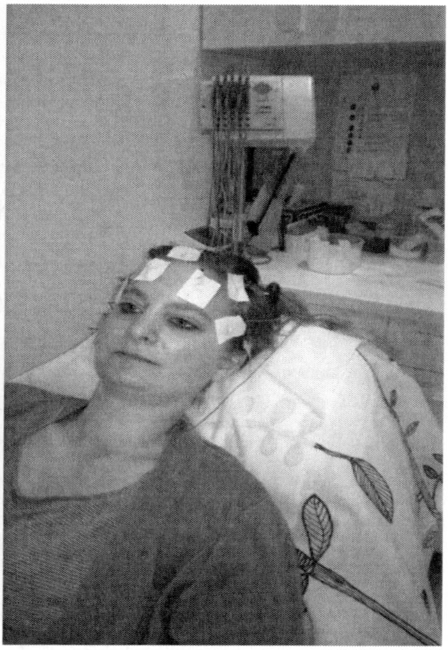

Figure 2. Neurology Center: ASMR research EEG measuring.

The research showed that the longer the research participants were exposed to sound (the sound of chewing gum/some even disliking the sound at first) the more they relaxed. The eyeball movement was measured too so it became obvious that the participants were still awake but came down and only gradually fell asleep (in some cases).

Electroencephalography (EEG) is a non-invasive method to record electrical activity of the brain along the scalp.

My own research measuring my brain activity showed that I was conscious during the entire 30 min session, yet, my brain activity was low as if the brain was switched off. All stress was forgotten and a sense of peace was achieved.

Further research participants were diagnosed as having anxiety and psychosomatic disorder. When the ASMR sounds were applied they became relaxed, became drowsy and then went into stage 1 sleep. Slight twitching of arms and legs was minimized.

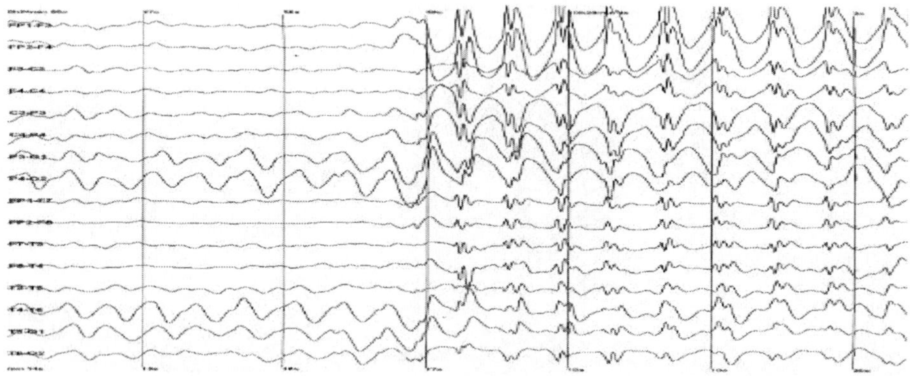

Figure 3. EEG Epileptic spike- ASMR opposite.

Further research participants had history of panic attacks and anxiety – after ASMR their minds were relaxed. Others were suffering from headaches and migraine for years – ASMR made their bodies and mind relaxed even though they still had slight headache.

Others were suffering from depression and through ASMR fully relaxed and fell into stage 2 sleep.

The research participants were asking for the link of ASMR videos and some have even replaced medication for ASMR. I believe that is worth researching and spreading the gospel [7].

It comes as no surprise that the use of ASMR within social media results in fierce critical confrontation (as everything does on social media). Nevertheless, it is up to us to see it as a serious answer to the ever-rising serious issue of anxiety and depression.

It seems impossible to write about ASMR without mentioning its great power on the social media generation and the outlet that was so needed to calm down. When silence and overwhelming information are disturbing – ASMR kicks in. There is not great power in silence anymore- but there is great power in ASMR. It seems as if the social media generation cannot stand silence anymore- it is alien to them. There was always a switched on TV, radio, mobile phone – constant flow of information to be processed. They have to be entertained. Also it means getting entertained to relax.

The challenge is to see ASMR as what it is. In fact, we do not know what it is we can just feel it. But most of what we feel cannot be explained or pinned down. This does not mean that we should ignore it; it should be explored, to be enjoyed or even used as treatment of anxiety and depression. For us to explore the brain would be an endless and never ending task. How about we recognising when we feel calm and explore it the best we can for now? We can shape progress, behaviour and outcome.

CONCLUSION

ASMR has often been dismissed as nothing more than sexualized whispering that somehow gained popularity among the social media generation; theorists however accuse it as being submissive. Very little supporting evidence of ASMR has been condemned without a fair trial to the footnotes of any academic study. It is true that when ASMR was first introduced to social media it was guilty of sexualizing experimentation to achieve views and subscribers, which had been gradually liberating itself from the suggestive narrative, divorced from sexual assumptions but celebrate the psychological effect and reality of ASMS which has outgrown its bad reputation. It must be remembered that ASMR is still a new art form (as I see it). It is only in its early years and therefore absolutes about its medium and content have to be regarded as premature. The revolution of social media highlights many of the arguments and concerns expressed at the arrival of sound in cinema and this new development will provide new insights previously held absolutes concerning what ASMR is, how it is created, perceived and how it is distributed and the effects it might have for the social media generation.

An overwhelming content supply and pressure of interactivity and availability and an economic subscription exploration of the unique qualities of the medium characterized the social media era. ASMR artists such as Maria of Gentle Whispering.com continue to extend these experiments in isolation of sexualized content. She has challenged ASMR content and revealed its unique expressive potential within the social media environment and more recent artists realized greater sophistication through using ASMR creatively [8].

Synchronized nurturing, dialogue-led whispering sounds remain the most dominant representation in ASMRs. Is this because the audience can understand and feels reminded of the nurturing sound of their own mother at home? Is it companionship without the impression of selling anything?

Whereas many critics argue that ASMR is similar to meditation, I argue that it is a complete sense of peace and calm as if "switching off your brain from the billions of daily impressions" [9]. Meditation in contrast is an out-of-body experience whereas the ASMR effect is an in-body calm. ASMR's original motivation is to nurture, bring people together who share the experience with each other and stimulate. Undoubtedly ASMR's representation of the world and the media was uniquely fenced in by people who did not understand its purpose and in my belief that never have enjoyed the benefits of ASMR. Only if you know what it is and how it feels will you be open to it and celebrate it.

No doubt, my research has shown that people with great anxiety came down by the simple sound of chewing gum. A phenomenon that was new to the neurologist and nursing team. It was extraordinary to interview the candidates (who were new to ASMR) and the waxing and whining amplitude of their result. They were conscious but free of thought. Some of them fell asleep…normally they reported that this was only possible with sleeping pills. The audience is learning how to interpret and relax with ASMR – similar to meditation – yet it is not that you leave the body, it is more a conscious cleaning of the brain and absence of thought within a happy space.

I wonder what the future will bring to ASMR. I wonder if ASMR will disappear and be replaced by even more effective relaxation method or if it will be continued and more widely accepted as what it is - a huge breakthrough of relaxation of our social media generation.

Theorists seem to ignore the audience's newly gained codes of perception of ASMR, which are a result of the social-media forums we inhabit. Never before in history were we as exposed to media and content as we are now. ASMR is a learned language of relaxation resonated by social media. If ASMR were a unique language then I would argue here that it reaches its greatest sophistication in the communication between artist and audience. Maybe, it is the frequency that we are used to by our mothers during our early years, maybe it is the sounds that we hear as embryos [10].

Similar to all social media content, traditional and mainstream ASMR needs to continually reinvent itself; embodying contemporary cultural and technical developments and advancements. In my belief, ASMR has to remain indefinable, unpredictable so that it can be experienced and enjoyed. The brain is still very much unexplored. The fact is, it works and brings down people.

In contrast to many theorists, I would strongly argue that ASMR is valid to be considered as a historical and psychological phenomenon. I believe that we have to embrace the new born ASMR content and allow it to gestate within an evolving, sophisticated and innovative social media environment. It is this innovative approach that allows it the means to continue to develop and move towards a notion of relaxation. ASMR is a new art form. It is an art that is dependent on technology, social media - yet it is not being exclusively perceived on social media (but also among individuals) but gained mainstream popularity at ASMR forums. The advances in ASMR, in its very nature, is in a constant state of evolution and the informed critical and practical response to this evolution will, I believe, result in an extension of the artistic palette of ASMR artists and will bring us closer to the essence of how social media can be used not only as a demanding tool but also a given platform.

REFERENCES

[1] Marsden, Rhodri (21 July 2012). "'Maria spends 20 minutes folding towels': Why millions are mesmerized by ASMR videos." *The Independent*. Retrieved 28 November 2012.

[2] "ASMR Triggers – Common ASMR triggers that cause tingles." *The ASMR Lab*. Retrieved 27 March 2015.

[3] Iqbal, Maneeza (6 May 2013). "ASMR artists: Videos not for sex, but for relaxation." *News10.net*. Retrieved 9 May 2013.

[4] Cheadle, Harry (31 July 2012). "ASMR, the Good Feeling No One Can Explain." *Vice.com*. Retrieved 2 December 2012.

[5] Mendonsa, Cristina (6 May 2013). "ASMR: The sound that massages your brain." *News10.net*. Retrieved 8 May 2013.

[6] Hudelson, Joshua (10 December 2012). "Listening to Whisperers: Performance, ASMR Community and Fetish on YouTube." *Sound Studies Blog*. Retrieved 13 February 2013.

[7] Novella, Steven (12 March 2012). "ASMR." *NeuroLogica*. New England Skeptical Society. Retrieved 2 December 2012.

[8] Overton, Emma (22 October 2012). "That Funny Feeling." *The McGill Daily*. Retrieved 2 December 2012.

[9] Hockridge, Stephanie (16 May 2013). "ASMR Whisper Therapy: Does it work? Relaxing, healing with sounds and a whisper." *ABC15.com*. Retrieved 28 July 2013.

[10] Jones, Lucy (12 September 2012). "Which Moments In Songs Give You Chills?." *NME*. Retrieved 23 December 2012.

In: Media Anthology
Editor: Theophilus Kofi Gokah
ISBN: 978-1-63484-931-9

Chapter 3

THE IRONY OF THE INDIAN EDUCATION SYSTEM PORTRAYED IN THE NOVEL OF CHETAN BHAGAT: FIVE POINT SOMEONE

***Saheel Iqbal*[1,*], *Lajwanti Kishnani*[1,†] *and Vipul Parmarthi*[2,‡]**
[1]School of Engineering
Birla Institute of Technology and Science, Pilani, Dubai
Academic City, Dubai, UAE
[2]Senior Lecturer
Govt Polytechnic College Gwalior
Gwalior, Madhya Pradesh, India

ABSTRACT

Chetan Bhagat is a prolific Indian writer who has dealt with key problems of the youth in India. His novels are spun around various social and cultural pressures in the society and above all to add to the dressing he adds a romantic twist to the entire story. He uses his writing as a proactive pill which stimulates the mind to find or ponder over the desired innovative changes in a patriarchal society. In his novel *Five Point Someone* he subtly questions the orthodox Indian Education System

* Email id: saheel438@gmail.com.
† Email id: sanjanakishnani@gmail.com.
‡ Email id: vipul.parmarthi@gmail.com.

which identifies knowledge of students in terms of the grades and CGPA they score. The novel is set at the backdrop of the premiere Engineering Institute of India, the IIT and makes us think that there is a need to improve our education system. The ideologies of Chetan Bhagat fantasize the vitality of pursuing one's dreams. His books are an impeccable reflection of his life. Relating to his own personal experiences, Chetan Bhagat presents his novel in a simple, yet very powerful way that never fails to impress the audience and most importantly the media. His novel was regarded with great favour that he gained a prominent status in various media platforms, like news channels, radio shows, and other social media platforms. The present paper tries to underline the attempts made by the author to highlight the study pressure and other performance related stress put on engineering students and the plaudits of the media that the book acknowledged.

INTRODUCTION

Five Point Someone: What Not To Do At IIT by Chetan Bhagat remains to be one of the biggest selling and most widely read English novels published in India since its release in the year 2004, and is one of the two main focuses of this project. This was Bhagat's debut novel, and is written majorly out of his own experiences at IIT Delhi. As the title of the book suggests, it is not a guide on how to get into IIT, and this is the note on which the author begins his novel. Through this novel, he has tried to bring out a lot of his concerns regarding the present education system and how it is failing the purpose of its original existence. He has also made an attempt to explain to his readers how screwed up and haywire your life can get in college if you lose sight of what you want to do and try to mess with the "system." Though he lived through 4 years at IIT and then 2 at IIM, the author's true passion dwelled in literature, and to bring about a change in the society through his written word. He is very much against a lot of the stereotypical mentalities people tend to have. More than the admission process of getting into the biggest educational institute in India, it is the education and learning process itself that he is concerned with. In fact, he suggests that getting into IIT isn't that a big a deal contrary to usual beliefs. As he mentioned in the book, he believes that if one can lock himself up in a room with book for two years and throw away the key, one can probably make it there.

In this novel, Chetan Bhagat has explored youth cultures and their issues. Through the characters of Hari Kumar, Ryan Oberoi and Alok Gupta, he has depicted the world of the youth, their cultures, challenges, difficulties, attitudes, contrasting interests, tastes, their expectations, ambitions, rebelliousness, their ways of dealing with stress, troubles, love, friendship, family and the many more issues they face on a daily basis. In addition to their personal woes, a lot of light is also thrown on college-life-culture, fresher-senior categorization, ragging sessions, hostel life, the sick education system, stressful exams and GPA, competition among students, and classification based on marks.

The novel is centered around major autobiographical elements. Through this story, Chetan Bhagat has managed to reflect his personal belief and the biblical concept of "Believe in thyself." It weighs the importance of the more important things in life over the mediocre things such as marks and GPAs. In the present day world, in the era of knowledge-based economy, where knowledge is transmitted at a rapid pace, those who have the knowledge are the winners. To prove his/her own talents and in order to succeed in this age of globalization with cut-throat competition, one should have a combination of multifarious potentialities. Advancements in technology, innovation, adventurous spirits and initiatives are the keys to success nowadays. It is evident that education is the cradle of talented people and human resources.

THE WAKE UP CALL

Through his novel, Bhagat has indirectly conveyed a very serious message in a humorous tone. This is a wakeup call for the elite technical institutions to replace the traditional style of "I teach; you listen" with the more sensible methodologies, say for example the age-old ideology of the Kurukshetra, where the primary motive of education was for a student to gain knowledge and values to survive in the world, something he will carry with him to his grave. He wishes for the educational institutes to inculcate a technique that will widen students' own potential to gather, choose, filter and incorporate information that inspires their ingenuity by developing their life-long capabilities; and teaches them how to learn proficiently and dynamically. The prominence should be on placed more on learning methods, rather than mere accumulation of knowledge to outsmart the other. Students need to be taught how to turn their knowledge, however great or little, into innovative ability and knowledge application ability. The book, in a not-so-subtle, but also in a sort of mild tone points out how our technical institutions have become so lifeless and mark-oriented and have lost the actual purpose of education, and how they need reformation.

The Stars of Our Show

- ***Set Location:*** The novel is set in the Indian Institute of Technology, Delhi, between the years 1991 to 1995.
- ***The Cast:*** The story is about the three heroes of the book:-
  - *The Cool Dude* - Ryan Oberoi,
  - *The Narrator* - Hari Kumar, and
  - *The Cry Baby* -Alok Gupta.
  - *The Girl-* Neha Cherian (daughter of The Evil Professor)
  - *The Evil Professor* - Dr. Cherian, Head of the Mechanical Engineering Department at IIT-D.

The Story Line:

The book begins off with the customary "ragging sessions" in the hostel at night. The rowdy senior Baku and his minion followers ragged the freshers in every extreme way, and on the first night, it was Hari, Alok and Ryan's turn. They were called out to the lawn in the center of the Kumaon hostel, and the seniors made these guys strip their clothes off. And just when what was supposed to be a friendly way of getting to know the juniors was about to turn into something very bad, Ryan saves Hari and Alok. He beats up Baku's minions and threatens to do worse if they don't let them go. And there began the friendship of the three. It was a very filmy but amazing start to a friendship that would take them through their entire four years of engineering at IIT, Delhi.

Right in their first lecture Manufacturing Processes, Prof. Dubey asks them to define a "machine." He then defines it as,

> The definition of a machine is simple. It is anything that reduced human effort. Anything. So see, the world around you is full of machines." [1]

To this, Ryan asks,

> "Sir, what about a gym machine, like a bench press or something? That doesn't reduce human effort. In fact, it increases it. Perhaps it yours is too simple a definition then?" [2]

Prof. Dubey then replies,

> What are you trying to do? Are you saying that I am wrong? What it son. In my class, just watch it." [3]

This very clearly depicts the typical attitude of professors who think they know it all, and don't even consider that the students' approach may be a correct in a way. It also shows the helplessness of the Professors' to handle the brilliant students who can pose challenging questions based on their common sense. This kind of mentality of professors is a way of stifling a student's ideas, just to make himself look smarter and the student stupider.

"It's a Damn Jail!"

As mentioned earlier, Ryan didn't like the whole aspect of "mugging," the studying trend at IIT. When he saw his friends sitting and studying all evening, he gets frustrated with it all. He prefers the idea of actually learning something through practical experiences rather than just writing notes mechanically all morning and mugging them up all evening. He expresses himself in the words

> "You call this a life? I think it is a jail. It really is. Damn jail." [4]

Alok, to this responds by saying,

> "Call it what you want, but that is not going to change it. Maybe you're forgetting that you're in IIT, the best college in the country. You expect a certain standard." [5]

Ryan replies saying

> "This is high standard? Working like moronic drones until midnight? ManPro yesterday, ApMech day before, Quanto today… it never ends." [6]

He is the exact depiction of what Chetan Bhagat wishes every student would have the freedom to be in India. Alok on the other hand, is what lakhs of students in India are forced to become, due to immense pressure right from their childhood from their parents, friends, school, teachers, and then from their university and professors. Just because they study in IIT, they believe that they should mug all night to score more, rather than gain some real knowledge and learn something through practical experiences and creating something with it. A lot of the students, like Venkat from the book and maybe even Alok develop the attitude of "More Marks, Better Reputation." This is also the primary attitude of majority of the professors. A lot of students in India face this issue where their creativity and ideas get stifled just because they don't have an impressive academic grade sheet to show off. So much of the potential of our youth goes unused, because due to continuous degradation from family and faculty, they lose every tiny bit of spark they have within them to achieve their ambitions, leaving them frustrated and lost. This exactly is what Bhagat wishes to point out.

Further in the book, the boys mess up their first quiz at IIT as they lose out on time to study and their marks drop way below the class average, leaving them unknowingly taking their first steps into becoming five pointers. After that they decide to cooperate with each other and help in terms of doing assignments and also enjoying. But all efforts fail and Alok how has family pressures decides to involve more with intelligent students to get good CGPAs. Although, inspite of the distance maintained by Alok, Ryan remains a faithful friend and helps Alok''s father to get hospitalized during a heart attack. Alok the returns to the trio and they enjoy a party with all five pointers. At this party Ryan comes with a "MICE THEORY," which he explains in his own words:

> "This IIT system is nothing but a mice race. It is not a rat race, mind you, as rats sound somewhat shrewd and clever. So it is not about that. It is about mindlessly running a race for four years, in every class, every assignment and every test. It is a race where profs judge you every ten steps, with a GPA stamped on you every semester. Profs who have no idea what science and learning are about. Yes, that is what I think of the profs, I mean, what have IITs given to this country? Name one invention in the last three decades. This system is an unfair race. If you are a mouse who thinks or pauses to make friends with other runners, or stops to figure out what you want to do in life, or drag baggage from the past, then you will be pushed behind. We can change all that. By living on our own terms. By being rats, not mice, work together and beat the system. I will not give up my friends for this system. In fact, my friendships will beat the system." [7]

"More Marks, More Money"

"More Marks, More Money." And in order to get there, student end up giving into unfair practices. They cheat, lie, copy and do whatever it takes to be better than the other. It is all about the competition now. People are ready to do anything it takes to outsmart the rest and then be a topper. It may be for mere fame, or like Alok of our story, to get a good placement with a good salary. You will find a very very small fraction of people learning just for the sake of gaining actual knowledge. The book *Five Point Someone* was adapted into a Bollywood movie called *3 Idiots.* In that movie, the role of Ryan Oberoi was played by Ranchodhdas Chanchadh. The boy never studied, never slogged, never mugged like the rest. He enjoyed every topic he studied and things like "coming first in class," or "being better than the others" were the last things on his mind. Though he never studied a lot, he came first in class for all the three years of his college life. And just like Ryan of the book, Rancho too was against the education system in his college, the disgusting grading system that is partial to the toppers and underestimates the average performers. Even in the movie there was a character called Chatur Ramalingam who was the depiction of Venkat from the book. He was a very serious competitor who did not believe in gaining actual knowledge, but just wanted to mug all day in order to be better than the others. These characters give us such a clear idea of how things have become nowadays. Parents themselves teach their children how to be selfish when it comes to studies and not help the others, just so that they can be the better ones. They teach kids how not to share the knowledge that they have so that they can get better marks and inculcate all the wrong habits in the kids at a very young age. By the time kids join school, they realize how important marks are, and how much more popularity they gain if they are the toppers, so in order to get there they become selfish, cheat, lie, copy and what not just to get those few extra marks. No matter how severe the "punishments" get in school, the kids never stop resorting to such activities. The children are not made to understand the more serious and valuable things in life that matter more than just getting those few extra marks. Their relatives, families, teachers and friends pressurize them from a very young age, making them believe that it is most important to outsmart others rather than gaining knowledge for themselves. This kind of influence from everyone affects their line of thought from a young age. And when they get to college, everything just gets heightened. These again can be considered as results of Social and Developmental Psychology, which as a result affect the cognitive skills of a person. Cognitive skills means the way a

person thinks, perceives and approaches a particular situation in life. In this case, these situations affect students in such a negative way that entirely change their cognitive skills. So instead of making them strong dignified individuals, the system is making students turn into selfish unfair people. In short, education is supposed to empower mankind, but instead it is ruining them. Ryan rightly remarks

> "1. It suppresses talent and individual spirit.
> 2. It extracts the best years of one's life from the country's brightest minds.
> 3. It judges you with a draconian system that destroys relationships.
> 4. The profs don't care for the students.
> 5. IIT's have hardly contributed to the country." [8]

The novel ends on a very positive note when Dr. Cherian identifies their talent when they submit a research proposal on Lubricants. He in fact confesses that this proposal would be invited by any investor and would do a good deal of business too.

"It has gained sufficient Media acclaim"

Chetan Bhagat has a strong flair for the written word. His writing style is appealing, and creates an exclusive first-time expression among the reading crowd. The present era doesn't expect superhero comic tales, or framed love stories. *Five Point Someone* justifies the wistfulness and its story background is written in such a succulent manner that the common youth can relate to it. It talks about the loopholes in the Indian Education System, and how students should focus on pursuing one's own dreams. It also provides a vibrant insight on various cultural backgrounds of Indians, how we meet people from different parts of the country under one roof in Hostels and how life changes. These are things that happen in the everyday life of a youth and thus, every youth undergoes a plethora of emotions. Not only the cult college group, but even the adult class tend to reminisce their college life days, and the various other happenings in life. His books have often been made into super-hit Bollywood movies, with *Five Point Someone* being made as the multi-million grossing movie '3-Idiots.' 3-Idiots beautifully depicted the honest and relatable emotions portrayed in the novel. Chetan Bhagat's novel is a popular cult among the youth, and thus, it naturally gains humongous attention of the media. Due to the popularity of the novel, he has gradually gained importance in various media platforms, like news channels, radio shows, and other social media platforms as well. He has a huge fan-following on Facebook and Twitter, and also makes frequent appearances on News Channels to discuss about the importance of writing and reading. The movies based on his novels have been nothing less than a "SUPER-HIT." They have received worldwide critical media acclaim and still continue to trend among various other movies.

CONCLUSION

Through his book, *Five Point Someone,* Chetan Bhagat has given a call for the pedagogues to come out of their traditional text book theories and face the challenges propounded by their pupils. Another prominent aspect of the book is that the whole background of the story is set in an engineering college where a student should be encouraged to bring forth his ideas or concepts in an innovative way so that he has an opportunity to have hands-on experience. Only by going about with this kind of an approach will help the country advance both technically and economically. Though it may not seem too significant, this plays a big role in this aspect. Every individual is bestowed with a unique set of skills and qualities, and something as little as a CGPA should not be the criteria to judge them and determine their future potential. Just holding a few exams at the end of a semester is not enough in any way to evaluate the intelligence level of any student. Someone who is a five pointer may reach the highest peaks of success at some point in life and may become an inspiration to hundreds of students who are like what he once was.

> "Though the trio suffers the ridicule of the teachers as well as the classmates, they avow to reform the patriarchal system of education" [9].

They thoroughly dislike the age-old teaching system and the grading system. the system demands them to endlessly mug books after books in order to get the good grades needed to be considered "smart," but none of the emphasis is given on gaining practical experience rather than just bookish knowledge. The author gives emphasis on the practical method of "learning by doing," just as he wished things would have been back in his college days. He intends to bring about a change in this system, which helps students get rid of the tedious tasks of mugging day in and day out. He believes that this method will help students face and solve issues in a more natural kind of way which utilizes their thinking and implementing skills. They learn innovative methods to solve problems put before them, and should they go wrong some time, they can always discuss with their classmates which will just broaden their horizons and help them improve their knowledge. Bhagat grieves for the sterile dogmatism of the education system.

Chetan Bhagat has a very straightforward approach to life. He strongly believes in the voice of his soul, which he never fails to listen to. Though he may face losses at the initial stages of his life, the man how listens to his inner voice always emerges out victorious. This is very clear in the life of the three boys. They under perform in their exams, are seen as losers by the other students and are considered useless by their professors. They are the exact opposite of the other people they study with. They are free thinkers, true lovers of life, harbingers of inventive ideas, images of freedom and precursors of youth-calling-approach. Despite all the failures they faced in the four years of their college life, they never gave up their confidence. They worked harder than ever on their project and towards the end got it accepted and emerged successful and achieved a good name among the professors and students.

Though Bhagat studied at the IIT himself, and emerged as the Best Outgoing Student when he graduated from the IIM, he thoroughly hated the teaching techniques employed in these colleges in India. He gave up his highly paid job to carry forward his dream of bringing a change in the Indian society through his written word. He is not just a novel writer, but also a motivational speaker and column writer, and through the years has stuck by his principles and philosophy in all this books, speeches and articles.

His work might not go down in history, but he definitely sets an example and till today, stands as an inspiration to every youth. His education in the top educational institutions of India, like IIT and IIM didn't deter his determination towards his writing desire. He continues writing about the everyday experiences he underwent in various horizons of life.

REFERENCES

[1] Bhagat, C. (2004). Five Point Someone. *Rupa and Co., New Delhi,* pp-9.

[2] Ibid, pp-10.

[3] Ibid, pp -11.

[4] Ibid, pp -14.

[5] Ibid, pp -14.

[6] Ibid, pp -14.

[7] Ibid, pp-101.
[8] Ibid, pp-107-108.
[9] Biswas, M.D. (2013, April). The Criterion: Depiction of Youth in Chetan Bhagat's Five Point Someone. pp-6.

ABOUT THE AUTHORS

Saheel Iqbal. Student, BITS Pilani Dubai Campus. Pursuing B.E (hons) Mechanical. He hails from Kashmir India and has completed his school studies amidst the beautiful valley of Kashmir. This is the author's first publication. A frequent speaker at various events in BITS Pilani Dubai, he looks forward to gain more experience in the real world. The author is involved in drama and sports at college level and is highly interested in sales and marketing.

Email id: saheel438@gmail.com.

Phone No: +971526740765

Dr. Lajwanti Kishnani. Assistant Professor, BITS Pilani Dubai Campus.

Ph.D. in English Literature by Devi Ahilya Vishwavidyalaya, Indore on the topic – "China Perceived through Christianity in the Fiction of Pearl S. Buck." (March. 2009). In the field of English teaching since fifteen years. Has written around 15 research papers and guided several UG projects. Keen interest in psychology, music and travelling.

Email id: sanjanakishnani@gmail.com.

Phone No: 9685808318

Vipul Parmarthi. Senior Lecturer, Govt Polytechnic College Gwalior. M. Phil in English Literature and has authored around 18 research papers. Keen interest in Hindu Philosophy,Astrology and spirituality.

Email id: vipul.parmarthi@gmail.com.

Phone No: 9425125576

In: Media Anthology
Editor: Theophilus Kofi Gokah

ISBN: 978-1-63484-931-9

Chapter 4

VIRALITY OF THE MALE GAZE: THE SELFIE AND COMMODIFICATION OF WOMEN

Meena T. Pillai*

Director, Centre for Cultural Studies
Director, School of English and Foreign Languages
University of Kerala, Trivandrum, India

ABSTRACT

This paper seeks to analyse how the representational politics of the selfie implicates the gendered gaze as a significant theme. In a culture obsessed with visibility and images, the 'selfie' is no longer read as an apolitical act confined to the relative isolation of virtual spaces. It further argues that in traditional societies, which nevertheless have been inculcated into neoliberal economies, the selfie becomes the metaphor for the rise of individual self in contrast to earlier valorization of tradition and community, with its entailing strategies of production, distribution and promotion of the self. Within a capitalist economy that encourages heightened levels of commodification of bodies, desires and new economies of consumption, women might themselves have imbibed and internalized the male gaze in their wresting of agency in constructions of the selfie. Between this double bind of surveillance and freedom, is it possible for a woman to take place within a selfie?

---

* meenatpillai@gmail.com.

> Producing a reflection of your image in Instagram always involves an awareness of the presence of others, the knowledge that your selfie is flaking and refracting in their phones. Labelling this reflection #selfie tacitly recognizes the horizontal proliferation of reflections, the dissolution of personhood in the network. The real narcissists are the ones who never take selfies. They imagine their self as autonomous, hermetic—too precious to be shared.
>
> (Brian Droitcour)

SELFIE AND THE SELF

Jacques Lacan speaks of the 'Mirror Stage' as one of the most dramatic of phases in the development of the human psyche. Somewhere between 6 and 18 months of age, the child for the first time looks into a mirror and recognizes his or her own image. This is the first connection made between the human body's corporeality and its specular possibilities. Within this context, it is interesting to note that the subject of the selfie is a contradictory pseudo-self mired in Lacanian misrecognition. The selfie is ultimately the public projection of a constructed figure intended to symbolize the self in a particular scenario. As with a child gazing into a mirror, the subject gazes into the specular selfie and identifies with it but is also alienated and othered by its status as an object of the controlling gaze. The child realizes that the image is 'I' but also 'not I.' Thus, the mirror stage talks about a fundamental gap between the subject and its own self or *imago*, which can never be bridged. An *imago* is not a simple image; it is an unconscious idealized mental image of someone. The function of all narratives in human history and art, whether literary, visual, oral or cinematic, has been to bridge this gap between the subject and its ideal image, in essence revealing the travails of the subject to reintegrate his or her alienated image. In the age of endless mechanical reproduction of images, this is what the selfie, as the postmodern avatar of the politics and aesthetics of self-representation, seeks to do. The subjecthood conferred by the selfie is also thus a fragmentary one where the self is reified for social approval.

There is a perceived need today not to mistake the selfie simply as an 'innocent' picture of one's own self, but to place it squarely in its context, of being a purely digital object and therefore evincing the characteristic features of innumerable and unknown circuits of circulation, storage and leakage (Shah 2015). However, as a digital object the selfie also slides elusively beyond cartographies of the state panopticon, poising itself in ambivalent spaces between technologies of the self and technologies of power. In traditional societies, which nevertheless have been inculcated into neoliberal economies, the selfie becomes the metaphor for the rise of the individual self in contrast to the earlier valorization of tradition and community, with its entailing strategies of production, distribution and promotion of the self. This process, supposedly operating within a neoliberal governmentality is however characterized by an 'omniopticon,' the many surveilling the many. The governmentality of digital objects and the bodies associated with them being a virtual impossibility leads to the entry of new regulatory regimes that are both internal and external to the state. The new and complex relationships forged between state policies, ideological state apparatus, civil society, corporate agendas and individual actors in evolving new forms of surveillance and punishment of offending bodies, and their gendered implications need to be studied.

Gender and Digital Cultures of Misogyny

In a culture obsessed with visibility and images, the 'selfie' is no longer read as an apolitical act confined to the relative isolation of virtual spaces. This paper seeks to analyse how the representational politics of the selfie implicates the gendered gaze as a significant theme. Therefore, the possibility that within a capitalist economy that encourages heightened levels of commodification of bodies and desires and new economies of consumption, women might themselves have imbibed and internalized the male gaze in their wresting of agency in constructions of the selfie. Between this double bind of surveillance and freedom, is it all possible for a woman to take place within a selfie?

"I am my body. I am not ONLY my body, but I am what I look like, too. And I find it powerful to represent myself, as I am, to the rest of the world (or whoever gives a cuss enough to notice). I like the colours, angles and intricacies of my physicality. I'm okay with what I look like today, and that's a big of a massive leap for me-kind" (Chrissy Par. 4). She goes on to say "Selfies are NOT, by their nature, unfeminist. Self-representation is hugely powerful for women. Blogging gives the average person, indeed the average woman a huge voice and reach. And you'd be amazed just how awesome a lot of these 'average' women are" (Par. 5). So here you have women who feel that they have been puppets in others stories, that men have represented them, whether it be art or culture, shaped and sculpted by the hands of men. The blogger goes on to say for example " Sure, the selfie has set its own precedents that are not always challenging to the cultural standard for how women are told they 'should' be represented, but at least the camera is in the hands of the woman herself. It's a starting point, people. One of the things that my instinct is often to be ashamed of is that I like to try on a nice dress now and then and take a photo of myself in it. It's like it suggests a level of self-acceptance that's a bit, well, unacceptable for the average woman" (Par. 6). This woman is here retaliating to a lot of the selfie shaming that seems to be part of the discourses around the selfie.

So even as the self gets circulated through the selfie, the self is stored and its privacy is indeterminably destroyed and leaked, there are a lot of regulatory regimes operating at each of the steps in this process. The gendered selfie invites an incredible amount of violence in the digital public sphere. This reiterates the gender violence that are explicitly there in our own ordinary and mundane day-to-day lives. Most often, as has been pointed out by many (Shah 2015), there is the tag of a slut associated with a woman's selfie giving strong clues on how patriarchal languages and structures mimic themselves in digital cultures too. Thus you see how our imagoes or idealised images of the self are also disrupted and spoilt by violent sexual language and sexist bullying. The word slut here is not used literally but has interesting cultural markers. It means "a woman who is dirty, unkempt, and unmarked by her belonging to a man and his home; a woman out in public" (Shah 89). For me the most important part of this description is the last part, a woman unmarked by her belonging, a woman out in public. Thus one can see here how a woman's body out in public spaces is an offending body and it has to be punished by society. This is often a social and cultural punishment sanctioned by the majority of the community and legal validity is never either invoked or felt to be binding. However as already pointed out the selfie can itself be seen as a subversive attempt to reclaim public and digital spaces by daring to make the private public and in that sense celebrating 'sluttiness.' But it also explicated how digital stripping, digital shaming, hate speeches, and digital rape make online spaces continue the very same misogyny found offline, more importantly without recourse to many regulatory mechanisms that can contain or punish such offences.

The representational ethos of the selfie implicates gender politics as a significant theme in its analysis. Sarah Gram argues that "the selfie, in the end is about the gendered labour of young girls under capitalism" in order to model their bodies as objects under "economies of attention" (Par. 14). The ability of the genre to generate self-image, and to grant freedom of expression is part of the provocation it engenders; women's selfies do claim agency to present their bodies as they deem fit. *The Guardian* reports that "selfie culture is a new battleground for the Iranian regime," highlighting the role of self-photography in women's movements across patriarchal countries (Tehran Bureau Correspondent Par. 1). Yet, as John Berger explains in *Ways of Seeing:* "A woman must continually watch herself. She is almost continually accompanied by her own image of herself" (qtd. in Gram Par. 1). Ingrained in sexist patterns of viewing, the woman's self-representation is never entirely emancipated from the male gaze. One disturbing dimension of the selfie is that it celebrates the overt sexualizing of female bodies for the pleasure of male voyeurism, and plays into the notion that a woman's public visibility hinges on her sexual attractiveness. A new study of young people's media behaviour in Sweden shows that girls as young as ten market themselves using manipulated selfies with 'duck face' poses where the lips are pouted and the body is held in sexually titillating poses unlike boys who take selfies playing computer games and strike passive, stony faced masculine poses. Thus the selfie replicates conventional macho masculinity and sexy femininity.

THE MARKET

The selfie, by virtue of the social forces that act upon it, move beyond the realm of photography and aesthetics to inhabit the niche of a rich cultural commentary on the self; it is a site where the capitalist market moulds citizens but also a zone of challenge to the stereotypical notions of selfhood thus cultivated. Amidst the explosion of images on the TV that is the hallmark of the late twentieth and of the twenty-first centuries, and the steady expansion of accessible visuals on the Internet, selfies function as promotional pieces for the self, rendered flawless and artistic with the aid of photo editing softwares. Each frame delineates personal theories and mainstream ideologies – the revelation of positions on concepts like beauty, power, money, gender, society and so on. The selfie allows an opportunity to flaunt buying power, create desire and envy, to market values and attitudes; all in the ambit of the market economy where the individual in the selfie is recast as a faithful consumerist subject whose body is marked with recognizable products. In a sense, representation of an individual in these terms completes the capitalist myth of 'wholesome living,' of the happiness, peace and joy that is to be had from the possession and purchase of goods. As management guru, Tom Peters articulates, "We are CEOs of our own companies: Me, Inc. To be in business today, our most important job is head marketer for the brand called you" (qtd.

in Davis 48). Intersecting both private and public spheres at a crucial juncture where identity is being constructed and declared, the selfie also denotes what Ralph Turner identified as "a shift in the locus of the self" – movement along a spectrum that ranges from "institution" to "impulse" (989). Breaking away from conventional expressions based on traditional institutions such as religion, family etc., the paradigm of the selfie is the representation of the 'real,' spontaneous and supposedly unmediated self (Davis 44). Self-image is saliently transformed into a monument of commoditization and consumerism, in turn directing the subject to relate to the self in terms of the market – as something that is defined by the consumption of goods and capital. In an age of liberalization and globalization we see how women groom themselves up to market orientations, turning themselves into spectacles, using their bodies as ageless, size zero objects that are ready to be consumed.

Selfie and a Pornographic Public Sphere

It is interesting to think of the concept of the pornographic public sphere (Agger 36) where the very word pornographic speaks of cultures of over sharing, where everything is shared and laid bare. For example you have naked selfies on dating sites. Invisibility has become an impossibility Ben Agger has commented on how the selfie is about presence and absence and how internet makes possible a viral presence (47). However, like pornography, there are disembodied bodies that we see on the screen, bodies that are dehumanized. So even when women like Chrissy feel that the selfie gives them control over their own representation and makes what was merely an object through the lens of a photographic into a subject, there are however very little instances of gender play or attempts to destabilise gender politics. Most of the selfies I looked at actually strengthened gendered representations and gender stereotypes. Also it is imperative that we read the selfie not simply as a cultural object but as "an object of relationships between the different sites of storage, practices of circulation, and bodies that leak," which makes it difficult to pin it down "because it is not one object but a series of circulating objects that are constantly replicating, being stored beyond the intentions of the user, and exposing the subjects of the selfies to unintended audiences and advances" (Shah 88). Therefore, at one level there is the celebration of the selfie as the ultimate symbol of the right over representations of the self, while at another level you have selfies strengthening gender stereotypes and objectification, in the process exposing themselves to more and more pornographic intentions and having new regimes of the gaze scrutinizing and punishing them in the process.

Little Histories and Pseudo Social Mobility

Selfies always project the democratisation ideal, claiming to narrate little histories of average men and women. In a neoliberal economy where the market is open, images are in excess and goods are mobile, people who lack social mobility achieve a semblance of it through the social media where identities seem to be in circulation, which can create a feeling of mobility and liberation. However this is also based on a miscognisance, because only those 'I's that are predicated on a consumable 'I' are in circulation, explicating how social hierarchies, dominant hegemonic assumptions regarding colour, sexuality, desirability and 'coolness' are replicated and strengthened in digital spaces. As one avid anonymous blogger points out "The selfie may be a bid to break out the cage of identity and let go of anxious control over it, but when others consume and comment on the selfie, they aren't helping you destroy that cage but are shoving you back in it. They are affirming that you are a discrete self, one baseball card in the pack, and your statistics alone will always be printed on the back" (Marginal Utility Annex Par. 17). Thus the selfie as a moment of breaking free, proclaiming your independence over your right to representation, is actually capitulating to the very same logic of the market and the network, where you make yourself into a 'tradeable image,' one that can be put into circulation in the digital network.

Moreover the body that speaks through a selfie is not an innocent body. It is always already codified and structured by numerous ideological markers like class, caste, race, and ethnicity. The so-called liberated subject that the selfie articulates is not spoken in any original or authentic language of identity (the self has not invented a language) but is written in a language already inscribed by the multiple poles of affective identity politics. So there are multiple emotive risks involved in creating an image of the self as body, the risk of being 'less feminine,' of being 'less white,' of being 'too black,' 'too fat' etc. So the hierarchies of racial, gender, ethnic stereotypes are often seen to be replicated in the selfie.

Selfies in fact can help question the singular definitions of beauty that cultures and societies lay down and to the attribution of women's primary function as sex objects. The aesthetics of the body and the beauty ideals seem however to be heightened by the majority of selfies where at the most fundamental level of the apparatus, resolution with dark skin in dark light continues to pose problems in smartphone cameras. The photo apps, the filters and other editing modes continue to emphasise the hegemonic Americanised paradigms of beauty that have become so homogenously commodified in the global market today. Even as feminist selfies, which flout the standard definitions of hegemonic beauty, flood the digital world, there is nevertheless a digital marginalization of selfies that do not conform to the racially biased model of socially acceptable feminine beauty. Thus such selfies remain ossified in their private spaces and might not get the circulation or viewer ship that feminine selfies get. The digital privilege accorded to whiteness or fair-skinned women and sexy, toned bodies as symbols of femininity create a backlash in having a negative impact upon the self-image of non-White females, particular Black and Brown women. Many of the selfies engage in playful and ironic dialogues both with the ideas of women's emancipation and freedom from stereotypes as also the celebration of sexual power and liberation from the male gaze. Many of the feminist selfies also try to generate a critique of women who have agency and choice but choose to exercise them to turn themselves into commodified sexual objects constructed in tune to male gaze. I find especially useful in this context Susan Browmiller's contention that the origins of femininity can be found in the borrowed affectations of upper class status, its relationship to the seductive glamour of the biologically female body, and in the historical subjugation of women through sexual violence, religion and law where the myths around women were propagated as biological facts.

So from women who remain insecure and unfinished products in the long process to femininity, to women who are scrambling to meet the endless demands of a market driven hyper-femininity, to feminists who are striving to sabotage the male gaze, what defines the modern woman's attempt to represent themselves amidst complex historical, political and market forces is both the centrality of the gaze and its more promiscuous contemporary digital virality.

The gendered questions around the politics of women's self representation in the selfies are mired in a tenuous postfeminist terrain characterised by the complex dynamics of women's agency, women's desire, consumption and a proliferation of everyday images of the ideal feminine and the feminist. (Yvonne Tasker and Diane Negris 2007) in their introduction to *Interrogating Postfeminism* speaks of how a postfeminist culture "works in part to incorporate, assume, or naturalize aspects of feminism," crucially also working to "commodify feminism via the figure of the woman as empowered consumer" (2). Emphatically "White and middle class by default" postfeminism is anchored in "consumption as a strategy (and leisure as a site) for the production of the self" (Tasker and Negris 2). Thus while remaining mired in a consumerist economy, it nevertheless invokes the rhetoric of feminism for its support. The selfie often becomes the most apt digital metaphor for the marginalisation of feminist politics within postfeminist cultures. Both the construction and rejection of femininity, its celebration and renegotiation, are predicated upon the male gaze that seeks to create a binary opposition between feminism and femininity or subsumes the former in the latter. In its enabling and delimiting potential the selfie is symptomatic of the gendered coding, regulation and control of women's bodies, the disconnect between female agency and social power, the disjuncture between postfeminist cultures and feminist politics, and the 'severe feminine neurosis' that cultures of misogyny engender in both digital spaces and consumer societies.

In: Media Anthology
Editor: Theophilus Kofi Gokah

ISBN: 978-1-63484-931-9

Chapter 5

COMPARISON OF CRIME SOLVING PROCEDURES BETWEEN INDIAN AND WESTERN TELEVISION CRIME SHOWS

Revathy Rajan*
School of Media and Communication
Manipal University Dubai, Dubai, UAE

ABSTRACT

This research paper aims to analyse and study the difference in crime solving processes between Western and Indian crime shows. It is no hidden fact that television plays an important role when it comes to informing and communicating to people about such procedural occurrences in crime genre. While there are established commonalities that are observed at all crime scenes, there are notable differences between the ways crime investigation is handled in the Indian subcontinent and the Western world. It clarifies how contemporary and previous television crime shows reflect those differences to a wide scale audience. To further understand these differences, a content analysis of episodes from both Western and Indian shows was conducted, to help give further insight into the portrayal of investigative procedures in these shows. The coding structure used revolves around certain factors such as, characterization, usage of technology, and types of violence and conviction rate of criminals in the episodes. The results shows that there

* revathy.rajan@hotmail.com.

were significant differences between the two sets of crime shows, ranging from a high level of portrayal of violence in the Western sample to solving crimes without much technological assistance in the Indian sample.

INTRODUCTION

Be it Western or Indian, there is fascination with law and crime television. This is where mass media, more specifically, television, takes advantage of this curiosity and attempts to 'educate' the population. Television has since been one of the sources of sharing news and series, ranging from fictional to reality (Gerbner, 1986). While television has been a medium of providing a lot of information and knowledge on many topics, it is a little disconcerting to note just how much of an impact crime procedurals have on audiences. This has been the primary topic of many researches, which indicate that public knowledge about crime and related processes has been gathered from the media. It has also been indicated there is a direct proportionality between prolonged exposure to television crime shows and fear of crime amongst the public (Brown, 2012). Other researchers have also noted that the perception of audiences often get altered from too much exposure to various kinds of crime shows and begin to expect investigative procedures to occur with the same accuracy in reality as well (Lutfy, 2013).

Regardless, serial dramas of this particular genre have always been rather popular amongst people, with pretty high ratings. It is this kind of success that has brought in the need to analyse just how crime related procedures are portrayed and how varied it is in different shows that makes audiences so hypnotised.

One cause of this fascination could be because shows like 'Law and Order,' make use of actual crime incidents and fictionalize it for their episodes (Eschholz, Images of Prime Time Justice: A Content Analysis OF 'NYPD Blue' and 'Law and Order,' 2004). Apart from the effect on audiences, there has also been an impact on courtroom jurors as well. Due to prolonged exposure to idealized portrayal of forensic science capabilities on television, many jurors often tended to expect the same kind of staggering capabilities in real-life criminal system (Cole, 2009). It is also noted that these unrealistic perceptions end up affecting the jury's final verdicts in actual case trials, simply because forensic evidences aren't presented in a way that is expected.

This is an all too serious cause, since it raises doubts, as observers, even attorneys, would begin to question the law and their faith in the jury.

Described further along are the different television shows that were taken as research sample, the first two from Western and the other two from Indian subcontinent.

'Criminal Minds' is different from the typical investigative procedurals, due to the fact that the crimes are solved, mainly by trying to understand the psychology of the criminal, a technique known as 'profiling the criminal.' Rather than focusing solely on the forensic clues and evidence, the FBI agents analyze the criminal's initial kill and anticipate the UNSUB'S (unknown subject) next move before the criminal resorts to murder once more.

On the other hand, *'CSI: Crime Scene Investigation'* is a standard crime show in the sense that much like many police procedurals, the forensic specialists in this particular television drama find the serial killer by applying heavy emphasis onto the crime and all the clues left behind at the crime scene. The characters do not attempt to go towards the behavioral aspect of the criminal, and rather only rely on facts and scientific testing conducted with the clues. Instead of employing the method of getting 'inside the perpetrator's head,' these forensic specialists working for Las Vegas Police Department examine and collect evidence from the crime scene and find the trail that will lead to the criminal.

'C.I.D. (Crime Investigation Department)' is one of the most popular crime detective series in India and also one that's been on air for eighteen years. The plot revolves around a team of investigators who track down the perpetrators by simply following up on the clues discovered at the scene of the crime. This is an anthology series, wherein there are not only different cases in each episode and season, but even a different set of characters as well. The protagonists are a group of police officers belonging to the Crime Investigation Department of police force, set in the state of Mumbai, India.

A more recent Indian television crime show that was aired in the year 2012 is '*Police Files.*' This particular show has more of a realistic sense to it since there is a display of cases that have occurred in a few North Indian states. Added to that, the audience is also provided with in-depth explanations regarding details of various crimes that have been committed such as why and how could the criminal have gone about committing those acts of violence.

It is no hidden fact that on more than one occasion, the media played an influential role in shaping the public's opinions on a variety of topics, including politics, economy, law and so on (A. Baum, 2008). Keeping that in mind, it would be highly safe to assume that their perceptions about crime and criminals are shaped by many television serials, much like the ones that are mentioned above. (K. P. Chan, 2012). For the time being, this may not seem like a major issue to be concerned about but in terms of the effect that these forms of media have on the public, there are two issues; does regular exposure to brutal crime shows create fear amongst the audience and does this fear influence attitudes about various criminal justice policies? (Dowler, 2003).

Quite a number of researches (Gerbner, 1986) have indicated that the public tends to develop a 'mean world syndrome' and an unnaturally horrific conception of reality as a result of frequently viewing crime related serials. Keeping at par with that, there is also a direct and strong relationship between television viewing and fear of crime. (Heath, 1987) Furthermore, it is not uncommon to find that many of the audience members who are exposed to forensic science and crime genre shows on a regular basis do not possess a science background (Cavender, 2007). This makes it all the more easy for the crime shows and serials to bend or accurately shape the public's viewpoint about law related policies and processes.

The topic of this study was grey and not much information was known on this particular topic so there has been the usage of adjoining literature in order for further explanations.

Keywords and Operational Definitions

Crime: An act committed in violation of law where the consequence of conviction by a court is punishment, especially where the punishment is a serious one such as imprisonment (American Heritage, 2011).

Perpetrator: Someone who has committed a crime or a violent or harmful act (Cambridge Dictionaries, Undated).

Profiling: The analysis of a person's psychological and behavioral characteristics, so as to assess whether they are likely to have committed a crime under investigation (Collins Dictionary, 2015).

Investigative: To inquire in detail in order to learn the facts about something hidden or complex, especially in an attempt to find motive, cause or culprit (Dictionary, 2011).

Conceptual Understanding

It is becoming increasingly evident that public knowledge related to crime genre, has been derived from the media, in the form of both fictional television and reality shows. Be it violence, the portrayal of crime solving procedure, or simply the characters, there has always been an intrigue amongst audiences of the world about crime and this has been made obvious by the high successes of television crime dramas.

Ultimately, these are the types of shows that can give people a false impression about the legal system and it's works (Dowler, 2003). This sort of impact that these crime dramas have on the public has been given the term, 'CSI effect,' coined by legal authorities (Cavender, 2007). The television drama, CSI: Crime Scene Investigation has always been highly popular, along with its related series, CSI: Miami and CSI: New York. In Indian television, a lot of shows have played quite a role in providing viewers with all sorts of information regarding crime related topics, and still continue to do so. Television serials like CID and Crime Patrol have been on air for more than a decade, broadcasting all sorts of violent and not-so-violent crimes and even showing to audiences the various methods applied to catch criminals.

Types of Crimes

Most episodes, however, focus on forensic techniques that are more reminiscent of science fiction than true investigative practice (Tyler, 2006). Having watched some of the episodes, it is indeed evident that the whole process they portray in order to find the killer seems a little too good to be true. Mentioning in connection with that, in certain shows like Criminal Minds, not only is the crime being committed at the beginning of the episode, but the identity of the criminal is shown to the viewers as well. Since the audience is already aware of this identity, they feel it's perfectly acceptable if the legal system acts in an unjust way towards the suspect. Additionally, they may also not like to know that judges are protecting the criminal's rights, even though that is how the legal system works in reality (McNeely, 1995).

Even when it comes to the time rate of the forensic procedures, especially in the collection of clues against the suspect and receiving results, shows like CSI provide unrealistic episodes in terms of the speed at which the forensic analysts get the results (Hughes, 2007). Another related observation that is to be noted is that, the shows televise all sorts of violent acts in places that are more of an urban setting (Heath, 1987). This is all the more obvious from the CSI franchise, wherein the series take place in Las Vegas, Miami and New York, which are some of the most prominent and high class places in the United States.

Judiciary and Execution

In courtrooms as well, jurors were often confused when versions were portrayed of scientific methods of collection of results with the actual scientific processes (Cole, 2009). It is also noted that these 'unrealistic' perceptions end up affecting the jury's final verdicts in actual case trials, simply because forensic evidences aren't presented in a way that they would have expected. One of the other notable side effects due to influential views of these crime dramas has been: rapid rate of increase in forensics and criminology undergraduate students across the States (Heinrick, 2006). Apart from criminals and the techniques, when it comes to showcasing violent crimes, there is a high rate of exaggeration in serial crime dramas (Eschholz, Crime on Television, 2003). The killings are televised in a brutal manner, more than the extent of what happens in reality, thereby initiating and increasing fear amongst audiences as well. This in turn led to a fear of victimisation of crimes amongst many members of the audience, even though they may not have actually been victims of a crime, simply by being exposed to these kind of shows (Williams, 2000). This is not only true for viewers of fictional crime shows, but for reality television as well. There is a bit more interest in this type of reality viewing, for these dramas portray the actuality of police work to the public and for this reason, the stories do not become stale (Prosise, 2004).

Crime Genres in Indian and Western TV

While there have been such extensive researches on the crime genre and its effects in the States, it is to be observed that such integrated researches have not been found on the study of Indian television crime dramas. Taking into consideration this as a research gap, the content exploration of certain Indian shows, which is being done for this particular research paper, will give an exact idea as to how the crime procedurals in the Indian dramas is showcased differently from that of the Western style, thereby providing a method to understand the content televised in Indian serials.

Regardless of this, it is seen that many of the both Indian and Western crime show episodes have a recurring feature of emphasizing on more of violent crimes, than non-violent ones. Due to this kind of frequent exposure, viewers may either get desensitized to violent displays even in real life or they may start wanting more, much like a drug of sorts. But despite these so called media effects, it is no lie that there is indeed a flow of information about various crimes and how they are solved differently in the Indian subcontinent and the Western part of the world.

Objectives

- To compare the crime solving procedurals between Indian and Western crime shows
- To explore how much of reality related to crime is exaggerated in the shows
- To analyse the crime shows based on certain criteria

RESEARCH DESIGN

The design in this study was by watching two Western crime television shows and two Indian crime shows and then, observing the differences. This approach was chosen as it was deemed best-suited in order to properly analyse the content in these shows. It also gave me (the author) a wider view of understanding as to how various crimes are solved in both types of shows and will further assist me with the analysis. A list of comparisons was made based on certain factors such as, the duration taken to catch the criminal, usage of high tech gadgets and technological procedures, whether there is more focus on the clues in the crime scene or profiling based on the crime and amount of violence that is shown.

Taking up the procedure of purposive sampling, four shows from both the West as well as Indian ones, based on high ratings of viewership were selected. My sample consists of two Western shows, CSI: Crime Scene Investigation and the second one being Criminal Minds. With these two choices, I noted different perspectives especially from the Western drama.

From the Indian shows, I selected 'CID,' being one of the oldest crime shows released in India and is still being aired on television. My second choice was Police Files, the reason being that it is a relatively newer show.

Annexure

Shows	Episodes	Duration Of Each Episode
CSI:Crime Scene Investigation	3	45 minutes
CID	3	50 minutes
Police Files	3	45 minutes
Criminal Minds	3	45 minutes

Coding Structure

Factors for Analysis: (Western and Indian Crime Shows)

USAGE OF TECHNOLOGY
MAJOR FOCUS ON CLUES OR PROFILING OF CRIMINAL THROUGH VICTIMOLOGY
TYPES OF VIOLENCE
CHARACTERIZATION
TERMINOLOGY
DURATION TAKEN TO APPREHEND THE CRIMINAL

Analysis

Usage of Technology

Having watched episodes of both CSI and Criminal Minds, it is observed that there is reliance on technology by the protagonists in order to catch the perpetrator. This is very much evident in Criminal Minds, wherein the BAU (Behavioral Analysis Unit) have their own computer specialist and she uses her skills to hack into systems or even trace down all existing records of the particular suspect. In the CSI season one episode, 'Pledging Mr. Johnson,' one of the forensic specialists himself uses an equipment known as an 'assimilation tank' in order to recreate the entire setting of the lake where the victim had been drowned, in order to get a clue. Additionally, in an episode of season two, 'For the Bully,' one of the lab technicians used a software in order to identify words from a faded notebook, that helped lead the forensic team to the killer.

In the episodes of both Indian shows, there is minimal reliance on technology by the investigators to apprehend the villain. In fact, in certain episodes, there is no technical assistance at all. But apart from using this factor to point out the intelligence of the investigators, the reason that equipment is not needed is possibly because of the simplicity of the crime. The protagonists do not seem to face as many difficulties as seen in the Western shows, thereby not requiring any sophisticated gadgets to find the killer.

Duration Taken to Apprehend the Criminal

In both Western shows, (CSI and Criminal Minds), the perpetrator is captured within the duration of one episode. Starting off with the crime being committed, the episode proceeds with the investigators following the clues or profiling the criminal, and by the end of the episode, they managed to apprehend the murderer. However, there are certain cases that extend onto a two-part episode, as can be seen at the end of season one of Criminal Minds. The last episode was titled, 'The Fisher King: Part 1,' by the end of which, the UNSUB was still on the loose, and so the case was extended onto the beginning of season two, which was titled, 'The Fisher King: Part 2.' It was only at the closing of this episode, that the perpetrator was apprehended. There is also another special situation, wherein the seventh season of the show, CSI: Crime Scene Investigation, one particular villain 'The Miniature Killer' was the main antagonist throughout the season and was only identified and caught at the end of the season.

Whilst there may be certain shows in the Indian subcontinent that portray a long delay in capturing the criminal, this was not the case in CID or CID: Special Bureau. The villain was apprehended by the end of the episode, which in relevance to the storyline in the show, lasted for a couple of days. Unlike in the Western shows, there were no unique circumstances where investigators were after the same criminal or killer for months. There are certain cases, which get continued onto another episode, like in the show CID, the episode 'Varun Dhawan Khatre Mein' was extended as another episode and only at the end of it, was the criminal captured.

Types of Violence

One of the stable features evident in the Western shows is the frequent emphasis on violent crimes, like torture and murder. Even in terms of the killings, it is shown that in most episodes, the murder techniques aren't simple like a gunshot wound or getting stabbed with a weapon. Rather, the victims are often tied up and tortured or in some cases, even raped, before their bodies are dumped either at a public location or at an inconspicuous place, depending on whether the criminal wants to send out a particular message. The continuous portrayal of murder in the crime shows is hardly a surprise, considering the emotional thread that it carries: depicting a loss of life, leading to those who mourn for that individual, which is highly relatable to the audience and keeps them hooked on. Being exposed to this kind of violence may also tend to make the audience more cautious in their day to day activities as to who they interact with and so on.

The display of violence and sheer brute force when it comes to torturing or killing the victims is very much minimal in the Indian shows, as compared to the Western counterpart. Yes, the crimes being committed in both CID and CID: Special Bureau include that of murder and kidnapping, but instead of directly portraying to the audience the gory scenes of how the victim was killed, it is only the dead body that is shown to viewers. If there is one negative point that is to be noted, it is that the emotional pain experienced by the loved ones of the victim does not appear obvious; this makes it difficult for me as a viewer to completely feel the loss of that one life.

Major Focus on Clues or Profiling of Criminals through Victimology

In the Western show, CSI: Crime Scene Investigation, the protagonists are a team of forensic investigators, who apprehend criminals by simply following the clues and finding the trail. They do not attempt to understand the psychosis of the criminal and instead, purely unite with the forces of forensic science to help them solve the cases. Whilst this is the typical fashion of showcasing a crime series, the other show-Criminal Minds-varies from this in a distinguishable manner. In this particular television show, the protagonists work for the FBI and are a part of the BAU (Behavioral Analysis Unit), a specialized department that employs behavioral psychology in order to solve crimes and catch the criminal. They are usually called upon to close up time-sensitive crimes, especially ones that involve a string of murders or in other words, serial killing. This is why the forensic specialists and investigators on these shows are shown to be working with a sense of urgency, knowing that they cannot let the criminal's pace get ahead of them and their tactics.

In the Indian shows, there isn't much of an importance on the profiling of the criminal, and it is just the team of investigators and officers, examining and analyzing the crime scene in order to apprehend the perpetrator. The characters also draw on the assistance of medical examiners, in order to receive details about the corpse that could help them track down the criminal by figuring out his or her M.O., which is a Latin phrase 'Modus operandi' and roughly translates into '*mode of operation*' applied by the criminal to commit to crime. Neither of the shows dwells on the psychology of the offender nor analyzes the psychosis of the perpetrator as to whether he could have committed the crime due to some mental illness. Instead, they only look for means and motive and once it is established, they arrest the offender.

CHARACTERIZATION

In the Western show, Criminal Minds, the main protagonists involve four male characters and three female ones. This is quite a good number since it goes on to show that there is no emphasized preference to representing only males in the crime genre television shows. All the characters roughly get the same amount of screen time as well and there is no evident discrimination. In terms of having protagonists of different races, one of the characters, Derek Morgan, is an African American, and is the only one whereas the rest of the team doesn't divert from the traditional American representation. This typical scenario is noted even in the case of the investigative team from the other Western show, CSI: Crime Scene Investigation. From these two observations, it can be rightly stated that there is an under-representation of other races. The representation of criminals is also quite similar as well, the most notable point being that the violent perpetrators all come from middle-class background, and furthermore, they have spouses and children of their own. In a way, this sends a message to viewers, one that says even the most ordinary and normal people have violent tendencies and the audience must be cautious when interacting with people in their everyday lives.

In the Indian shows, there is a similar over-representation of male lead characters, which is either portraying that not a lot of females apply for investigative related careers, or it is reaching out to the viewers' thinking that men are more efficient than woman when it comes to this kind of an occupation. Additionally, the investigators who are constantly working on the field are not shown to be as physically fit and robust as the protagonists in the Western shows. If there is a need for the show creators to keep in touch with realism, it shouldn't be that way, since field investigators will find it difficult to keep up with the criminal in a chase, if they are not fit enough. The criminals and killers represented here possess lesser violent tendencies and instead of displaying excruciating and torturous methods of murdering someone, the shows' criminals execute basic killing techniques, such as gunshots, stabbings and road accidents. The perpetrators either come from a middle-class background or a lower-class status, those that happen to get involved with the wrong sort of people.

TERMINOLOGY

In both the Western shows, there is heavy usage of terms that are completely crime genre specific in every episode. Be it the criminal's methodology of committing the crime, or the technique employed by the investigators to solve it, there is a mention of various terms. Some of these include, *embezzlement*[1], *larceny*[2], *assault and battery*[3], *forgery*[4], and so on. The creators perhaps work with the notion that the audience have a background in science and are already familiar with the terms, hence the exchange of the exact meaning of the terms does not happen between the protagonists. These happen to be common terms in the crime world, but when talking to the victim's loved ones, the language and terms are toned down a bit.

However, the terminology scenario is different in the case of the Indian shows. There is not much mention of a crime related vocabulary; rather, everything is stated in a simplistic fashion. Granted, the forensic investigators give a proper explanation as to how the crime was committed but they do so without delving into jargons and not giving much importance to the specific words. There is both an advantage and disadvantage here; the former being that it is very much easy for viewers to understand and the latter being that the

---

[1] Withholding assets in a dishonest fashion for the purpose of theft of such assets.

[2] Unlawfully taking hold of a person's private property.

[3] A combination consisting of threat of violence and actually inflicting physical violence.

[4] The act of making imitations of objects or documents with the intent to deceive and alter public perception.

show ends up playing not much of a big role in educating the audience more about the crime genre.

CONCLUSION

Television shows play a major role when it comes to influencing the perception of audiences when it comes to the genre of crime. But as was seen from the above analysis, it is not just about the display of cold-hearted murder and other acts of violence, but indicates deep emotional hooks as well. Both Western shows rely heavily on usage of pure science and believe that every crime, violent or not, has a scientific methodology that needs to be applied when it comes to apprehending the offender. The analysis also establishes that this sort of increasing crime shows, both Western and Indian types, have always played a role in entertaining and informing audiences about the crime genre, and will possibly continue to do so.

Furthermore, it has also been noted that the Indian shows have not reached the level of technological sophistication that is seen in Western depictions. With the ever increasing developments in the field of forensic technology, it is becoming easier and easier to identify perpetrators but neither Indian television programs have taken advantage of this particular factor. The direct involvement of the police department and their officers in solving crimes and finding justice is also emphasized upon in Indian shows, whereas in the Western portrayals, it is rather a different section of law enforcement (BAU, Forensic Specialists), that are responsible for capturing the criminal and not 'policemen' as such. This goes on to show that all crimes do not fall under the same criteria of 'importance' and depending on the jurisdiction of authority that the law enforcers possess, each violent or non-violent crime will be dealt with in a different manner.

Be it an Indian or a Western show, crime genre television programs have exaggerated the accuracies and speed with which villains have been captured, thereby leading the audience to believe the same phenomenon happens in reality. The Indian shows make the investigative procedures appear easier, in comparison to the style of the Western shows, wherein the protagonists face a wider range of complexities that hinders their process every now and then. All this plays a huge role when it comes to understanding just how and why investigative procedures vary in the Western and the Indian subcontinent.

Further research in the qualitative field may explain the observations that were found using quantitative methodology.

In: Media Anthology
Editor: Theophilus Kofi Gokah
ISBN: 978-1-63484-931-9

Chapter 6

CELEBRITY ENDORSEMENTS ON YOUTH BUYING BEHAVIOUR

*Kanika Mathur**
Manipal University Dubai,
School of Media and Communication,
Dubai, UAE

ABSTRACT

Celebrity endorsements are believed to greatly influence the buying behaviour of consumers. Many leading firms use celebrities as endorsers to sell their products. Celebrities are often used as endorsers because they are seen as credible and reliable sources. They serve as a bridge between the brands themselves and the image of the brands in the minds of consumers. It is also believed that celebrity endorsements enhance certain characteristics of products, which makes them more desirable. Celebrity endorsements have therefore been used extensively over the years because of the benefits they offer. The emergence of youth as an integral part of the consumer sector makes them a primary target for most celebrity endorsements. This research paper thus focused on the impact of celebrity endorsements on youth buying behaviour. This paper also aimed to find out the factors, which determine the extent to which, celebrity endorsements influence buying behavior of youths. Some of the factors that were taken into consideration were monthly allowances of students,

* E-mail: kanikamathur46@gmail.com.

spending habits, relatability to celebrity endorsers and exposure to celebrity endorsements.

It was found that students were neutral to celebrity endorsements, which meant that there was no significant impact of celebrity endorsements on youth buying behaviour. Data was collected through questionnaires, the results of which are discussed.

INTRODUCTION

In modern competitive market marketers need to come up with different techniques to stand out from their competitors. Marketers have thus developed celebrity endorsements wherein well-recognized celebrities associate themselves with products and advertise it. Celebrities could be athletes, film stars, television actors and so on.

Since celebrities use their public recognition to endorse a product, their association with the product makes its presence more noticeable in the market. Furthermore, the use of celebrities in screen advertisements helps to grab the attention of viewers since viewers can relate to their favourite celebrities. Consumers try to purchase those products and services that correspond to their own self-image or personality (Kasana and Chaudhary 2014). For example, a person who imagines him/herself as a well-dressed sports-person like David Beckham may consider purchasing products endorsed by him, such as Police sunglasses.

Celebrities are also used in advertisements because it is believed that they lend their credibility to a product (Escalas and Bettman 2015). All may not trust a brand or product that is newly released in the market; but as soon as a celebrity is associated with the product, consumers begin to view the product as reliable and may choose to purchase it. Therefore, celebrity endorsement is perceived to be an effective marketing strategy. This is especially true in the case of youth as consumers.

The youth looks for products that allow them to express their individuality. Celebrity endorsements introduce them to products that give them the opportunity to do the same. The youth will, as a result, gradually becomes well informed since information regarding current trends in the market is readily available to them. This increases their influence on parent's buying decision. Targeting young people in their early years also makes them potential brand loyal consumers in the long run. This makes the youth a target audience for most celebrity endorsements.

REVIEW OF LITERATURE

Over the years, advertising has become more prominent across all forms of media and is used by marketers for the promotion of various products and services. In recent times, celebrity endorsements have become a part of the promotional strategy for advertisers.

The definition of a celebrity according to McCracken (1989) is, "… any individual who enjoys public recognition and who uses this on behalf of a consumer good by appearing with it in an advertisement" (see also Byrne, Whitehead and Breen 2003). The term Celebrity could also refer to an individual who is known to the public (actor, sports figure, entertainer, etc.) for his or her achievements in areas other than that of the product class endorsed (Friedman 1979).

Endorsement is a medium of communication in which a celebrity is appointed as the spokesperson for a particular brand, and thereby communicates about the brand itself by associating himself/herself with the brand. The selected celebrity extends his/her name, popularity and status in the society or knowledge in a specific area (Roll 2014). Therefore, when one uses the term 'Celebrity Endorsements,' it refers to companies using celebrities as spokespersons with the intention of informing consumers about a particular product in the market, by linking the characteristics of the celebrity with the characteristics of a product.

Marketers target youths as they serve as potential consumers. In a large market where there are endless options to choose from, youths are more likely to choose those products that they can best be used to describe themselves. Celebrities are often used by companies as they are known to have "stopping power," where celebrities are used to attract attention of publics to messages that are aimed at them (Poturak and Kadric 2013).

Marketers may also use celebrity endorsements as a means to build trust in the minds of young consumers. It is important to build trust among consumers rather than simply persuading consumers to buy a product. Due to the wide variety of choices consumers have, consumers tend to buy only those products which are tried and tested by them and have lived up to their expectations. Celebrities see this as an opportunity to connect with their fans in a different way and better establish their position in their respective fields, as well as gain acceptability from consumers as reliable product endorsers (Manjusha and Segar 2013).

For any kind of marketing strategy to work, it is important to analyze consumer-buying behaviour. Understanding consumer buying behaviour helps serves as a vital tool for marketers to predict changes in consumer tastes and preferences and develop those strategies, which would effectively influence their buying behaviour. Brand awareness is one of the key factors, which impact a consumer's decision to buy a product. This ensures that consumers are aware of the existence of a particular brand in the market and are able to recall the brand name (Brosekhan and Velayutham 2008).

Celebrity endorsements are thus used to create a brand image and help potential consumers recognize a particular brand, given the wide variety of brands consumers can choose from. It is important to understand the conditions for effective celebrity endorsements. A celebrity should have the quality of being liked by all, should be physically attractive and have a desirable personality which creates impact on another person (Agarwal, Kumar, and Kumar 2013).

However, there have been cases where the outward appearance of a celebrity is not a matter of concern. There are youth members who remain unaffected by the physical appearance of celebrity endorsers. According to an article in a UAE based newspaper, *The National Swan* (2014) which published the research findings of Mari Ouhan, youth consumers rely more on the expertise of the endorser rather than the endorser's physical appearances.

Celebrities who seem to be credible endorsers also have an impact on the purchase decisions of consumers and brand loyalty (Rashid, Nallamuthu and Sidin 2002). Brand loyalty refers to preference of a brand over other brands and repeat purchases of products or services from the same brand (Urde 1994). Endorsers who concentrated on portraying themselves as knowledgeable in advertisements were able to influence the purchasing decision of consumers and ensure repeat purchases by them.

Consumers also tend to believe the notion that a company has good reputation and credibility if a celebrity is endorsing their product. It makes it easier for consumers to remember the brand. According to the research findings of Apejoye (2013), youth consumers can recall those advertisements which are endorsed by celebrities more easily than those advertisements which are not endorsed by celebrities. For example, Lakme - a cosmetic brand is easier to identify and recall since it was endorsed by a celebrity (Kareena Kapoor), as opposed to other cosmetic brands which were non-celebrity endorsed (Dengra 2014).

A study conducted by Ghani and Kakakhel (2011) shows that the relationship between the product to be endorsed and the choice of the celebrity endorsing the product is directly proportional. Students would prefer to choose only those products, which are endorsed by celebrities they can relate to. An appropriate example to substantiate this statement would be the Indian drinking chocolate brand, Boost, which is endorsed by celebrity sportsperson Sachin Tendulkar. If a student who wants to be a cricketer with high stamina, he would prefer to buy Boost drinking chocolate, in place of another brand.

Apart from relatability, another factor that influences consumers is quality. People tend to perceive products endorsed by celebrities as superior in quality, as opposed to non-celebrity endorsed products. So even if there is no difference between one brand of soap from the other, the brand of soap, which is endorsed by a celebrity, will be considered as of a greater quality.

Social status is another factor that can influence consumer-buying behavior. It refers to the position of an individual in a social hierarchy. Different sections of the society who form diverse social groups serve as the target audience for most advertisements. Consumers in different social groups have different opinions on products and services that may or may not be of use to them. Marketers use this to their advantage and highlight certain features of products and services that show that the use of the product or service will increase their social status in the society (Dzisah and Ocloo 2013). For example, advertisements may show that by owning an expensive watch, you can easily fit into the crowd that considers you to be "cool."

Some consumers may have a tendency to believe that celebrities endorse products because of their liking for the product, disregarding the thought that celebrities may also take up endorsements in return for a big fee (Silvera and Austad 2004).

It is also important to highlight the drawbacks of celebrity endorsements. Many a times, the same celebrity endorses several other brands. This can lead to confusion about which brands the celebrity actually likes. Consumers may also mistake one brand for another in case they forget the brands' name, which the celebrity has endorsed. Furthermore, with many competitors resorting to this technique of advertising, it is hard for consumers to realize which brand is better than the other.

However, the fact that celebrity endorsements have a major role to play in affecting consumer's buying behaviour is evident, from the above discussion. Due to this phenomenon, consumers find it easier to recall brands, remain brand loyal, and be aware of the products available in the market. Celebrity Endorsements are also beneficial for celebrities as they can reach out to their audience and gain their trust.

It is however important to find out the extent to which celebrity endorsements impact youth buying behaviour in order to judge the real power of this tool.

OBJECTIVE OF THE STUDY

To find out the extent to which celebrity endorsements have an impact on youth buying behavior.

Two criteria were taken into consideration while finding out the extent of impact celebrity endorsements have on the youth –

1. Influence on purchasing decision.
2. Belief in claims made by celebrity endorsements.

- To find out if the youth considers celebrity endorsements to be positive or negative.
- To find out if the impact of youth buying behaviour is dependent on the following factors-
    - Exposure to celebrity endorsements
    - Income
    - Gender of the celebrity endorsing the product
    - Relatability of self to the celebrity endorsing the product

RESEARCH DESIGN

This research paper was exploratory in nature since its objective of this paper was to study how the youth is affected by celebrity endorsements. Since data collected was statistical and involved numbers and percentages, systematic methods were used to collect data. Thus, the data was quantitative in nature.

Data Collection Source

Primary Data: Primary sources of data came from university students. A questionnaire with a list of 10 questions was distributed among the sample population. This data was then represented in the forms of tables and graphs.

Secondary Data: Secondary sources of data included pre-existing research papers, which were published in journals. Sources also included newspaper and web articles.

Questionnaire Design

The questionnaire was designed with the help of expert opinion. The questions were designed to focus on the factors affecting the way in which the youth reacts to celebrity endorsements and their buying behavior thereof. The questionnaire was distributed among students studying in different departments in Manipal University Dubai.

Sampling Design

The sampling method chosen for the purpose of this research was Purposive Sampling Method. The chosen target population for the purpose of this research was the different departments at Manipal University Dubai.

FINDINGS AND ANALYSIS

Students from various departments at Manipal University Dubai responded to the survey that was distributed to them. The total number of students that responded to the questionnaire was 105. The following pages will discuss the results of the questionnaire.

Age

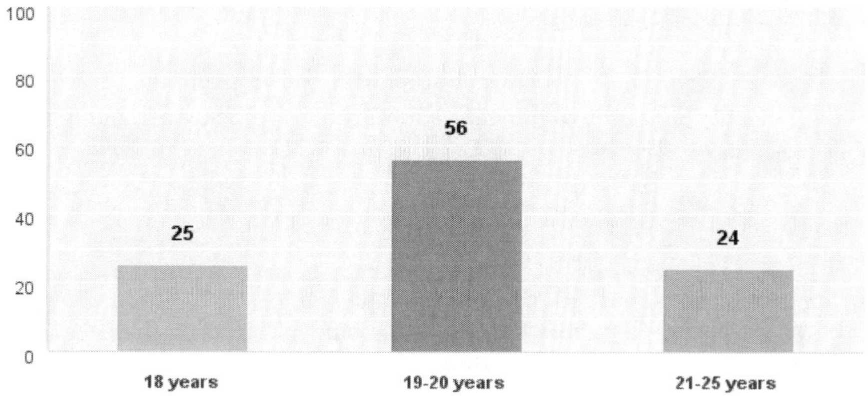

Figure 1. Age of students.

Figure 2. Gender of students.

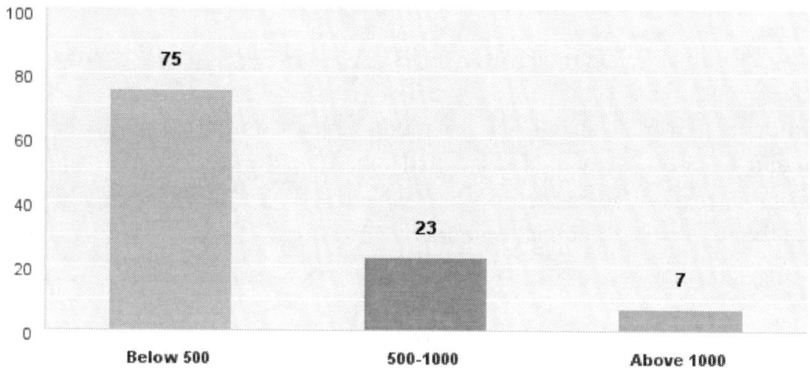

Figure 3. Monthly allowance of students.

Majority of the students who answered the survey belonged to the age group of 19-20 years, followed by 18 year olds, and students belonging to the age group of 21 – 25 years.

Gender

From the above chart almost 60% of the students who participated in the survey were females. The distribution was not biased as more females than males were willing participants (Defeo 2013).

Monthly Allowance

Monthly allowance was a key element of youth buying behaviour. The more allowance the youth has, the more purchasing power they have. This provides them greater opportunity to spend more. The monthly allowance of most students was below 500 Dirhams, as can be seen from the above graph in figure 3.

BUYING BEHAVIOUR PATTERN

The buying pattern of participants in the study was also examined (figure 4). According to the results obtained from the questionnaire, majority of the students spent their monthly allowance on food (63%). Students spend the least of their allowance on music/movies (< 1%).

This revelation is in line with Lane and Fisher's (2015) study, which suggests that students are not overly influenced in spending on celebrity-endorsed products. Although they do watch celebrity promotion shows on television, it was only for the sake of entertainment.

Purchasing Decision

As we can see from figure 5, 51 students were neutral when asked if their monthly allowance influenced their purchasing decision in case of celebrity endorsements.

Answer Choices	Responses	
Electronics / Gadgets / Video Games	8.57%	9
Car (Petrol, servicing)	4.76%	5
Food	62.86%	66
Accessories / Personal Care (Clothing, handbags, beauty products)	16.19%	17
Music / Movies	1.90%	2
Concerts & Events	0.95%	1
Other (please specify)	4.76%	5
Total		105

Figure 4. Buying behaviour pattern.

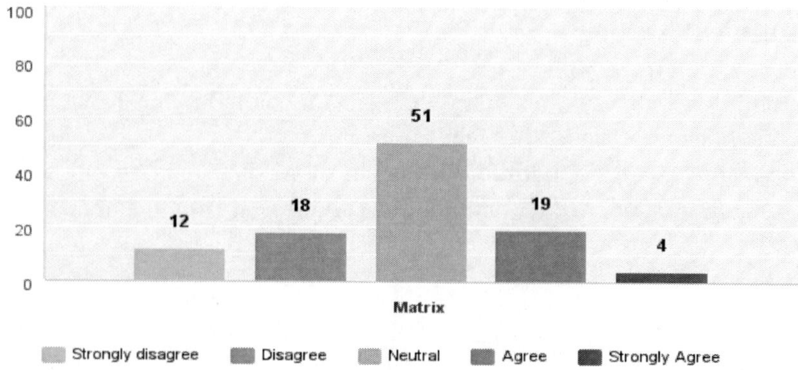

Figure 5. Relationship between monthly allowance and purchasing decision in case of celebrity endorsements.

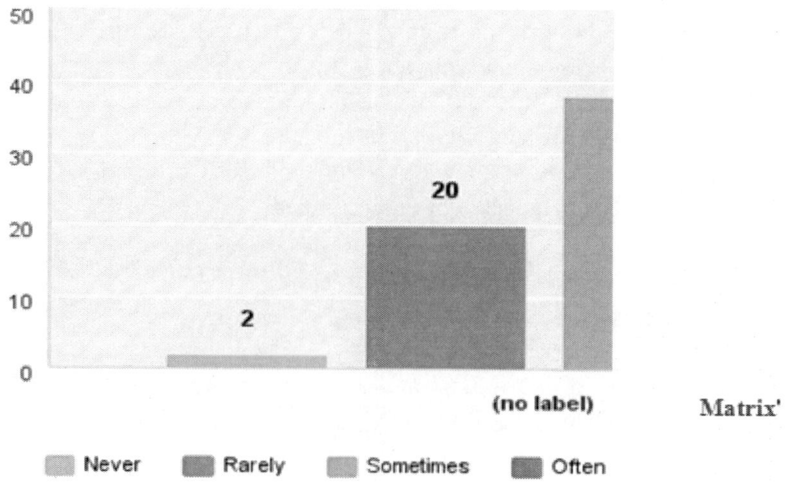

Figure 6. Exposure to celebrity endorsements.

This indicates that monthly allowance may or may not affect their purchasing decision.

EXPOSURE TO CELEBRITY ENDORSEMENTS

Figure 6 shows that 44 students come across endorsements, which feature celebrities. This indicates that the chances for students to be influenced by celebrity endorsements also increase.

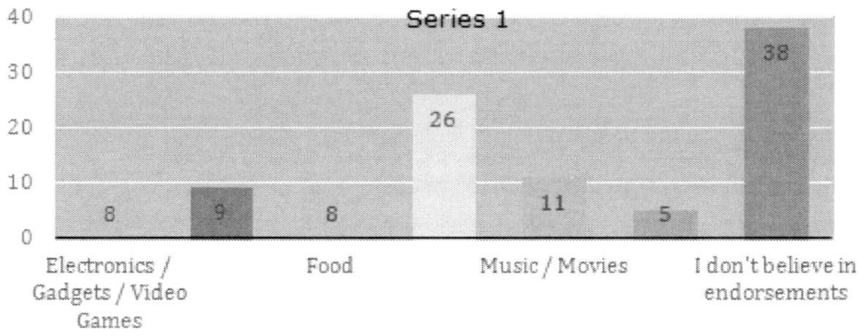

Figure 7. Belief in celebrity endorsements and type of product being endorsed.

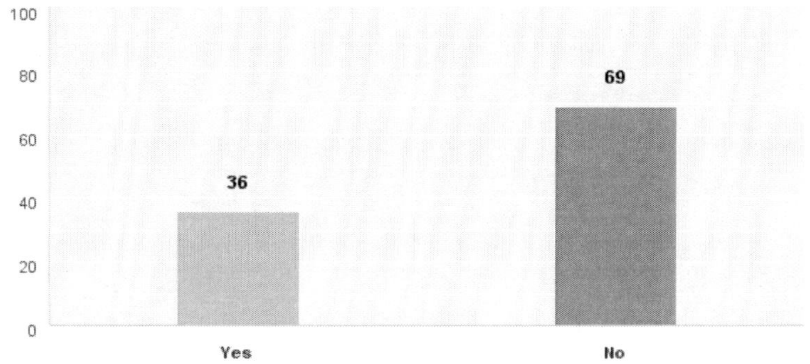

Figure 8. Gender of celebrity endorsers.

Belief in Celebrity Endorsements and Type of Product Being Endorsed

This question is integral for the research paper as it was designed to measure the extent to which celebrity endorsements have an impact on youth buying behaviour. Figure 7 shows that 38 students do not believe in celebrity endorsements. This indicates that the students are not affected by endorsements, as compared to those students who have listed their preferred product to be endorsed from the choices that were given to them.

Gender of the Celebrity Endorser

The data in Figure 8 implies that the impact of celebrity endorsement is not dependent on gender of the celebrity endorser. As many as 69 respondents were of this view as opposed to 36 who thought the gender of endorsers is relevant in influencing their decision to buy or consume a product.

Relatability of Self to the Endorser

Celebrity endorsements use certain features of celebrities to enhance essential characteristics of products. The above graph (figure 9) reveals that 69 students are more likely to a buy the endorsed product if they are able to relate themselves with the endorser. This indicates that students have increased chances of purchasing those products that are endorsed by celebrities who possess characteristics, which students can relate to.

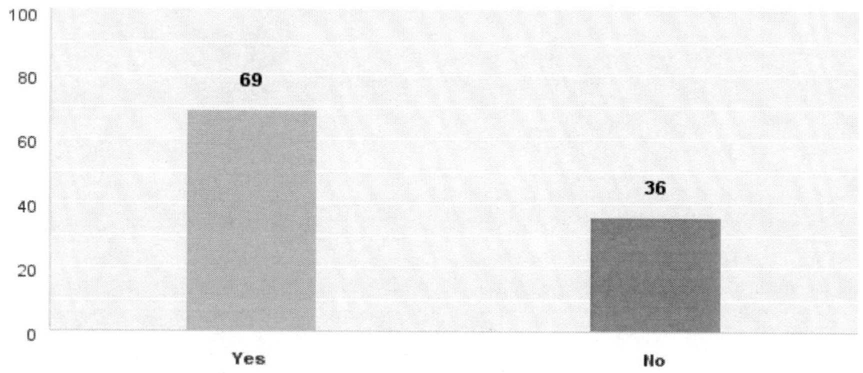

Figure 9. Relatability of self to the endorser.

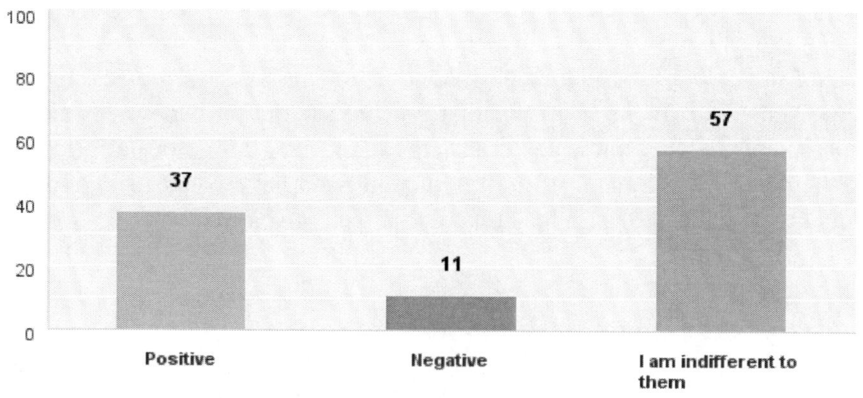

Figure 10. Are celebrity endorsements positive or negative?

Positive or Negative

Celebrity endorsements could either have a positive or negative impact. 57 out of 105 students are indifferent to celebrity endorsements, according to the data in figure 10. From this, we can infer that the majority of respondents are neither affected nor unaffected by celebrity endorsements.

CONCLUSION

In today's world, celebrity endorsements are considered to be extremely helpful in the promotion of a brand, product, or service. The youth is more often than not, the target population of celebrity endorsements. Big companies are willing to spend billions to differentiate their product from the rest and gain a good share of the market.

According to the results obtained, at least 50 respondents agreed that celebrity endorsements help them remember a brand. This ensures brand loyalty in the long run since students would be able to recall one brand over the other while they make purchasing decisions.

Contrary to the readings from previous studies on the same topic when tested against views from a local context revealed that celebrity endorsements may not be as effective as they were thought to be. This implies that generalizing celebrity endorsement in relation to youth consumerism can be tricky and ought to be done with care in order not to mislead. Although they do play a role in enabling brand recollection, young people, such as respondents in my study, do not necessarily buy the same product. Other factors such as quality, price, and special offers also affect a student's purchasing decisions. 42 students would not buy any product endorsed by a celebrity if the quality does not meet their standards.

Celebrity endorsements can be made more effective by choosing the right medium to showcase them on. Findings revealed that 46 of students have more exposure to the Internet as an advertising medium. Students are also more likely to buy those products, which are endorsed by celebrities who they can relate to. The gender of the celebrity endorser is irrelevant, as inferred from the results, which showed that 69 of students thought that the impact of celebrity endorsements is not dependent on the gender of the celebrity endorser.

55 students also prefer actors as endorsers as opposed to politicians, actors, subject matter experts (example, doctors), and sportspersons. The

extent to which the students believe the claims made by celebrity endorsers is also essential. 45 students were neutral towards the claims made by celebrity endorsers.

37 students think that celebrity endorsements have a positive impact on them. A large portion of the students 57 was indifferent to celebrity endorsements, while the remaining thought that celebrity endorsements had a negative impact on them.

Overall, there seemed to be no significant impact of celebrity endorsements on youth buying behaviour, as most students remain neutral.

Majority of the students appeared to be indifferent to celebrity endorsements and do not find them to be positive or negative. The impact of celebrity endorsements on youth buying behaviour is not dependent on the gender of the celebrity endorser, but it is dependent on relatability to the endorser. Most students were neutral towards their allowance affecting their purchasing decision. The views shared here, no doubt, is contrary to the ones found by Chan et al. (2013) whose study among 76 Chinese adolescents aged 13 to 19 revealed that their interviewees were best able to recall celebrity endorsers whom they considered attractive, funny and expressive (as with respondents in Manipal University Dubai). They identified popularity, a good image, and congruence between the celebrity's image and that of the brand as important factors for marketers to consider in selecting celebrity endorsers. A majority of the interviewees perceived that using a celebrity in an *ad* would increase brand awareness, attract the celebrity's fans, encourage trial, and enhance purchase confidence.

Further studies can be conducted on individuals of diverse age groups. Since the target population in this study was limited to a particular demographic i.e., students belonging to different departments of Manipal University Dubai, the target population can be widened to include students from different universities. Future studies could also target specific mediums through which students are exposed to celebrity endorsements and also examine limitations associated with celebrity endorsement, first proposed by Byrne, et al. (2003). This in my view would provide a broader understanding of celebrity endorsements.

In: Media Anthology
Editor: Theophilus Kofi Gokah
ISBN: 978-1-63484-931-9

Chapter 7

BEHIND THE TURNTABLES IN A DESERT: EXPERIENCING EDM CULTURE IN DUBAI

Seidon Alexis [*]
School of Media and Communication,
Manipal University Dubai, Dubai, UAE

ABSTRACT

The research paper investigates the Electronic Dance Music (EDM) culture, from casual producers to club DJs to the fans of this specific genre. The Study objective is to (a) find out the local EDM culture, has EDM been popularized amongst DJs and fans? (b) The type of music being produced by local artists. (c) To find out how Dubai stands when it comes to competition with other countries and (d) to find out what it takes to become a top notch DJ/producer in the region. This Dubai based study finds that youth in the region follow commercial music more than underground music and tracks from emerging or local producers. A rich mix of heterogeneous music artists from diverse nationalities dominates the EDM scenario within the region. However, strong compartmentalization[1] of the expat population leads to polarized music catering to fixed genres like Desi Music, Top 40 and Billboard Hits. The peculiarity of the region is reflected in small fan base and narrow understanding of EDM as opposed to the global fan base. This often leads

[*] E-mail: seidon.alexis13@live.co.uk.

[1] Desi – It is a term for the people, cultures, and products of the Indian subcontinent or South Asia and their diaspora.

to commercial pressures. The paper will also peak into the works and lives of promising producers/DJs asking them what it takes to make it big within the region. Understanding whether the people associated with this culture know the significance of EDM; its growing state, evolving productions and never ending list of emerging talented artists.

INTRODUCTION

One of the obvious problems concerning EDM movement in Dubai is the lack of awareness concerning the different genres and artists of electronic music, internationally as well as locally. Over the past 20 years or so, many genres related to EDM have evolved but its impact to the local party scene here has been very slow (Batran 2013). Given the fact that the amount of academic information (in relation to EDM culture in Dubai) available at my disposal is limited, it was imperative to know what was happening around the world in relation to EDM culture. So what makes an EDM track? Or what are the components needed for a song to make it EDM? Most of the commercialized EDM tracks are composed from 4/4 beats. The track then builds up to a single and catchy powerful loop that goes on to become the focus of the entire song also known as the "drop" (FL BEAT Tutorials 2015). The various production techniques used in EDM, generally known as the "build-up" and "drop," which are produced to create tension and a sharp emotional intensity among clubbers and listeners has been peaked into by Ragnhild Torvanger Solberg. She carried this out by descriptive and interpretive music analysis, where she used spectrograms and a schematic model to visually represent the dominant production techniques (Solber 2014). But then, what about the production aspect of this genre? How does an evolving producer know what to do and from where to start? This type of music was first introduced to the public in the late 1970s and the term 'EDM' gained popularity only in the second half of the 1990s yet still the term remains misunderstood (EDM Junkies 2015). It is very important to know that EDM is used as an umbrella term for various genres that make up for something called 'dance music' (Zach 2014). There are many sub-genres that fall under the term 'EDM' which obviously vary in terms of components, style, production technique, origin and hardware/instruments[2] used. For example, there lies a difference in the tempo of an 'Electro House' track,

[2] Hardware: Production equipments like DDJ controllers, synthesizers, physical playable pads (Launchpad).

which is around 128 BPM, and the tempo of a 'Deep House' track, which lies around 120 BPM. Moreover, that just accounts for one of the differences between these genres, while the differential list is a long one (TALA 2014).

As Batran (op. cit.) earlier mentioned, the evolution of local party scene, in terms of genre awareness, is comparatively slow in relation to the global scenario. Does that pose a problem for emerging and local talent then? Yes, there are major event companies bringing their famous festivals to the local scene and clubs having local DJ residencies and guest appearances by international DJs. But is that where the movement ends? I guess not, it just keeps evolving. Dubai's first take on something with underground music and something different from the mainstream came with the Analog Room. This club is one of the few places in Dubai where the city's loud expats who are "living the dream" get a taste of the different genres of EDM. The club has done justice to its type by bringing down some big names to play on their roster (Whats On, 2015). In the past few years, EDM has been reaching out to many new ears and the very rapid arrival of the genre has many people confused as to where it begins and where it ends. The study will mainly focus on this theme with emphasis on producers, DJs and the festival scene.

WHAT IS ALREADY KNOWN?

EDM, a term that did not really exist until a few years ago is now being used to describe one of the most popular and commercial genres around (O'Malley 2015). A quick flashback to 20 years from now, and EDM in its very roots sounding nothing like how it sounds today. The music was different, the vibe was different, the festivals were different, the energy was different; everything was at a low (Whittle 2014) The very funny thing about the commercialization of this genre is that, EDM has been around for quite a few decades now but without the three-letter abbreviation. The synth beats being played to us by disco tracks and the acid drops in techno tracks, were in fact all under the genre of EDM (Garrat 2014).

Like every other type of music having a different pattern and different elements/instruments involved is the same with EDM. Starting with an ideal dance element, whether its bass music, house, or techno: the 808 kick, then a melody made by the house organ/piano with a few electronic fifths and then for the main drop, side chaining it without a compressor (Preve 2014). Obviously, those are not the only elements involved, but the list of instruments grows with an evolving list of artists and their creative minds.

Now, taking Dubai in perspective what do we so far know about the scene here? The city definitely is a major hub for international artists and major festivals with annual festivals held by top eventers every year. The list of festivals hosted by the region continues to grow in appearance and with the number of artists included. In 2013 alone, the confirmed artists for different festivals had been; DJ Baeur, ATB, Marco V and Tiesto (Garrat R. 2013). A state likes EDM when they call out major DJs/producers such as those. Artists like Calvin Harris, Duke Dumont, Syn Cole, Martin Garrix to name a few are dubbed as the big players of EDM. They have their tracks persistent on the Billboard charts in the TOP10 or TOP40 (Chau 2014).

Just to drift for a moment and to pose a question, has EDM reached the professional level, at least globally. YES! One very good example is the tie up with YouTube and SiriusXM, with the launch of their weekly show on the video sharing platform called; The YouTube EDM 15 (PR Newswire 2014). EDM is a catchall header that includes a vast array of electronic genres that revolve around working with samples, loops, and beats including techno, bass, electro, trance, house, dubstep, and numerous others. The rupture of commercial radio and the beginning of personalized download services has covered the five-year growth course of EDM. Having said all this, one can easily say that EDM might be the fastest growing genre (Music Trades 2013). According to Music Trades, a well-known magazine covering all sorts of music related news, reported that the famous hit "Wake Me Up" by Swedish DJ Avicii had almost 130 million views on YouTube whilst hitting number one on the Billboard charts. That's not all; it also reported that SFX Entertainment, the largest promoter for EDM, disclosed that they had an IPO, which valued their company at a staggering $1.0 billon. In the Q4 of 2014 Forbes' top 10 EDM artists have racked up a combined $268 million this year, an 11% increase from 2013, with top earner Calvin Harris bringing in $66 million.

A recent report (Alvarado 2014) found out that EDM is a $6.2 billion global industry. Most of this money comes from festivals, Las Vegas club dates and other global club gigs. All of these staggering numbers have sought the interest of big brands. Moreover, some have major brands and have already made moves and are sponsoring festivals, events, and others have featured DJs in their commercials.

These numbers are huge and they definitely mean something, EDM might have been around for a long time now but it has recently gained popularity due to the commercialization of their music through radio channels and EDM festivals.

RESEARCH DESIGN

In order to find out the likes and dislikes of EDM fans, the awareness of local artists and music and their perception of EDM, a questionnaire was created. This questionnaire gave me answers to the above mentioned and indicate the popularity of EDM by local fan following.

It was important that I found out about the artists themselves, as this would give me a detailed view into how the EDM industry within the region works. Conducting an expert opinion was the only way I could find out about the passion that drives these artists, their own opinion about the local EDM movement and what the future had in store for Dubai. The following experts opinions were sampled:

Mangal Suvarnan - a very talented Electro House producer who is about to close a deal with a huge recording label.

DJ Varun Sharma - a DESI and Progressive House DJ who has played at events like Club West and Atlantis Dubai (to name a few).

Aayush Thukral (DJ AK) - a DJ who specializes in all types of house music and has played at clubs like Velvet Underground and China White.

Brendan Lopez - a budding DJ who has his own radio show on an online radio channel and specializes in Progressive and Electro House.

Zohaib Naveed, DJ turned Producer, - an underground producer who recently launched his first EP '1992.'

Mahesh Raghvan - a Dubstep producer and DJ currently working on a new project.

The artistes were chosen based on the type of music they specialize in, venues they played at and diversity in their style and approach. What do all these talented people have in common? The unified passion to create and share electronic dance music. Most of these artists have more or less similar influences, either successful international DJs or other music genres that eventually led them to EDM.

Primary Data:

- Primary sources of data include EDM fans and DJs from Dubai. Online questionnaire with a list of eleven (11) questions was placed on a dedicated site and respondents invited to respond to the questions. This data was then analyzed and represented in the forms of tables and graphs.

- For Experts Opinion, DJs and Producers who are well versed with the EDM movement within the region and who have played at notable venues were interviewed. Sample size was six (6).

Secondary Data: Secondary sources of data include pre-existing research papers, which are published in journals. Sources also include newspaper and web articles.

Questionnaire Design: The questions in the survey revolve around the type of music fans listen to and their understanding of the local EDM movement. The questionnaire mainly targeted EDM fan following within the region. This questionnaire was also circulated within a Facebook page called 'EDM Dubai'; a Facebook page with almost 5000 hits covering all sorts of local festival news, international artists and track releases. This gave me a very closely related representative sample to work with. The sampling method chosen for the purpose of this research is Convenience Sampling (Bailey 2012).

RESULT AND ANALYSIS

EDM fans from Dubai responded to the online survey that they were invited to fill-in. The total number of fans that responded to the questionnaire was eighty (80). The following pages will discuss the results from the questionnaire. Most of my representative sample comprised of expats and a few local people.

Around 60% of my representative sample gave the definition of EDM being 'Electronic Dance Music.' The other 30% were very personal with their answers some saying it was a personality to them and to some it meant more than music, being a lifestyle to them. The remaining 10% either ignored the answer or gave an irrelevant answer.

From table 1, more than 75% of the fans listen to music that they have either bought or downloaded, 50% of them listen to music through the radio or podcasts and 40% of them listen to music through streaming services available at their disposal. While the others mentioned 'Live shows.'

From table 2, Majority of the sample size (54%) listens to Progressive House followed by Trance (46%) and Electro House (47%) followed by the rest of the genres.

The other specific genres were Trap, Chillstep, Bigroom House and Psy Trance.

Table 1. EDM Music Listening Pattern

Answer Choices	Responses	
Streaming Services	41.25%	33
Downloaded/Bought Music	76.25%	61
Radio/Mixes/Podcasts	51.25%	41
Other (please specify)	5.00%	4
Total Respondents: 80		

Table 2. Electronic genre preference (the most popular ones)

Answer Choices	Responses	
Techno	24.05%	19
Trance	45.57%	36
Dubstep	31.65%	25
Deep House	31.65%	25
Progressive House	54.43%	43
Future House	15.19%	12
Electro House	46.84%	37
Other (please specify)	18.99%	15
Total Respondents: 79		

Table 3. Rating the last EDM festival you attended. (1 being the least impressive and 5 being the most)

1	2	3	4	5	Total	Weighted Average
8.45% 6	8.45% 6	21.13% 15	28.17% 20	33.80% 24	71	3.70

Nearly 62% of the population said that they were impressed with the last festival the attended while 16% thought otherwise and around 20% were neutral about it. Almost 42% of the people were satisfied with the type of music being produced by local artists while nearly 26% were impressed while the remaining 31% thought otherwise.

Respondents in the study provided a broad spectrum of artists in terms of their favourite international EDM DJs/Producers. They mentioned the top 4 artists were Hardwell (25%), Armin Van Burren (20%), Martin Garrix/Dimitri Vegas and Like Mike (15%). The other responses provided a wide spectrum of artists from different genres and different styles. This just goes on to say that, nearly 40% of my representatives simply have a very wide choice of artists from different genres, proving diversity within EDM subgenres and artists amongst them. Nearly 10% of my sample skipped this answer indicating that a few of them have no favourites in this EDM culture.

When asked to name their favourite local artists, almost 60% of respondents sampled ignored this question. Only 28% of the sample gave all 3 responses to the question indicating that just 1/3rd of the EDM fan following in Dubai knows about the local culture whereas the others are unaware of the culture surrounding them. Half of the sample said that they were not affected by the commercialization of EDM while nearly 30% of them liked it and the remaining did not. From table 6 we observe that more than 80% of the representative sample used Facebook as their source for EDM related news followed by SoundCloud (53%) and Blogs (35%).

Table 4. Quality of music produced by local artists (1 being least impressive and 5 most)

1	2	3	4	5	Total	Weighted Average
13.16% 10	18.42% 14	42.11% 32	25.00% 19	1.32% 1	76	2.83

Table 5. Commercialization of EDM?

Answer Choices	Responses	
Yes	29.11%	23
No	20.25%	16
Neutral	50.63%	40
Total		79

Table 6. New releases/artists/festivals/and other related news?

Answer Choices	Responses	
Facebook	80.52%	62
Newsletter	12.99%	10
Twitter	18.18%	14
Magazines	14.29%	11
Blogs	35.06%	27
Soundcloud	53.25%	41
Other (please specify)	23.38%	18
Total Respondents: 77		

While newsletter, twitter and magazines collectively accounted as a news source for 45% of the representative sample.

Discussion and Conclusion

No matter how successful you get as a producer or DJ, the initial start-up stage is always a difficult phase for anyone. There are many challenges that one would face in terms of reaching to their audience, in terms of users' expectations or perception of what they are seeking (Gessner, Chandler and Wilcox 2015); promoting their music or just in terms of sharing their love for music. Some of the experts pointed out that promoting their music to the right audience was a difficult task, as not everyone understood music as they did. They also pointed out that the popularization of radio hits and 'DESI' music has killed the potential of good EDM tracks to be played at parties or clubs.

Any profitable industry has competition involved, that's how new ideas arise and that's what keeps the market going (Parkman, Holloway and Sebastiao 2012). The competition in EDM can be seen from various aspects, in terms of music, crowd appreciation or even the superiority of one DJ over the other. Most of the experts pointed out that having the right amount of 'contacts' in the right places was more important than the type or quality of music you played (Madureira 2005). For this very reason, any new upcoming artist with a possible better style in music may go unnoticed. There were also comments made as to how 'DESI' music was mandatory in most of the top clubs in the region, setting a sort of boundary to which the DJs have to fall within.

A region like Dubai boasts certainly about talented local artists but how do they stand in comparison with the other international artists? Almost all of the respondent experts said Dubai was only in its 'baby' stages in terms of the EDM movement. As most of the artists here are less of producers and more of DJs, meaning there is less original productions and a lot of remixes to already created tracks. This just means the artists within the region have a lot more to explore and have to show more of their originality and creativity (Martens 2011). Dubai is growing though, with nearly weekly parties featuring major international DJs. There was very specific comment made by Mangal Suvarnan about this statement that I would like to quote,

> "There's also the restriction of Dubai itself. You are only entitled to stay here in Dubai if you have an economic purpose. i.e., you need to have a job (or be a student) to legally stay in Dubai. This tends to hamper talented individuals from pursuing their dreams. In order to really be able to pursue a career in music, you really do need to have a stable income, and plenty of time."

With every new and emerging market, everyone wants to know what is next! All the talented artists on the panel said the potential for the growth of EDM within Dubai is a lot but unfortunately at a very low rate. They mostly blamed the lack of creativity of artists and the popularization of radio hits by most of the fan following which curbed the way for new styles within the genre.

My expert opinion findings indicated that DJs/Producers within this region face a serious problem when it comes to promoting their music and instilling that same kind of understanding of the culture that they have among fans. All of their influences have been other major EDM artists or a different genre of music that eventually directed them towards EDM. Talking about completion within the local movement, there lacks real competition as most clubs and top notch local DJs have risen to fame due to contact with the right sources or having a preference in another subgenre, as 'DESI MUSIC' is the mostly preferred type of music in Dubai. The panel also went on to say that actual talent is hidden due to these reasons. They found Dubai to be lagging behind in terms of the EDM movement when compared to the international platform saying it all has to start from the minds of the fans. They were also very ambitious with their response to the future in store for the local movement, saying Dubai has all the potential to grow but a very slow rate, a rhetoric earlier touted by Balakrishnan (2008).

In retrospect, it has been established that people in Dubai definitely know what EDM is and what type of music comes under its classification. Their subgenre preference within this culture is very mainstream as 80% of my representative sample opted for the commercial genres while 20% of them opted for underground and upcoming genres. So, there is a small set of people within the local culture that do follow the underground and non-commercialized music and actually like it!

When talking about artists, nearly 90% of my representative sample gave all 3 of their favourite artists, most of them being commercial DJs while around 15% of the sample within this number (90%) mentioned underground artists. It was a very different scenario when they had to mention their favourite local artists, as nearly 60% left all the 3 options blank. Only 28% were able to name all 3 DJs, which was also a very diverse set of names. This just indicates that the fans within this region are not completely aware of the EDM artists within the region.

The quality of music being produced by local artists was only appreciated by 50% of the culture while the remaining thought otherwise. The EDM festivals were very much appreciated by the fans, as nearly 62% of them mentioned that they enjoyed their last attended festival.

The commercialization of EDM simply means the popularization of this type of music. Did the local fans like it? My findings indicate that only 30% of them liked the commercialization of the music while 50% of them were neutral about it and 20% disliked it.

Most of respondents found out about EDM related news through Facebook, nearly 80%, while others relied on Sound cloud and Blogs to find out about other EDM related news. Further research work may have to be conducted on the 'DESI' EDM movement with expectations of better responses, due to the popularization of DESI music within the region. Also there is a huge scope for researchers interested in this field to find out why local EDM music is not that popularized among fans and the obstacles that a producer faces to promote his/her music.

In: Media Anthology
Editor: Theophilus Kofi Gokah
ISBN: 978-1-63484-931-9

Chapter 8

THE REPRESENTATION OF NATURE, GENDER ROLES AND POST-COLONIAL MEDIATORS IN *POCAHONTAS* (1995) AND *PRINCESS MONONOKE* (1997)

Hansabye Luximan*
School of Media and Communication, Manipal University,
Dubai, UAE

ABSTRACT

Pocahontas and Princess Mononoke reinterpret historical figures and stories, while presenting them to a younger audience. This paper draws a bridge between two cultural products based on the following themes: nature, gender portrayals and voices of colonial centric viewpoint. The paper evaluates how both cultural artefacts use the 'other' in defining non-European civilization, initial stages of colonial subjugation, role of nature in depicting conflict or subservience, subsequent human consequences of establishing settlers and exploitation of the country's resources by the 'outsider.'

Keywords: nature, gender, post-colonialism, animation, culture

---

* E-mail: hansa.luximan@gmail.com.

INTRODUCTION

This study intends to uncover, synthesize and summarize the analysis conducted in the last twenty years on both *Pocahontas* and *Princess Mononoke*, so as to find a substantial correlation between the two. The study intends to do so by attempting to answer to the following questions: (a) what is the role and representation of nature in *Princess Mononoke* and *Pocahontas*? (b) How are gender roles portrayed in *Princess Mononoke* and *Pocahontas*? Do they stick to a specific culture's conventions? (c) Is the theme of colonization prominent in both films? How do the characters respond to colonization and what are their roles in it? Understanding these three themes will help in determining whether there are gaps in the literature that can be further explored and if a new conversation can be started about the impact of the films' content on this generation of young adults.

The content reviewed in this study has been gathered through EBSCOhost Online Research Databases, which includes academic journals, scholarly articles, essays and e-books. Google Scholar, although containing content that requires authorization and payment to be accessed, has also been a source for academic papers, reviews, e-journals and e-books. The Manipal University Dubai Campus Library was a third source for content, however the number of books pertaining to the subject were limited.

The following is a list of the main components that make up this research paper and their respective definitions and descriptions, as a way to demarcate the areas that will be focused upon.

Pocahontas is an animated film released in 1995 by Walt Disney Pictures and produced by Walt Disney Feature Animation in the United States of America. The plot is loosely based on the historic character Pocahontas and is a fictional depiction of her encounter with Captain John Smith, a settler traveling from the Virginia Company. The story is set in 1607, in the New World, where John Smith intends to build a new town. He meets Pocahontas, the daughter of Chief Powhatan. The storyline revolves around their fictional 'love' story and their short exchange depicting their respective ways of life. They both help to avert a war after one of the tribesmen is shot dead by a settler. Smith is blamed for the death and brought to the tribe leader, Chief Powhatan. To retaliate, the settlers attack the Chief, and John Smith throws himself in front of the Chief. Smith is wounded in the process and has to be treated. He returns to England while Pocahontas stays back to lead her people.

Princess Mononoke is a 1997 anime film written and directed by Hayao Miyazaki and produced by Studio Ghibli in Japan. The plot is set in the feudal period of Muromachi (1337 to 1573). It is the story of the Emishi warrior Ashitaka who, while in search of a way to cure himself from a deadly curse, gets caught in the struggle between Lady Eboshi, leader of Irontown, in which she harvests iron from the forest, and San, the eponymous heroine of the film. He falls in love with San, a human girl who was adopted by the wolf god clan. Ashitaka tries to help both parties by deflecting as much violence as possible, however Eboshi's objective is to behead the Forest Spirit so that she may continue to harvest iron. She successfully does so but invokes the wrath of the Forest Spirit. Ashitaka and San appease the Forest Spirit, averting a massacre. After Eboshi realizes her mistake, she decides to build a better town. San and Ashitaka, while being in love, cannot be together, as San resents humankind and decides to stay with her clan.

The two aforementioned films belong to the genre of Animation, a process by which one can create motion and the illusion of shape changes. It is done by rapidly displaying a sequence of static images. The word 'animation' finds its roots in Latin 'animatio' which is the "act of bringing to life." Both Pocahontas and Princess Mononoke use traditional animation, however Princess Mononoke is the first animated film that integrated digital art with hand drawn art.

Princess Mononoke and Pocahontas share many themes, however the themes of Nature, Gender Roles and Post-Colonial Mediators will be focused on.

The word 'nature' in Latin 'natura' means birth or character. Nature, in the broadest sense, encompasses all the aspects of the natural, physical or material world. According to the Oxford Dictionaries, it is the 'phenomena of the physical world collectively, including plants, animals, the landscape and other features and products of the earth, as opposed to humans or human creations.'

Nature is also defined as the 'physical force regarded as causing and regulating the phenomena of the world.' In Amerindian mythology, Mother Nature is a goddess of life, feeding plans, animals and humans. In Southeast Asia, earth is also personified, although her role is slightly different and it is unclear how. In Western history, the term 'Mother Nature' is only considered a personification, and not a goddess. We will study its representation in both films. In Pocahontas, the main character is connected to her surroundings and is repeatedly given advice by Grandmother Willow, a willow tree. In Princess Mononoke, the animals of the forest are under the protection of the Forest Spirit, which has a deer-like appearance with odd features, such as a beard, that set him apart. The Forest Spirit is also seen as male throughout the film.

Gender Roles are norms set by members of a society dictating how a person's behavior should be based on their actual or perceived sex. These norms determine what is considered 'masculine' and 'feminine' and are deeply ingrained into the cognitive framework of a society's members. These roles can be transferred through education and repeating exposure to models that represent the roles.

Films play a big role in educating masses and provide members with these representations. In Pocahontas, the protagonist is an Amerindian young woman who experiences the settlers' arrival in her country. She is promised to the best warrior in the tribe, an arrangement made by her father. She falls in love with one of the settlers, John Smith, and has to decide whether to follow her heart or serve her people.

In Princess Mononoke, Prince Ashitaka meets three central female characters: San, the wolf girl, Lady Eboshi, the leader of Irontown and Toki, an ex-prostitute who takes up leadership in Irontown when Eboshi is gone. Prince Ashitaka falls in love with San and wants peace between her and her sworn enemy, Lady Eboshi.

Pocahontas imagines the first encounter between gold-hungry settlers led by Ratcliffe and an indigenous people, the Powhatan. Ratcliffe declares the Powhatan as 'savages' and orders his soldiers to shoot them on sight. John Smith, on the other hand, is seduced by the idea of 'conquering the land.' Princess Mononoke narrates the conquest of the forest and its inhabitants by the people of Irontown through Western weapons for the increased industrial production of iron.

The Powhatan first made contact with settlers in the beginning of the seventeenth century and The Portuguese brought guns and gunpowder to Japan in the mid-sixteenth century, however, both of these films have been produced and released in the twentieth century and it is thus possible for us to qualify both as part of the post-colonial discourse. Post-colonial studies is a discipline in which intellectual discourse that analyzes, explores and responds to the cultural, political and social legacies of colonialism is examined. It describes the human consequences of establishing settlers and exploiting the available resources of a country.

One of the prevailing concepts of these two films is mediation between two cultures, between two sets of people and between two countries. Pocahontas tries to establish peace between her people and the settlers and to come to an understanding.

Ashitaka wants to stop the fight between the Forest gods and Irontown and in-between, attempts to undo the curse.

ROLE AND REPRESENTATION OF NATURE IN *POCAHONTAS* AND *PRINCESS MONONOKE*

Both Pocahontas and Princess Mononoke give substantial importance to Nature in terms of visual presence and character importance. In fact, Nature is a central theme explored in both films. The many clues will be uncovered in the following paragraphs.

In *Pocahontas*, the Amerindians are portrayed practicing farming and fishing. They are seen as near vegetarian and respect all of Nature's creations. For example, Pocahontas stops John Smith from firing at animals during one of their meetings. According to Whitley (2012), their attitude towards earth and life forms are revealed when Pocahontas sings the Colors of the Wind. The song is explained by Edgerton and Jackson (1996) to have been inspired by Chief Seattle's famous speech challenging white ascendency and land appropriate. The film removes the mystique around the innocence of virgin nature, which is compared by Whitley (2012) to *Bambi*'s pristine, immaculate nature, however that mystique is shifted to the virgin daughter of the tribe. Whitley (2012) concludes that it is a selective representation of nature. He also remarks that animals are seen as human pets, such as the hummingbird and raccoon accompanying Pocahontas, and become comic sideshows. Pina (2013) characterizes these animals as anthropomorphic, as having distinct human characteristics and mannerisms. For example, the pet raccoon displays gluttony and curiosity in a most human way, including licking his claws after a meal, nodding and pointing to his muzzle when he demands a snack. Naess (1989) argues that this representative can do some good, as empathy towards life forms is the first step to reestablishing a relationship with nature. According to Aidman and Reese (1996), Pocahontas being motherless finds the wind to be her mother. The wind becomes a key metaphor for freedom and fluidity (Whitley 2012).

In Princess Mononoke, Nature is seen as less forgiving. The main animal characters are no comic sideshows, but are gods whose main trait is vengefulness. According to McHugh (2010), the curses that are inflicted between the gods and to Prince Ashitaka are direct proof of this. There are no cute animals here; the animal gods are oozing with discharge and blood. Smith and Parsons (1992) understandably state that the Forest Spirit is terrifying as the Nightwalker, the creature it turns into after the sunsets. The humans and animals are willing to preserve their habitats at the expense of each other. Miyazaki shows fearful respect of the natural world. He conveys the idea that the forest is not just a beautiful place to play with and desire, but is to be shown for its true colors: that, it is unforgiving, vengeful and terrifying. Smith and Parsons (1992) explain the importance of death in Miyazaki's film as an aspect of nature: beautiful and disturbing yet essential and inevitable. In the film, we are shown what happens when these elements of nature are taken away from humanity and the earth. When Lady Eboshi beheads the Forest Spirit, McHugh (2010) argues that this is a critique of the destruction of Nature in modern Japan. Usually, films show that people lose most when nature is destroyed but the film shows that even though the residents of Irontown had the most to lose when the Forest Spirit destroys the forest, they are given an opportunity as they can harvest more iron from now on (Smith and Parsons 1992). Napier (2001) explains that when the Spirit is given his head back and explodes, decimating everything in its way, he disappears into the cycles of nature, of growth and regeneration. This uncertainty for the future and this lack of reassurance is what Miyazaki is all about, and is a definite factor that stands out from American films.

According to Smith and Parsons (1992), Miyazaki rejects the extreme form of ecocentrism, where nature is not to be a source to be exploited. Instead, the film insists that preservation is a must so that humans can benefit from it. In Pocahontas, there is a message about balance and imbalance in nature, however it is lost in the magic and the historical inexactness (Pina 2013). The Japanese have an ambivalent attitude towards Nature, where the two dimensions are love and fear, explains Kalland (2002). In Pocahontas, there is a clear usage of Reductionism, whereby removing the offensive and displeasing elements to enhance some elements of nature. Lee (1984) compares this to framing a shot or a photograph. However Miyazaki's work seems to be closer to gardening, where his intervention allows nature to express itself in a louder voice (Kalland and Asquith 1997). Indeed, Nature becomes an agent and an acting individual in Princess Mononoke. This contrasts greatly with many western films such as James Cameron's *Avatar* (2009), in which Neytiri proclaims, "Our great Mother does not take sides, Jake, only protects the balance of life." Similarly, in Pocahontas, Nature is seen as a third party, that does not act through individuals and seems not be one with its offspring.

How are these perspectives reflected within the audiences in the United States and Japan? Kalland (2002) points out the dichotomy of western dualism and non-western monism, as well as of western anthropocentrism and non-western ecocentrism. Kalland explains that the Japanese either see themselves as part of Nature or see Nature as a source to be exploited, and declare themselves as superior to other creatures. Guha (1989) challenges the myth of the ecologically noble Oriental and says that the dichotomy should not be applied to the Japanese, as the polarity is in itself a western concept. Kalland (2002) suggests that by bringing Nature in the social life, an interest to protect Nature can be created. The Japanese, despite long periods of deforestation, still have the largest forest to land ratio. Koh (1954) further says that Tokyo, being one of the most polluted cities, went on to become one of the cleanest. Kalland (2002) explains these changes by pointing to the Japanese's painful experience, confrontations and political pressures to better their environment.

Cocks and Simpson (2015) differentiate strong anthropocentrism from weak anthropocentrism, where the first one indicates that Man sees the environment as a commodity to be used, whereas the second one is Man still measuring Nature by its value to human beings but while it allowing people to feel good about themselves and allowing them to grow. In this case, Pocahontas looks down upon strong anthropocentrism by denouncing the actions of the settlers, and promotes weak anthropocentrism by developing the relationship between Pocahontas and Nature. Cocks and Simpson (2015) question whether it matters if a person possesses an anthropocentric or ecocentric perspective, as humans' experiences of nature are different, yet equal.

Taking into account Bandura's (2009) social cognitive theory, by which people learn social behavior through direct observations and Gerbner's (1998) cultivation theory, by which people create a (distorted) perspective of reality; we can analyze the effect of these films on young minds. From the point of view of an educator, filmmakers can simulate a discussion on the role of Nature in our lives and reinforce their perspective through repetitive reinforcement of their message. In Pocahontas, the message is clear: Nature is helpless, does not manifest discontentment when settlers try to exploit it, and is a third party that solely guides and advises the human, but takes no direct part in the actions advancing the story. Princess Mononoke teaches its audience that Nature is a force to be reckoned with, and has agents to carry out its bidding, advancing the story as they do. However, Nature is not everything and its resources can be exploited with moderation.

A theme that is constantly repeated and stressed upon in Ghibli films (Nausicäa of the Valley of the Wind, My Neighbor Totoro, Ponyo, Arrietty), Nature isn't a subject explored in depth by Disney (The Little Mermaid, Bambi, Brother Bear, The Jungle Book) but is more often a backdrop intended to enhance the story of the human characters. Another theme explored by both studios is Gender Roles, which will be tackled in the upcoming chapter.

GENDER ROLES IN *POCAHONTAS* AND *PRINCESS MONONOKE*

Pocahontas is the eponymous heroine of the Disney film, and like for many other animated female characters (Snow White and the Seven Dwarves, Cinderella, Alice in Wonderland), her point of view should triumph in this film. However, Borthaiser (2008) notes that Pocahontas was drawn from a Western male point of view. Her hair is long and flowing in the wind, her eyes are heavy with 'mascara' and are doll-like, she is tall and has muscular legs (Edgerton and Jackson, 1996). Yoshida (2011) explains that the character developer had used supermodels, a typically western concept of beauty, for inspiration while creating her Barbie-like figure. Smith and Parsons (2012) first see her through water, through Western gaze and imply that he continues to see her through it throughout the film. Dundes (2001) notes that she is one of the few Disney princesses whose story does not end in matrimony. Dundes summarizes that 'this marks the metamorphosis of the usual docile heroin into an adventurous young woman who stands up for her beliefs' (Gabriel 1995; Henke, Birnie, Zimmerman and Smith 1996; James 1995; Riemenschneider 1995). She rescues the male protagonist and uses the love for him as a rationale. However, at the end of the film, she abandons her own desires to serve her people. While this is fundamentally different from other Disney films, there is a shift from egocentric relationships to setting aside one's desires for other's needs (Brown 1992). Whitley (2012) explains that although her decision was sentimental, the protagonist decides to stay back, ensuring that her values survive the force and attraction of the colonizers. Dundes (2001) criticizes this 'strength' and explains that although Pocahontas' story stands out amongst Disney princesses, her actions are still based on emotions, not rational thought. This stays true to gender stereotyping and her simple response at the end of the film "I'm needed here" throws her back to patriarchal values of family and the suppression of her own goals for the benefit of others. Aidman and Reese (1996) add that Pocahontas pays for her strong character but that the realization seems to be an afterthought. The film could also be a critique of classes, as Pocahontas and John were denied their interracial relationship. This problem is usually solved in other Disney films through magic, such as Cinderella going to the ball or the Beast turning back to his human form. The character of San is not stereotypical, in comparison.

Yoshida (2011) says that San is not the typical 'shojo' character, which is seen as 'kawaii' and shy, a characteristic desired by Japanese anime standards.

Napier (2005) writes that she is seen to have an aggressive sexuality rather than an appealing one as her first appearance on screen is her spitting out venom with a blood-covered face. Princess Mononoke involves many strong female characters such as San, who is the only one willing to stand up and save the forest; Lady Eboshi, who is a self-made woman, running her own business; one of the Lady's protégées, Toki, who takes up leadership when it is needed the most in times of crisis; and San's mother, the wolf god Moro who is a mother of three (Smith and Parsons 1992). While Ashitaka is the hero of the film, San is the eponymous character, gaining importance in the events of the film. The prince obviously has feelings for her, but the reverse isn't obvious. She takes care of him, but never expresses the desire to be with him. She goes back to the forest as the end of the film, which is seen as more heroic than Ashitaka's decision, which is to stay with the people of Irontown and help build a better future (Tucker 2003).

Pocahontas rescues the male protagonist as well, showing strength. While she is obviously attracted to Smith at first sight while her friend is horrified and surprised, she resists his attempts and efforts to be kissed. Dundes (2001) quotes Coontz (1992) to explain this: 'it's okay to be swept away, but nice girls don't plan for sex.' This leads us to believe that Pocahontas is still deeply affected by traditional gender roles and does not attempt to break free completely. San, in comparison, is a strong character that does not let her emotions affect her judgment or decisions.

Are these roles reflected in media and in reality? Day and Mackey (1986), while studying the primary roles of men and women, found that men were usually represented as soldiers and protectors and women as primary child caretakers. He justifies this by quoting Merton's (1968) anticipatory socialization that allows the masses to rehearse roles before behaving socially. Brown (1970) further classifies activities not performed by women in most cultures as: (a) Activities that take participants far from home (b) Activities that require consistent high levels of concentration (c) Activities that are dangerous (d) Activities that require frequent interruptions, and are dysfunctional in performing the task.

Day and Mackey (1986) also points out that these gendered roles presented in the media are exclusive to their respective sexes, meaning that men are the sole protectors and women the sole caretakers. In Pocahontas, chief Powhatan is the father figure in his daughter's life and shows concern for her well being by enforcing his decisions onto her. He is absent in caretaking, unlike Grandmother Willow, who knows Pocahontas' dreams and ambitions and is close to her emotionally. The second caretaker is Pocahontas' mother as the wind, who guides her. However both these women do not engage as soldiers.

The period in which the films were released saw many changes, in the United States as well as in Japan. Yoshizumi (1995) noticed that 40.8% of the total Japanese workforce was constituted of women, and 46.2% of the labor force in the U.S. was made up of women (US Bureau of Census 1997). Harris and Long (1999) note that in Japan, the rate of education, the age of marriage, and the rate of divorces have increased. The rate of never-married women was at its highest. They also note that in the United States, the percentage of female managers increased from 14% (1950) to 42% (1992). Also, more men have sole custody of children and are the primary caregiving parent. This means that the audience is changing at a faster pace but the films that are meant to entertain the audience do not have accurate representations of the audience. In Princess Mononoke, most of the women hold power and are the primary characters that take the story forward. Sugihara and Katsurada (2000) note that Japan was originally a matriarchal society, and the current Japanese society is not as gender-centered. Kashiwagi (1972) and Ito (1978) say that men are less masculine than the expected stereotype and women less feminine than the expected stereotype. The stereotypical masculine man is aggressive, independent, dominant, competitive, confident, analytical leader, risk-taker, and decision-maker (Azuma 1979). Whereas the stereotypical feminine woman is tactful, gentle, affectionate, sensitive to feelings, quiet, has no harsh language, is less dominant, independent and risk-taking and more subjective, conceited and weaker than men. Azuma (1979) and Williams and Best (1950) agree on similar traits across cultures. These traits are reinforced in Pocahontas, through the male characters of Chief Powhatan, John Smith, Governor Ratcliffe and Kocoum; as well as through the female characters of Pocahontas, Grandmother Willow, Nakoma and Pocahontas' mother. On the other hand, it is difficult to box characters of Princess Mononoke in the masculine or feminine stereotypes, which reflects Kashiwagi's (1972) and Ito's (1978) findings.

To conclude, Pocahontas still holds gendered stereotypes, despite having a lead female character. We can only wonder if the audience can relate to these stereotypes, when they themselves are going through many societal changes. Princess Mononoke, in contrast, presents male and female characters that are not bound by stereotypes, and who reflect the changes present in the Japanese society. How historically accurate are these characters? And what are their roles? In the next chapter, the presence of post-colonial mediators will be discussed.

POST-COLONIAL MEDIATORS IN *POCAHONTAS* AND *PRINCESS MONONOKE*

Pocahontas imagines the first contact between English settlers and the Powhatan. The settlers scout the land and name it Virginia, claiming it for themselves. *Princess Mononoke* is based on the conquest of land through western weapons, however Tucker (2003) explains that the Japanese cannot play 'victim' and claim that they had no part in developing the weapons themselves.

Borthaiser (2008) explores *Pocahontas* through postcolonial theories and looks at the basic dialogue between culture and nature. He speaks of Anzaldúa's (1987) 'deviant' concept, which encompasses all characters that are deemed outcasts by their former community. He also quotes Bhabha (1994) while speaking on the space in between two communities, the interstitial space, where a feeling of unhomeliness is born. Borthaiser claims that the space in between the two communities can be called the borderlands, where Pocahontas and John Smith meet. The film makes of Pocahontas and John Smith outlaws, both disobeying direct orders, where Pocahontas isn't allowed outside the village and John is supposed to be hunting down the indigenous people. Yoshida (2011) adds that the way Pocahontas moves is important in discerning how she is viewed throughout the film. Animal-like, her movements are seen through low-angle shots, forcing the viewer to see through a different way. Yoshida concludes that there is a Self/Other dichotomy that we can watch this film from, a Eurocentric view that is imposed by animating techniques.

This other/self dichotomy can be observed in *Princess Mononoke* as well, where outsiders are heroes. Yoshida (2011) also quotes Bhabha (1994) in saying that the Irontown is a place 'in between,' where others take the whole story forward except for Lord Asano and the Emperor. There is little left of Self in the film. Ashitaka is a prince from a marginalized group, San is a human outsider with an animal god for a mother; the residents of Irontown are all outsiders, ranging from prostitutes to lepers (Tucker 2003). Lady Eboshi, while wanting to make money at the expense of the forest, cares deeply for her people. Their work is seen as heroic and invites empathy for the workers. This human complexity is characteristic of Miyazaki's work and his non-binary oppositions, which celebrate diversity (Smith and Parsons 1992). This human complexity is also seen through Prince Ashitaka, who refuses to take sides, which makes San and Eboshi both seem sympathetic. He a neutral mediator between the two female characters, and is fully aware of the capacity of violence to feed on violence. He is described by Kraemer (2004) to be a version of the Christ, a savior and martyr of the story. He kills two men while trying to save women and children, expressing regret. He carries the teaching of Shinto and Buddhism through his actions, which are fundamentally different from the binary system. Napier (2001) argues that these ideological differences contribute to national identities. This is the equivalent of finding oneself in the human experience and discovering one's purpose.

In *Pocahontas*, this is evident through the life choices that Pocahontas has to make. Pina (2013) describes how the Song Around the River Bend reveals Pocahontas' angst. She has to decide whether to do what is expected of her by listening to her father or to do the unexpected and find fulfillment. Edgerton and Jackson (1996) also write about her journey to find her true path, getting advice from Grandmother Willow. As she risks her life to save John Smith, she becomes more assertive and realizes her true purpose. She becomes a peacemaker. Unlike *Princess Mononoke*, *Pocahontas* is rooted in the good versus evil antagonism. The conflict between the tribesmen and the settlers is based on their differences. White men are seen as oppressive and violent fools, according to McHugh (2010). John Smith and Governor Ratcliffe are both driven by materialism, believing that they have the right to possess the land. Smith has a quest for adventure, whereas Ratcliffe solely wants to find gold (Pina 2013). However not all the settlers are seen as the evildoers. The King is portrayed as innocent, as being manipulated by Ratcliffe (Yoshida 2011).

As both of the protagonists become fully involved in the conflict, their paths are cut out for them as mediators and peacemakers. Borthaiser (2008) notes that violence is not actually shown in the film, but is represented in their chants as the two groups face each other. The natives are called "filthy little heaths" while the natives assume that "they're not like you and me, which means they must be evil." Despite the racism and intolerance, Belkhyr (2013) explains that the natives try to emulate in the conflict through mimicry. They not only fear the settlers but are in awe, as well. The notions of 'self' and 'other' are seen through the eyes of western ideology. Pocahontas plays a symbolic role, says Whitley, where she deflects violence, which is at the center of the cultural conflict by trying to demonstrate their similarities. The differences that are shown in the film are highly idealized according to Withley (2012). Strong (1996) says otherwise, that there is a clear-cut difference in the ideologies, where the natives utilize violence to politically subordinate and incorporate, whereas colonists use violence to exterminate and deprive others.

In *Princess Mononoke*, Freiberd (2006) notes that the characters at the forefront of the war are not a male versus female deadlock but are part of a generation conflict. Lady Eboshi is older and seen as more successful whereas younger San is true to her raw nature and recklessness. This can be seen as an empowering factor for the young audience of *Princess Mononoke*. San's conflict with herself is central to the plot, as she fights her own humanity. Ashitaka tries to tell San that she's a girl, not a wolf. They fight, but in the chaos, their necklaces are tied and her wolf cloak falls to the ground. It is here that San looses a large part of her wild image and turns into a 'normal' girl, now she allows herself to accept her own humanity and her own 'self'; her cloak of wolf fur does not come back later (De Vries 2010). In the film, technology is at the heart of the conflict. Napier (2001) elucidates why by saying that since technology cannot be erased, it is deemed unpleasant but permanent. The war between nature and technology reaches destructive levels in the film. While the film and the conflict are fictional, the medieval setting is factual. Tucker (2003) speaks of Japan's violent past and the many wars during feudal Japan. The animation portrays characters that are loosely based on historical figures. The conflict is rather idealized, as the ideologies are attributed inexactly to families and princes in the film. The Emishi, for example, were seen as savages, which is not unlike the Powhatan tribe in Pocahontas. Ashitaka embodies noble traits and takes on the Japanese legend, creating a fiction that Tucker describes as essential to teach ecological balance.

Conclusion and Suggestions for Further Study

While *Pocahontas* tries to establish a relationship with its audience through friendly characters and innocent landscapes, the natural elements lack dimension and their representation is selective. Nature is seen as magical and passive and takes a backseat to the romance between Pocahontas and John Smith. *Princess Mononoke* unleashes powerful animal characters and natural forces, all of which take the story forward. The destruction of the force that decides balance and imbalance is a statement that criticizes the destruction of nature in modern Japan, although a glint of hope and uncertainty reminds the audience that nature is to be preserved, but not revered. The film's uncertainty around the consequences of the destruction of Nature is something that Miyazaki leaves to the audience to ponder upon.

Pocahontas' protagonist seems original and avant-garde, but a deeper study into the character creation reveals that the character was created through a western gaze and still fits in the social norms of womanhood and femininity. Although the effort to break away from traditional Disney stories is appreciated, it is still rooted in patriarchal values and stereotypes. *Princess Mononoke* presents strong female characters that lead the plot. Independent and stubborn, they wage war against each other by standing for their respective beliefs. Romantic values are secondary in the film.

While colonialism is not a major theme of the film, questions about the historical context of colonialism in the films are raised. With the arrival of outsiders in Pocahontas, borderlands are drawn, where characters from both cultures meet, but are deemed outcasts. Violence between the clan and the settlers is understood but not shown on screen. While the notions of good and evil are extreme, not all settlers are seen as evil. Pocahontas finds her role as peacemaker and mediator, while fighting to be with the one she loves. In Princess Mononoke, Irontown is a symbol of the place where outcasts and outsiders are welcome. While there are no essentially good or evil characters, violence is the real enemy, and Ashitaka is the one fighting it. The film reflects Japan's violent past, although inaccurately, to teach its audience ecological balance. Pocahontas depicts a clear-cut dichotomy between the English settlers and the Powhatan while Princess Mononoke contains more complex concepts of Self and Other.

All of the studies mentioned and referred to in this study are of qualitative nature. Further studies could attempt to quantify these observations and support and contradict its findings. The review of the literature also indicates areas for further study. The questions that future studies could attempt to answer to are: (a) how are Patriarchal and Matriarchal systems represented? (b) How is the conflict between groups visually shown? (c) What are the gender roles for male characters in the films? (d) What is the visual presence of colonialism on-screen?

In: Media Anthology
Editor: Theophilus Kofi Gokah

ISBN: 978-1-63484-931-9

Chapter 9

CULTURAL APPROPRIATION AND THE MISREPRESENTATION OF PEOPLE OF COLOUR (POC) IN MAINSTREAM HOLLYWOOD MOVIES

Sayema Wasi*
School of Media and Communication,
Manipal University Dubai, United Arab Emirates

ABSTRACT

The objective of this presentation is to show how media misalign cultural identity[1], cultural appropriation[2], and the subsequent effects of racial and cultural stereotypes on People of Colour (PoC). To achieve this objective, three Hollywood movies: Breakfast at Tiffany's, Indiana Jones and the Temple of Doom, and The Lone Ranger is studied for their representation of PoC. This is backed by Focus groups interviews to

* Corresponding author: Sayema Wasi. E-mail: sayemawasi@gmail.com.

[1] Cultural identity is the identity or feeling of belonging to a group. It is part of a person's self-conception and self-perception and is related to nationality, ethnicity, religion, social class, generation, locality or any kind of social group that has its own distinct culture (Ennaji, 2005).

[2] Cultural appropriation is a sociological concept that views the adoption or use of elements of one culture by members of a different culture as a largely negative phenomenon (Young, 2010).

understand opinions amongst PoC and media consumers about issues relating to race, culture, and identity.

INTRODUCTION

Representation of PoC in Hollywood movies is an issue that is consistently relevant and worthy of repeated discussion. It stems from the understanding that America's wish-generating factory runs on the backs of people who, despite being an integral part of American society, continue to remain hidden in dense shadows (Fisher, Oddsson and Wada, 2013).

The fact that Hollywood has such a limited depiction of POC – where, it can be argued, they should technically find greater acceptance and representation, since art industries tend to present creative opportunities for people of all sorts – is not only proof of the continued existence of the inequality and bias non-White citizens face in America, it is also indicative of the sort of opinions dominant classes of Americans (i.e., rich, predominantly white) hold towards their differently-coloured counterparts. For instance, there are the widely acknowledged stereotypes in American movies, listed here through personal observation: *swarthy Middle Easterners*, *clever Far East Asians* (often grouped under the misleading blanket race of 'Asian'), *hypersexual Latinos*, *Irish Mafia men*, *unsophisticated Indians* and *shrewd Russians* – to name a few.

Adam Sandler, a Hollywood actor, comedian, screenwriter and film producer, was caught in a media storm during the shooting of his latest movie 'Ridiculous Six,' based on Native Americans. The content of the film is reported to have been so extremely racist and provocative that it led to a large number of Native extras walking off the movie sets, refusing to continue to be part of it.

One can question the logic behind consciously and intentionally alienating a significant portion of the movie-going audience for the sake of providing a contrast to the complex, many-layered, overwhelmingly white protagonists. It can be said that it is done to provide a context that will appeal to White audiences – since they form the majority of the American population (Cotton, O'Neill and Griffin, 2014). However, the need for more diverse content is consistently becoming more apparent. According to a report by the Ralph Bunche Center of the University of California, Los Angeles, although Western media has had a noticeable increase in racially diverse content over the years, audiences are continuing to demand more proportionate representation (see also Kinsky and Smith, 2013).

It has also been studied and documented that racially diverse content brings in more audiences, has a higher approval rating, and generates greater revenue (see for example Fam and Waller, 2006). The recent success of shows starring POC, such as ABC's Fresh Off the Boat (Asian American), *Black-ish* (Black American) and *Cristela* (Latin American) are proof of the same. Other shows that highlight POC are ABC's *Scandal* and *How to Get Away with Murder*, along with Fox's *Empire*. This sort of diversity is yet to be witnessed and documented in mainstream Hollywood cinema.

Although it seems as though content producers are beginning to put in a lot of thought into creating a controlled diversity in their content, it seems there is little thought spared when taking over the identity of coloured peoples and passing off their time-honoured culture and traditions as belonging to the dominant White American group. Examples of cultural appropriation and the subsequent birth of racial stereotypes that are a direct result of the appropriation are prevalent everywhere in pop culture (Little, Holmes and Grieco, 2001). This includes, but is not limited to, instances such as people all over the world dressing up as 'Chinese' for Halloween; Lady Gaga and Rihanna sporting burqas to make a fashion statement; Pharrell Williams wearing a Native American headdress; and Katy Perry performing one of her shows as a geisha, dressed in a kimono and a white-powdered face.

A very recent occurrence was the largely online backlash from Indian communities settled in America during the popular Coachella music festival, held annually in California. Many Indian women took to social media to express their resentment towards the trend of 'Indian'-inspired outfits amongst non-Indian attendees of the festival. It led the topic #ReclaimTheBindi to trend on Twitter and Tumblr, a hashtag which was principally created by Indians who believed they alone had the right to wear the bindi, as their non-Indian counterparts had little knowledge or appreciation for the history and context behind the adornment and how it is worn.

In a similar incident, Selena Gomez donned a bindi for debuting a new song, which, according to her, had a 'Hindu, tribal feel.' This led to Rajan Zed, President of the Universal Society for Hinduism to release this statement:

> The bindi on the forehead is an ancient tradition in Hinduism and has religious significance... [it] was not meant to be thrown around loosely for seductive effects as a fashion accessory aiming at mercantile greed.

Australian singer-rapper Iggy Azalea also angered the Indian community when a video for one of her songs was found to have extremely stereotypical and misinformed representation of Indian culture and beliefs. In one part of the video she also styles herself as the Hindu deity, Ganesha.

Cultural appropriation, in general and as seen by the examples illustrated above, is a deeply racist and insensitive practice, for the principal reason that the very same people that privileged groups 'borrow' culture from, are also the people who are, in a majority of the situations, also subjugated by the privileged groups. Thus, cultural appropriation is highly offensive because of the lack of equal balance of power (Das and Kumar, 2010).

REVIEW OF LITERATURE

In a 2012 paper presented by Stacy Smith at the University of Southern California, 500 popular movies were analyzed, and each speaking character was observed and coded according to traits such as race, ethnicity, hyper, sexualisation, etc.

The paper dealt with the representation of ethnic minorities and culture groups in mainstream Hollywood movies. Its key findings have to do with how African-American directors inject more diversity as a whole into the movies they produce and direct, instead of their white-skinned counterparts, who mostly overlook PoC completely.

Additionally, across 100 top-grossing films of 2012, only 10.8% of speaking characters are Black, 4.2% are Hispanic, 5% are Asian, and 3.6% are from other mixed race ethnicities. Just over three-quarters of all speaking characters are White (76.3%). These trends are relatively stable, as little deviation is observed across the 5-year sample (Smith, 2012).

Hispanic females (41.1%, 39.3%) are more likely to be depicted in sexy attire and partially naked than Black (31.8%, 30.5%) or White females (32.8%, 32.3%). Asian females (15.7%, 15.7%) are far less likely to be sexualized. Domestic roles did not vary for females by race or ethnicity, but differences emerged for males. Hispanic males are more likely to be depicted as fathers and relational partners than males in all other racial and ethnic groups. Black males, on the other hand, are the least likely to be depicted in these roles (Smith, 2012).

Briggs, Landry and Torres (2010) paper about the portrayal of minorities in media says the same. This paper states that minorities in the entertainment industries receive no proper representation. Their portrayal is biased and actors playing minorities characters supposed to be in minority groups are hardly ever the center of the narrative.

Kacie Shaeffer's paper for Alma College breaks down the type of portrayal each racial group has in mainstream media. It specifies the relationship America shares with several minority groups, such as Black Americans, Asian Americans, Arabs, Jews, Italian Americans, Native Americans and their representation in media content, which conform to existing stereotypes and further propagate these harmful, derisive beliefs amongst audiences.

In relation specifically to Americans of African origin, scholars point out that European Americans are not familiar with Black sub-culture (Hillard, 2001). They point out that Blacks are usually portrayed not within their own culture, but as beings that have been assimilated into the dominant Euro-American culture (Campbell, 1995: 22). Some have gone so far to define a 'new' racism, one which represents upper-middle class and wealthy Blacks, but in which the 'conditions of life for poor or working-class Blacks are discounted or avoided' (Artz, 1998). Kwak (2003: 274) also speaks of the representation of Italian Americans, Asian Americans, Arab Americans, and Jews as characterising American urban landscape. In all, several American minorities, including but not limited to African Americans, Italian Americans, Asian Americans, Native Americans, Arabs, and Jews, are sorely underrepresented in the US mass media.

Simon Cottle (2000) provides a slightly different perspective. His book, *Ethnic Minorities and the Media: Changing Cultural Boundaries* deals with definitions of race, racism and prejudice, and how these factors affect media content,production, news and entertainment.

In relation to the issue of proportionate representation of PoC in media, a report written by the Ralph Bunche Center of UCLA states that "Hollywood is not progressing at the same rate as America is diversifying" as found by Hunt, lead author of the second annual Hollywood Diversity Report and the Center's director and a sociology professor. The US population is about 40 percent minority and slightly more than half female, but women and minorities are represented on screen and behind the camera in drastically lesser proportion (Siegemund-Broka, 2015).

It is also necessary to consider cultural appropriation from Smith's (2012) perspective. Linda Smith is an indigenous woman from New Zealand, and is professor of indigenous education at the University of Waikato in Hamilton, New Zealand. She had a profound quote on the subject of cultural appropriation in her book, *Decolonizing Methodologies* – "It appalls us that the West can desire, extract and claim ownership of our ways of knowing, our imagery, the things we create and produce, and then simultaneously reject the people who created and developed those ideas and seek to deny them further opportunities to be creators of their own culture and own nations" (Smith, 2012).

METHODOLOGY

A case study method was adopted to investigate Cultural Appropriation and the Misrepresentation of People of Colour in mainstream Hollywood movies. Data was triangulated (Denzin, 1999) using different approaches – case study (Yin, 1994), focus group (Fagerheim and Weingart, 2005) and online survey (Evans and Mathur, 2005). In the focus group interview, three, 10 minutes focus groups were arranged. Participants of the focus group consist of people from various races: Indian, Pakistani, Nigerian and American. The first group with an age range of 17-21, the second with an age range of 32-38, and the third with an age range of 56-67. They were questioned about their opinion of Black, Asian, Latin and Native Americans and whether the media affects their opinion they consume.

A list of all mainstream Hollywood movies produced between 1955 and 2015 was made. This created a frame from which movies could be randomly selected for purposes of analysis based on defined benchmarks i.e., movies with noticeable and acknowledged forms of racial misrepresentation. Then, through simple random sampling, one movie was chosen from each period within a frame. The following were the selected movies:

- 1955-1975: Breakfast at Tiffany's
- 1975-1995: Indiana Jones and The Temple of Doom
- 1995-2015: The Lone Ranger

FINDINGS AND DISCUSSION

In this section we discuss each of the selected movies and how they are framed including its plot.

Breakfast at Tiffany's (1961)

Breakfast at Tiffany's is a much-loved American classic, starring Audrey Hepburn as a young New York socialite Holly Golightly in an iconic role that would go on to inspire many others.

However, one of the most memorable aspects of the movie is not sparkly jewellery or an elegant dress; it is Mr. Yunioshi, Golightly's 'Japanese' neighbour.

Despite the fact that the character is clearly supposed to be of 'Asian' descent, American actor, Mickey Rooney, plays Mr. Yunioshi.

On the face of it, the most noticeable critique of the casting and portrayal of Mr. Yunioshi can be said to be the use of 'yellowface' - the phenomenon of having Asia characters in a script or story, but employing white-skinned actors to play these characters because of a reluctance to employ coloured actors, and painting/making up their outward appearances to resemble the native skin tones of the people of the culture that is being represented, resulting in creative freedom for the content producers, and the creation of negative, offensive stereotypes.

Mr. Yunioshi is portrayed as being one of the many men in Holly Golightly's life who want to have some time alone with her – in his case; it is for a 'private' photography session. In context, the character is a thinly veiled manifestation of the reigning negative sentiment amongst Americans regarding the Japanese as a direct result of the events of the Second World War (1939-1945).

The physical appearance of Yunioshi can be described as Bucktoothed, eyes with noticeable epicanthic folds, Portly and short, clean-shaven and short sighted. His other traits are: constantly irritated, clumsy, loud; thick 'Japanese' accent and mildly perverted.

For years, there was no public outrage or backlash against this extremely insensitive depiction of Mr. Yunioshi that made a hurtful caricature out of the Asian, Asian-American and Japanese communities in America. Reviews of the movie soon after its release largely overlooked the existence of Mickey Rooney's character, and if Mr. Yunoishi was acknowledged, he was seen as being "broadly exotic" (Weiler, 1961).

In the 1990s, however, many leading publications such as the Boston Globe and Los Angeles Daily News had much harsher criticism for the character.

In more recent years screenings of the movie led to protests arranged by Asian American communities, strongly condemning the racist nature of the portrayal. In 2009, a re-release of Breakfast at Tiffany's on DVD featured a short extra about the Asian perspective on yellow face. In addition, the only other non-white aside from Mr. Yunoishi is a woman of unspecified Asian descent, seen at one of Golightly's parties, dressed.

Indiana Jones and the Temple of Doom, starring Harrison Ford, is another Hollywood classic. The plot follows swashbuckling archaeologist Indiana Jones as he saves a village and its people from an evil cult.

The film opens with a sequence shot in Shanghai. The movie makes use of mild 'yellowface,' as the opening performance by Indiana's arm candy Willie

Trott features a horde of white dancers dressed to look "Chinese." Despite being white and American, she sings in Mandarin.

The film features three distinct racial groups: the Americans, British (white); the Chinese, and Indians. Indiana Jones has a sidekick in the form of Chinese former pickpocket 'Short Round,' whom Jones saved from a terrible life on the streets. 'Short Round' now regards Jones as his best friend and is a constant companion and accomplice. His traits include broken English and constant gratitude/servitude to Jones.

The Chinese crime lords in the sequence are seen as being clever and dishonest, but despite their best efforts, the indomitable Jones and his small crew easily outsmart them. Chinese were thus portrayed in the movie as untrue to their word, violent, maniacal laughs and disregard for women.

The action then moves to 'India,' where Indiana Jones and his posse are shown as being appalled and scared at the mere sight of an Indian. They then proceed to a village where they are immediately crowded around, and the pathetic plight of the Indians (who are depicted at first as zombies speaking unintelligibly) is recounted to their to-be savior, Jones.

Similarly, Indians (in the frame above) are portrayed as savage, mostly poor, superstitious, have an appetite for snakes, insects, brains, eyeballs; Bad table manners (burp on screen, lick their fingers), people who wear turbans and helpless.

The movie then depicts a kingdom (Pankot Palace) directly responsible for the terrible condition of the 'Indian' villagers, where Jones and group head to next.

In the scene pictured above, the Prime Minister of the Maharajah of Pankot is seen introducing his liege as "Zalim Singh" – Zaalim, an Urdu word, translates to "cruel."

It is in the Pankot Palace that Indians are depicted as raw snake – insect – eyeball soup drinking – monkey brain eating savages with no table manners. This depiction is particularly problematic because of two reasons: (1) traditional Indian cuisine does not consist of these foods and (2) even if it did, these foods are seen as being 'disgusting' only because it is foreign to the largely white protagonists and target audiences of the movie.

Indian actor Amrish Puri plays the role of the sadistic, merciless temple priest who rips out hearts from chest cavities with his bare hands and makes human sacrifices to the Goddess Kali as part of the Thuggee cult, whose members were earlier killed by British colonial forces. He also enslaves children in mines to look for age-old displaced stones, which are said to have special powers when united.

The movie was intended to be shot primarily in India. However, due to the racist and deeply offensive nature of the depiction of Indians – their customs, religions, beliefs, food, language and clothing, the Indian government did not allow the big-budget.

Towards the end the movie makes a subtle reference to pro-colonialism, as the white protagonists (Indiana and group, along with a British officer featured briefly earlier) are able to save the day and kill the evil temple worshippers with the help of the colonial army (who seem to be 'Indians'). They are able to restore livelihood and return the enslaved children (from the Thuggee mines) belonging to the former impoverished Indian village, now rich and prosperous.

The Lone Ranger (2013) Directed by: Gore Verbinski

The Lone Ranger is a story about a masked man and his sidekick, as they become living legends through their work. Tonto, The Lone Ranger's sidekick, is a Comanche Indian. However, Hollywood A-list, white American actor Johnny Depp, plays him. The movie starts with a child visiting a mannequin booth in a running circus in 1930s America. He stops at an exhibit of an Indian man with a placard reading 'The Noble Savage – In His Natural Habitat.' It is then a very matter-of-factly revealed that the 'Noble Savage' is, in fact, an aged Tonto, who tells his story to the child – after trading the child's peanuts for a dead rat.

The Lone Ranger's trait is presented as broken English, face paint, Feathers in hair; lots of assorted items making up eccentric costume, can talk to animals, Stoic and unintentionally funny because of his "strangeness."

The stereotypical portrayal of a Comanche Indian can be seen in the way Tonto is portrayed as an "other" and not really part of the white - American community.

The Comanche Indians (Domínguez, 2014) believe in the existence of spirit animals – i.e., they believe in an animal's ability to 'cross over to the other side' and return.

This is referenced in the movie where a mysterious white horse 'converses' with Tonto and reveals that John Reid (Armie Hammer, who at the time is unconscious and nearly dead) is destined for great things, including bringing the notorious Butch Cavendish to justice. Thus, Tonto gets to work to help bring John back to consciousness.

Additionally, the first time Indians are featured in the movie (aside from Tonto), the depiction is stereotypical, with the Indians dancing around a fire at night. Analysts describe this representation of Indians in North America as commodified racism and "exotic other" (Merskin, 2009).

Prior to and post release, the movie faced criticism regarding the portrayal of Native Indians as well as the casting of Johnny Depp. In one of the scenes, actual Native Indian Gil Birmingham is present – however, he is given no speaking lines, a decision which greatly angered the Native American community.

The movie released to disappointing business and reviews, for issues that were found to be costume design, a drab, unappealing colour scheme and an unusually long running time (149 minutes). In terms of portrayal, however, the blatant cultural appropriation of the Comanche Indian peoples – their beliefs, get-up and face paint is the most apparent problem.

FOCUS GROUP

In Focus Group 1, participants were within the age group of 17-21, and included Indians and a Nigerian. None knew the meaning of the phrase cultural appropriation, however, when asked what they thought it could mean, they collectively answered "something to do with racism."

Their opinions of the following races were:

Black American: - Cool, funny, silly, strong, prone to violence
Asian American: - Smart, sometimes funny

Latin American: - Fun, good cooks, good looking
Native American: - Live in deserts, non-existent today.

None of the participants personally knew any people of the races mentioned. They agreed that their opinion is based on the media they consume.

In Focus Group 2, participants were within the age group of 32-38, and included Indians and a Pakistani. One knew the meaning of cultural appropriation. The others said it is "something offensive" or "something wrong."

Their opinions about the following races were registered:

1. Black American: Speak in slang, aggressive, violent, poorly educated
2. Asian American: Smart, disciplined, boring
3. Latin American: Blue collar workers, family-oriented
4. Native American: Aggressive

As with Focus Group 1, none of the participants personally knew any people of the races mentioned. They agreed that their opinion is based on the media they consume.

In Focus Group 3, participants were within the age group of 56-67, and included Indians and an American. One knew the meaning of cultural appropriation. The others said it is "cultural insensitivity" or "being faithful to your culture."

Their opinions of the following races were:

1. Black American: Goofy, financially weak, uneducated, aggressive
2. Asian American: Dull, no sense of humour, disciplined
3. Latin American: Fun loving, talkative
4. Native American: Financially weak

Two of the participants personally knew people of any races mentioned. One agreed that their opinion is based on the media they consume.

Quantitative Research Findings

In a survey of 100 respondents (63 female; 37 male) consisting of Hollywood movie buffs, People of Colour (Indian, Pakistani, Irani,

Bangladeshi, Nigerian, Sudanese, Russian) and young adult consumers of media, the following results were recorded.

Only 70% of respondents actually identified People of Colour. 80% of respondents were not aware of the meaning of the term cultural appropriation. When explained, 65% of the respondents said that they found it an offensive practice. The reasons why ranged from "it creates a misleading stereotype" to "members of the dominant group seldom understand the history, tradition and context of the culture of the other, less dominant group" to being "unethical."

Only 16% of respondent think that their culture is accurately represented in mainstream Hollywood movies. However, when asked if racial stereotypes were necessary in Hollywood movies, 60% of the respondents answered "Yes, but only to some degree," with 37% responding "No."

82% of respondents answered that they had, in some point in their lives, found racial stereotypes funny.

Only 14% of respondents believed that Hollywood is sensitive in its portrayal of different ethnic and racial groups. 35% answered "No," whereas 51% responded that it "Could be better."

47% of respondents believe that they would be accepted in Western society based on the representation of their cultures in Hollywood movies. However, 52% respondents answered "Yes" when asked whether the representation of their culture in mainstream Hollywood movies had ever made them feel embarrassed or ashamed of their cultural identity or origin.

Conclusion

The results of the case studies, focus groups and survey confirm that the existing type of PoC representation in American media, with special reference to movies, is damaging to the identity and self-image of PoC. The research has also revealed that most participants and media consumers were unaware of the meaning of the phrase cultural appropriation prior to participation in the research. However, after understanding the meaning of the term, most agreed that is an offensive practice.

It was found that stereotyping in movies greatly affects people's opinions of different racial groups, with most participants of the focus groups forming opinions of Black, Asian, Latin and Native Americans without knowing people of these races. Results of the study show that only 14% of respondents believe that Hollywood is sensitive in its portrayal of different social and ethnic groups, and 52% answered that the sort of representation they see of their cultures in mainstream Hollywood movies has, in some point in their lives, made them feel ashamed of their cultural identity or origin.

The case studies of the movies, as well as research about important news events related to these movies, have revealed that Hollywood representation of PoC is highly offensive, stereotypical and appropriative.

The research has been unable to determine whether misrepresentation and cultural appropriation are trends that have increased or decreased over time in mainstream Hollywood movies.

In: Media Anthology
Editor: Theophilus Kofi Gokah
ISBN: 978-1-63484-931-9

Chapter 10

MAD MARKETING: THE BOLLYWOOD BUSINESS IN THE UAE

*Disha Dadlani**
School of Media and Communication,
Manipal University Dubai, United Arab Emirates

ABSTRACT

The objectives of this Study are to examine the growth and progress of Bollywood cinema, its distribution and the various promotional activities executed by different companies in the UAE. Cinema is a business; filmmakers and businesspeople each compete to overtake the other in order to reach the '100 Crore Club.' India is a large movie producing country, releasing around 800 movies, each year. Some of the movies survive and make it through the audience's 'hearts and pockets' and some just have a blink-and-miss appearance. In order to understand how this success translates in the UAE market, a case study on two Bollywood movies marketed extensively in UAE was done with a focus on the marketing budget, the success rate, the promotional campaign executed and profits made. Expert Interviews was used to gather information on growth of Bollywood in the UAE. The result shows that there is a marked increase of 50% production, promotion and distribution of Bollywood films in UAE.

* Corresponding author: Disha Dadlani. E-mail: dishadadlani55@gmail.com.

Keywords: Bollywood, promotions, marketing, cinema, distribution, globalization

Introduction

Promotional activities initiated through the use of handmade posters and simple billboards have become an extensive business in marketing films. This is not surprising because the four P's of marketing (Promotion, Price, Product, Place) are the most important in marketing, and by extension, a movie (Garikaparthi, 2008). Promotional activities vary from posters to movie apps on smartphones. Online websites, blogs and games are the newest entries in the world of Bollywood marketing and the impact on moviegoers has proved to be tremendous. Existing research (Mukherjee-Das, 2013) suggest that 14 million Indians spend their leisure time at the cinemas on a daily basis and spend an amount that equates to an average Indian's daily wage, on viewing ticket, each year. Indian producers today make it a point to not only touch upon unique themes but they also employ experimental techniques of promotional methods. In previous years, Bollywood films' success was measured by the number of weeks the movie ran, unlike today where the measure is based on, first and foremost the amount the movie makes and then viewership. To reach that objective, prizes are often used as incentives to lure viewers and audiences with the aim of boosting box office sales of a film (Mukherjee-Das, ibid).

Sequels have also come to be identified as a way of promotion, rather than nostalgia marketing, of keeping the first movie alive, with the aid of the second, thus, inducing a sense of familiarity. Product placement in films has also grown over time and can be seen as an indirect and subtle way of promoting films (Kaur, 2014).

In Films like *Jaane Tu Yaa Jaane Na* and *Taare Zameen Par*, modern marketing strategies gradually opened the doors to new media marketing (Ahmed, 2011). Bollywood films are recognized globally but filmmakers still constantly compete in the rat race to promote their movies extensively and get them noticed. The bottom-line is that promotion and persuasion acts as powerful tools in influencing the decisions of cine goers.

EXISTING DISCOURSE

Globalized Bollywood

A global association in Bollywood has been discussed (see for example Desai, 2013). For example, songs like "*Mera joota hai japani...*" in the 1950s. Similar influences can be found in films like *Bombay Dreams, Moulin Rouge*, etc., wherein the Bollywood style was adapted (Shrestha, 2008). Compared to a meagre 607 films released annually in the United States, in the year 2006, the Indian film industry produced and released a total of 1090 films (Geoffery et al., 2014).

Bollywood is often confused with Indian cinema; however it is important to understand that it is a Hindi language cinema out of at least a dozen other language cinemas in the nation (Dudrah, 2012). Bollywood as a cinema may be powerful nationally but it is not the national cinema (Wilson, 2014). According to *The Economic Times of India*, the first highest grossing film of Bollywood that made it large was "larger than life" *Hum Aapke Hai Koun!* With a hint of effective marketing, it ran for almost a year, raking $30 million, in comparison to a mere $3 million made by an average film (Rajadhyaksha, 2007).

The Karan Johar directorial, *Kal Ho Naa Ho*, is noted to have been the first commercial Indian film set in America. Both US and British-based Indian directors such as Gurinder Chadha, Mira Nair purport to have filled the void between Indian and Western Cinema with their respective films (Thusu, 2012).

BOLLYWOOD AT THE BOX OFFICE

Compared to the United States and United Kingdom, the price of a ticket in the Indian theatre is 10 times lesser. $1/5^{th}$ of the profit earned by Indian cinema is generated from foreign markets (Bose, 2006). *Mission Kashmir*, Hrithik Roshan and Preity Zinta starrer was the first Bollywood film to be featured in *Times Square* in the big apple – New York. Sony had purchased the foreign market rights for a whopping 120 million rupees (Govil, 2007).

THE POWER OF PROMOTION

In this section, the power of promotional activities is highlighted, emphasizing on some Bollywood movies that made it big and the marketing techniques its filmmaker employed.

3 Idiots

With a great global response and an even greater box office sales 3 Idiots had indeed grabbed attention (Upadhyay, 2010). The film marketed itself with the joint effort of Reliance Life Insurance, using the tagline of the mantra on the film 'All is well,' which also went well with the insurance concept offering an 'All is well' secured life to their clients (Upadhyay, ibid).

Owned by the Ambanis, this collaboration between the corporation and filmmakers, speak volumes about its success. 3 Idiots hit 1750 screens and 1550 prints in total. Multiplexes raised the price by 25-30% for evening shows and the rate almost doubled for morning shows. The result was a higher revenue generation (ibid, 2010). The film also collaborated with Converse and Pantaloons, in order to reach out to the youth and to garner appeal.

MAD MARKETING: CATCH-ME-IF-YOU-CAN

Since the film revolved around the sudden disappearance of *Rancho*, Aamir Khan's character in the film, the actor tried to execute the same reel stunt. The actor hid in mysterious locations, in the country and his fans were allotted a time of 2 weeks to find him. In an attempt to indulge in new media marketing for the film, the marketers created a customized Facebook page called Pucca Idiot which offered fans who were awaiting the movie an opportunity to watch the film on this special platform (Nidhi Upadhyay, 2010).

In the ensuing section, I highlight the marketing strategies implemented by the biggest business tycoons of Bollywood, Shah Rukh Khan and Rohit Shetty, for their blockbuster *Chennai Express*. The film had all the elements of a Marketing Mix (Dasgupta, 2001).

Eid Release

The decision to release the film on a festive date, during a festive atmosphere was a very clever move by the marketers.

Language Diversity

The blockbuster was released in 10 different languages worldwide to reach out to a wider market and finally the decision to sell the TV rights of the movie to Zee Entertainment's new Hindi movie channel and pictures.

Social Media Marketing

Social media, mobile phones and TV (Reality shows such as *Jhalak Dikkhla Jaa*, *DID Supermoms*, *Comedy Nights With Kapil* and even TV soaps with high TRP and popularity such as *Madhubala* and *Taarak Mehta Ka Ooltah Chashmah*) were buzzing with Chennai Express promotions well in advance.

METHODOLOGY

The design in this study was exploratory. Interviews were held with 6 people whose views were considered as expert opinions on marketing and Bollywood films. These were purposively chosen because it was believed they hold the key to answers on the subject in review. After all, expert opinion is a purposive sampling bearing in mind the degree of accuracy required to study Bollywood promotions in UAE; Expert Opinion was thus deemed an effective method. This also afforded the opportunity to understand growth patterns of Bollywood film promotions, distribution and production in the UAE.

Participant Observation at Bollywood movie launches and promotions of movies gave an insight into film-marketing scenarios in the UAE. Along with this, a case study on two Bollywood films that were promoted on a large scale in the UAE helped to build a better understanding about Bollywood film marketing techniques in the UAE.

Findings and Discussions

Expert Opinion

Experts based in UAE, from varied fields of expertise were contacted for the study in order to get a wide spread of data. UAE has grown as a film market over the years and is considered as one of the most profitable overseas market. Typically, 50% of Bollywood films shares are generated from the region. Some of the influential factors that have contributed to the development of UAE as a film market are: Proximity to India, the standard of operating procedures offered by the government and comparative pricing in the global film market.

Bollywood Film Actors and Commentators: Ranveer Singh, Priyanka Chopra, Ali Abbas Zafar and Arjun Kapoor at the trailer launch of their film, Gunday at the Dubai International Film Festival.

There has been a gradual but positive increase in the production, distribution and promotion of Bollywood films in the UAE over the years. However, the degree or percentage increase is difficult to quantify in specific terms. However, experts estimate that there is a 40-50% increase in the growth of Bollywood films in UAE as observed by this respondent:

> There has surely been an increase (it would be difficult to quantify these metrics) and if the present is any indication we are looking at an upward trend in the future. As the audience for Bollywood films in this region grows and the cinema chains continue opening more cinemas

(which translates to more screens for Bollywood films) distribution of Bollywood films seems like a promising proposition. Promotion of Bollywood films in the UAE is evolving as well. In the UAE we are fortunate enough to have media outlets that have a wide reach and are immensely popular with the Bollywood audience. The Bollywood radio networks, TV Channels, etc. do a great job of supporting in promotions of Bollywood films. In the past year social media and social media influencers in UAE have also done a phenomenal job in promoting films in this region since majority of Bollywood films cater to the youth and social media is perhaps the best place to target them. (*Roshini, Expert Respondent* X1)

India is already familiar with the term 'Mad marketing,' which means out-of-the-box and innovative promotional activities that garner attention and appeal. It may be unlikely that this method of marketing will hit UAE soon. Marketing anything requires investment which most of the movie marketing companies won't advise for UAE because it exceeds the budget. However, it is looked upon as a successful strategy and may gather steam over the years as again suggested by Roshini:

Unsure of what the phrase 'Mad Marketing' means; if it means out of the box and fierce promotions leading up to the release of the film then yes I'd think that this is a successful strategy. The audiences these days are extremely selective about the media they consume and are time-deprived. In such a scenario, it only helps when a film comes up with a promotion that is different from the rest and gets everybody talking about it. There is a fine line between being edgy and being offensive so as long as the campaign promotes the film without belittling any person/place/institution there is no harm in trying newer forms of promotional campaigns. I already see this trend having entered the UAE markets. Filmmakers want cooler, fresher and edgier ideas to appeal to moviegoers. Hopefully this will gather more steam from 2015.

Among the successful promotional techniques adopted to promote a film in the region, the most effective is the 'Meet and Greet' with the cast of the movie. In a recent marketing stunt employed by Talent and PR agency, *Muse Dubai* with the help of *the Dubai Film and TV Commission*, thousands of extras from all over UAE were roped in and were an integral part of the blockbuster *Happy New Year*. This proved to be a major success. 70% of *Happy New Year* was shot in Atlantis, Dubai, which marked it as the longest shoot for a Bollywood movie in the UAE. The following opinions express this thinking:

> Opportunities that cannot be bought by money are always the ones that work the best. Hence, if a promotion allows fans to meet a star of a movie it is a sure shot guaranteed success. Another thing that works well is tie-ups with other media channels such as a radio partner and organizing word of mouth screenings/premieres. The hype created before, during and after such events usually sustains and works in favour of the movie. (*Rehaab, Expert Respondent*)

> "This campaign got people talking about Happy New Year months before the official launch of the first poster! It generates a lot of publicity for the film and gets people talking. It tied in perfectly with the fact that the film was shot here and SRK has a massive fan following here as well. It's imperative to have a comprehensive campaign that covers all forms of media that your target audiences are consuming. No point in spend hundreds of thousands of Dirhams on a billboard *ad* in a misplaced location; 'accurate targeting' is key. It could be a simple promotion but as long as it is executed effectively and targeted to the right people at the right time it will deliver positive results. (*Gagan, Expert Respondent*)

PARTICIPANT OBSERVATION

Participant Observation to gauge audience reaction produce a synonymous effect of what respondents make of Hollywood film promotion in UAE

> If you just place a camera in India, and then just place the same camera in Dubai, you will see the difference in the quality of air and quality of picture. The Khans choose to shoot often in the UAE since they get good governmental support. Dubai has become like an extended city of India for bigger films to promote... Indians in Dubai are very close knit and they all come to know about upcoming events, releases, etc. very quickly. One visit by the cast of a film is enough to get everyone aware in the city; which is absolutely not the case in India. So promoting films in Dubai gives an upper hand of a better opening for the film (Therefore, promoting a film in Dubai helps the makers to some extent). However, local audiences have a lot of variety with all English releases and I feel they will still watch whatever they want to and it's not easy to influence

and turn them towards Bollywood films just because UAE was a destination for that film; this turn can only be brought about by quality films, performances and stories regardless of which city they are shot in. If Dubai is a very integral part of the story and not just a mere location, then maybe it can stir some feelings in the local audiences, else not. (*Japinder, Expert Respondent*)

Expats (especially South East Asians) form a huge part of UAE's population. In order to get their films to reach a wider market (outside India) it is important for studios/distributors to promote their films in this market. Over the past couple of years, the landscape of Bollywood cinema has changed drastically with Bollywood stars themselves coming to UAE to promote their films since they've mapped the potential of Bollywood films here. Many filmmakers target this region even before the 'promotion stage.' Happy New Year was extensively shot in Dubai and hence the movie was fiercely promoted in UAE.

Filmmaker Japinder Kaur being interviewed on the red carpet about her film, in Novo Cinemas, Dubai.

Respondents in this study believe that one reason, if not the main reason, for the speedy growth of Bollywood film promotions, productions and distribution in Dubai should be credited to the News Media. This respondent also touches on other factors, which he considers as critical:

The first factor would be the south Asian population which is almost to 65% in UAE. The market is serving the high profiles and page 3 groups, which mean anything being discussed here, would be soon news.

The craze, glitz, glamour and nightlife in Dubai are discussed around the globe and attract attention easily. It is a signature opening if marked by the presence of any Bollywood celebrity, that's the trend which is now pulling up, when it comes to mega launch/openings. The media coverage they capture in Dubai caters to massive market meaning, target audience from multiple nationalities. The media here is not as huge as back in India BUT, it spreads the news not only in GCC but on a global network and social media as well. (*Asif, Show Producer and Expert Respondent*)

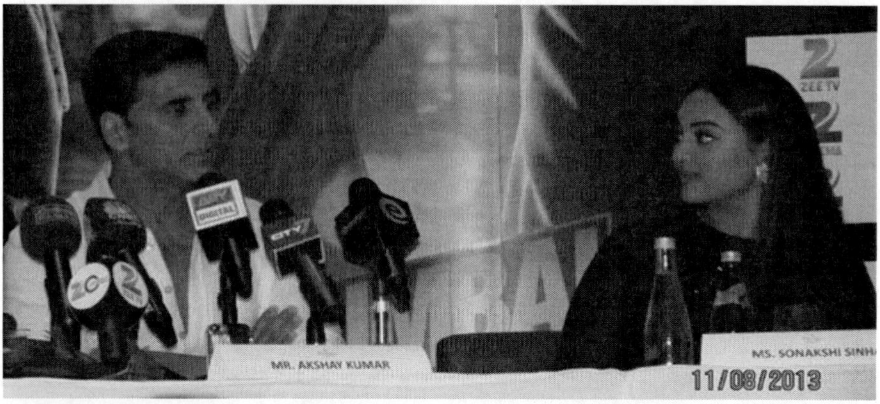

Akshay Kumar and Sonakshi Sinha address the media gathering at a press conference for their film Once Upon A Time In Mumbai Dobaara at the Oberoi Hotel, Dubai.

Left – Shahid Kapoor signs an autograph at the meet and greet event to promote his flick Chance Pe Dance at Ramee Royal Hotel, Dubai (Right) – Excited fans meet their idol Dharmendra when he was in Dubai to promote his film Yamla Pagla Deewana 2 in Meydan, Dubai.

The concept of Meet and Greet has become very common and is considered to be the strongest promotional tool because everyone wants to meet their favourite star and click a picture with them!

Public interaction is a small but genuine effort. Stars sometimes make it a point to interact with the public and brief them about the movie in the theatre before the movie is screened.

The cast and crew of Yamla Pagla Deewana 2 interacts with the public before the premiere screening of the film at Meydan, IMAX, Dubai.

Other promotional tools such as social media were mentioned and emphasized by Roshini:

> This is a trend that started a while ago and has only gotten stronger as time went by. Social media contributes the most since unlike most forms of traditional media (TV, newspapers, etc.), social media gives people a chance to create a direct dialogue with the film makers and the cast. They share their opinions about the movie with friends and help create buzz that is considerably higher than a magazine ad or a billboard banner. This is because of the added 'credibility' factor. I may have seen the trailer of a film on TV and heard a radio spot but still decided not to watch it. But if a friend tweets with a positive review about the film, that could change my perspective and create an intent to watch. New media makes that possible. Today if a film doesn't have an online presence (a website, a Facebook page or a Twitter profile) the buzz is highly affected because their rankings on Google are affected. This is not a good idea because in this day and age if one wants information about anything, they

> instantly hop on to Google. Facebook, Twitter and Instagram are growing at a very rapid speed in UAE and to engage with the youth on these platforms films are promoted actively on social networking sites as well (both Bollywood and Hollywood). I've seen and been a part of a lot of cool initiatives to promote Bollywood films in the UAE which include tools like interactive mobile applications, augmented reality and many more.

The importance of Social media marketing has received attention in academic discourse. Curtis (2011) for instance mentions that Facebook has more than 500 million users worldwide; Twitter has approximately 175 million users; LinkedIn has more than 90 million users; and MySpace has 57 million users, which makes it feasible to reach a huge market at the click of a button. Companies and firms are also tapping into these platforms as part of their strategies (Pradiptarini, 2011). It is not surprising that Bollywood is also using social media to expand its market base.

Daud, another respondent and a film maker adds to the commentary on UAE as a film market:

> Take for instance the film Happy New Year. A major portion of it was shot in Atlantis, Dubai. The grand locations offered by the UAE are definitely one of the factors that come to mind while considering UAE as a Bollywood movie hub. People prefer UAE because of its infrastructure and its large South East Asian diaspora. Over the years, locals have developed a love for Bollywood, as well, which serves as yet another factor... Bollywood production in UAE has increased a lot over the years. It is due to film festivals like the Dubai International Film Festival that more filmmakers are encouraged to shoot and produce films in the UAE. Though it may seem an expensive affair to shoot and produce in Dubai, the city's security and infrastructure is reason enough to influence filmmakers to film in the city. Today almost all big names fly down to UAE to shoot/promote their film.

Next, we focus our attention to some cases and their various promotional strategies in marketing Bollywood films in UAE.

The Case of Chennai Express and Jai Ho

Chennai Express promotional plan included a promotional tour of the 100 crore film which was brought to the UAE by Event and Advertising agencies, *Dream Advertising and Ministry of Events*. To achieve the 'wow effect' and to ensure that audiences flock to theatres in large numbers to watch the film, the makers and the event agencies concerned with the promotional campaign filled the agenda with a press conference, and a crowd engagement activity to generate public interaction, a niche activity, a store visit and an *Iftar* dinner.

Since it was the *holy month of Ramadan*, it was only apt to break the fast with the masses. Hence, there were two Iftars observed - a mass public *Iftar* that was open to everyone hosted by RJ Sid of City 101.6, *Chennai Express's* official media partners. The other *Iftar* was a grand exclusive *Iftar* dinner restricted to elites only.

The *Chennai Express* team estimated 500 posters, 5000 flyers, 25 roll-ups and 25 standees, *pre* and *post* event coverage in newspapers. An email blast was also conducted and emails were sent at random to a database of 70,000 active email addresses, with the promotional campaign included in each mail.

The team used *Twitter* and *Facebook* to spread awareness about the film. Mall activities were conducted on a large scale and special branding backdrops and promotional materials were displayed at the malls. Cut outs were also placed in the malls prior to the tour in order to create a buzz.

Albeit, *Jai Ho* did not only enjoy large scale promotions and a World premiere in Dubai, Meydan, IMAX, but it also enjoyed a small share of production in the UAE for which crew from India were flown down to the Emirate. *AURA Events (Hospitality and Food and Beverage) and Creative Angels (Advertising) and Pacific Ventures (Co-producer)* brought *Jai Ho* to the UAE bearing in mind the fact that blockbuster was to have its World Premiere in Dubai; the event management and advertising agencies concerned then decided to raise the level of their promotions. What then was their promotional plan?

Jai Ho promotional schedule included a chain of events starting from press conference to be followed by a red carpet event at Meydan, Imax. The screening and the after-party event was an invite-only to elites.

Choosing to promote the film extensively and to screen in Dubai definitely worked in the favour of Bollywood and its film crossed a whopping 200 crores+.

CONCLUSION

It is evident from the discussions that UAE has gradually evolved as a film market over the years. The major influential factors contributing to the production and promotion of Bollywood films in the region, as observed, are the proximity to India and a chunk of South East Asian population in the region.

Although it isn't easy to quantify the results, experts in the field of film and cinema are of the view that there has been a marked increase in the production, promotion and distribution of Bollywood films in UAE.

Bollywood has globalized and is now widespread across the globe. Typically, 50% of the total share of overseas market collections of Bollywood films comes from the UAE and this figure is more likely to increase in the coming years.

In: Media Anthology
Editor: Theophilus Kofi Gokah

ISBN: 978-1-63484-931-9

Chapter 11

TROLLING AND ONLINE AGGRESSION: A REVIEW OF UNDERLYING CONFLICTS AND VARIED DEFINITIONS

Lippy Ramchandani*
School of Media and Communication,
Manipal University Dubai, United Arab Emirates

ABSTRACT

This paper attempts to draw a clear distinction between trolling and other forms of online aggression. It also considers the many definitions of trolling and tries to eliminate those that are stereotypical and generic in nature. In this way, it aims to provide content for future research. The extensive popularization of trolling by the media has driven the masses to have incorrect notions about what constitutes trolling. Consequently, the term 'trolling' is used to define almost any situation of online aggression. This has led to ambiguity around the word "troll." All the attempted explanations proposed by researchers have assisted in distinguishing trolls from other cyber criminals. However, it is important to take into consideration, due to the deceptive nature of trolling, the subjectivity that comes along with it. All the proposed definitions of trolling, although overlapping with each other and other concepts, seem to have a redundant pattern. This paper does not only try to clear any ambiguity associated

* Corresponding author: Lippy Ramchandani. E-mail: lippy.lnr@gmail.com.

with the word trolling but also try to construct a working definition of what constitutes 'trolling' and who a 'troll' is?

INTRODUCTION

With the evolution of all the phases that synchronous and asynchronous Computer Mediated Communication (CMC) have been through, i.e., from its initial instigation in the 1980's as an aid to education, to where it is now, a thriving medium for viral videos and memes, it is quite expected that something of such a global scale will have some negative repercussions (Cuddy, 2006). It is important to state that CMC is far more complex as compared to face-to-face communication and should therefore be subject to greater critical and lexical analysis (Warschauer, 2001). Asynchronous CMC is communication that happens over the Internet but there is a delay between sending and receiving messages between multiple participants (Hirotani, 2013).

Social Media, described as "Internet-based applications that build on the ideological and technological foundations of Web 2.0 and that allow the creation and exchange of user-generated content" (Kaplan and Haenlein, 2010) is a good platform to analyse aggression. The key word here is "user-generated content" because one of the aims of this paper is to throw light on the irony of how it is "user-generated content" itself that distresses the other users.

For the sake of our better understanding, this paper will take examples of celebrity cases for the simple reason that celebrities, by their very nature and profession, are always placed under the scrutinizing and watchful eye of the media. Even though CMC is ephemeral in the online world, it has a sort of permanence if someone witnesses the action, and this is even more so in the case of celebrities because fanatics are always watching their every step. Celebrities have two personas: public and private. The public body is the one that they carefully presents in front of the camera, while the private body includes their personal lives – the ones that they try to hide away from the camera. The evolutionary upsurge of social mediums, as well as the ease with which one can access and peek into the life of a celebrity, has blurred the fine line between the public and private lives of celebrities (Harris, 2011). This has inevitably led to a lot of cases of 'celebrity harassment' (Watt, 2012).

The following case will help us to deconstruct what trolling is?

CASE STUDY

At the 55th Annual Grammy Awards, when pop-star Justin Bieber wasn't nominated, he admitted that he was disappointed, as he had worked hard enough to be at least nominated if not awarded (Rolling Stone, 2013).

On the other hand, the Black Keys, the American Rock Duo, won three awards for their hit single, "Lonely Boy." After the award ceremony, a TMZ reporter asked Patrick Carney, what he thought of Justin Bieber being snubbed by the Grammy's, he replied, "I don't know, he's rich right? Grammys are for like… I don't know, for music not for like money and he's making a lot of money. I don't know. He should be happy, I guess."

TMZ then broadcasted this on their website and YouTube channel. Justin was offended by the comment and he then tweeted to his 30 million strong fans the following:

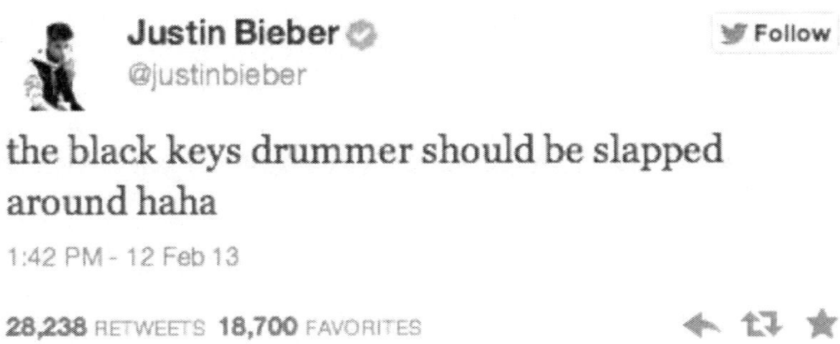

Credit: Twitter.com.

Patrick Carney justified himself by implying that the words were put into his mouth by TMZ and that his comment was purely innocuous. He even said that he was paying Bieber a "compliment he didn't understand."

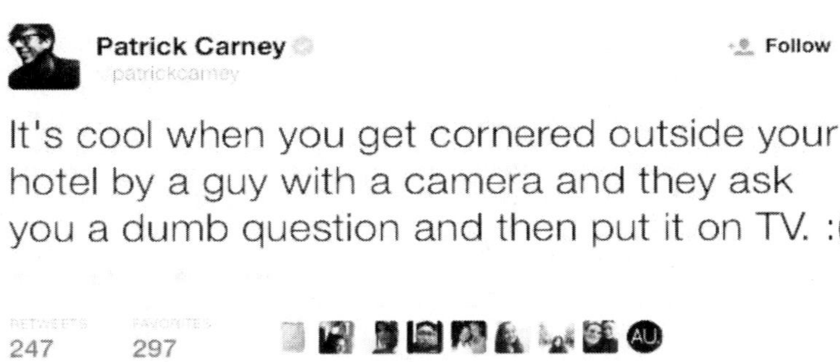

Millions of Justin Bieber's fans unleashed their fury on Patrick Carney's comment. To this Patrick Carney replied with his deadpan humor and sheer placidity, sometimes throwing a sad face emoticon in there, taking whatever came, in his stride. This didn't stop Bieber's fans from sending hate to Carney.

Carney then decided to take it to the next level and thus began the most iconic feud in the history of celebrity trolling on Twitter. He changed his name to Justin Bieber, his profile photo to a picture of Justin Bieber wearing black-rimmed glasses and his bio to "a official twitter for the actual verified Justin Bieber DOS virtual buddy." And, since he is a celebrity, his now turned Bieber profile had the verified tick, which essentially signifies that this is a famous figure's official account.

He then began posting as Bieber himself, parodying everything that Bieber embodies and stands for – even cyber bullying. This began a chain of tweets between Carney and Bieber fans. Bieber fans would insult Carney, and Carney would reply with nonchalance or funny, sarcastic remarks. This further infuriated not just Beiber's fans but also Carney's. Both the fan bases called him "childish" and "immature" for doing this but it didn't stop Carney.

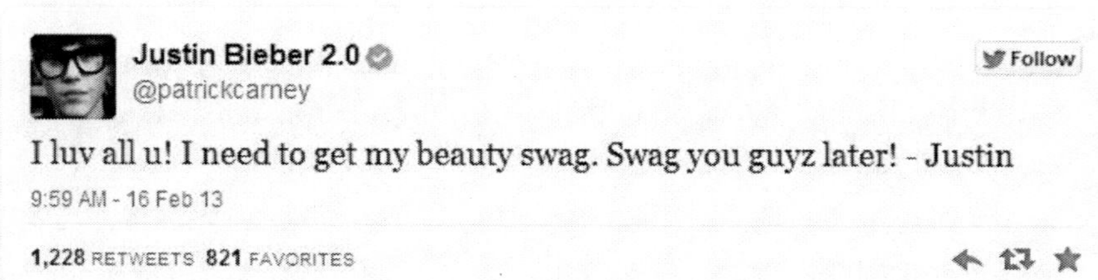

Then following year in an interview with Rolling Stones magazine, he let out more hate on Bieber by unapologetically cussing at him (Rolling Stone, 2014).

Note: For the sake of convenience and understanding, future reference in the paper linked back to the case study will be written in italics.

ANALYSIS

Hopkinson (2013) claims that the phenomenon of trolling hasn't been extensively studied. Hopkinson further points us to Hardarker's (2010) work, which seems to be an extensive and seemingly exclusive research dedicated towards obtaining a working definition of trolling. Hardarker (ibid) reaffirms this claim by stating that linguistic online aggression is occasionally perceived as trivial. However, this is not entirely true. With a significant rise in online forums there has been a corresponding increase in the interest for understanding how online communication has shaped the Internet to what it is today (Merritt, 2012).

Hardarker (2010) mentioned impolite flaming, trolling and other forms of online abuse, whether explicit or implicit, as their common denominator. Researchers who study impoliteness in CMC for research purposes are gradually shifting from a syntactical notion to pragmatic ones (Hardaker, 2010). Earlier researchers were more concerned with superficial qualities of online arguments such as the syntax and structure. Now, it is being realized that conflict and argument play a vital role in defining identity and "the-self" and are core contributions to dissemination of ideologies. This is where trolling comes in. Trolling, at the face of it, may not necessarily appear as trolling. On the other hand, contextual insight into seemingly innocent situations may, in fact, be a trolling situation. Thus, before trusting anything online, one must verify the sources and look for trustworthy certifiable information. But of course, this can't always be done and definitely not in the case of trolls since their purpose of existence itself is to deceive their victims and the spectators (Ficaras, vivas and Romo, 2009).

WHAT A TROLL IS NOT

Hardaker (2010) proposes a definition of a troll by first stressing on what a troll is not, i.e., trolling is not merely a situation of online impoliteness. Although impoliteness is an inherent outcome or characteristic of trolling, the following situations do not constitute trolling.

- Ritual or Mock Impoliteness: This form of impoliteness is meant to strengthen bonds between Speaker/Producer/Writer (Hereon S or She) and Hearer/Recipient/Reader (Hereon H or He) where by Speaker may deliberately offend or insult a recipient with their banter. This form of communication may be deemed as ritualistic or customary in order to enhance relationships and create a sense of belongingness to the novice participants. To an outsider, this form of communication may appear impolite. As its name 'mock impoliteness' suggests, it is not genuine impoliteness, it is just a mock performance.

- Non-malicious impoliteness: It is communication without any intent of antagonism by a Speaker as S/he may feel that she is in the position to offer constructive criticism and assumes the responsibility even though she knows it may offend the recipient.
- Rudeness/Faux Pas/Failed politeness: This refers to absence of politeness or a situation where the recipient, although innocent, takes a Sender's message, offensively. The Sender miscalculates the degree of politeness required by the recipient and this consequent lack of politeness offends him/her. This type of interaction is based on the recipient's interpretation of the sender's message, rather than the Sender's actual intention of the conveyed message.

Carney's comment regarding the lack of Beiber's nominations at the 55th Annual Grammy Awards ceremony, "… Grammys are for like… I don't know, for music not for like money and he's making a lot of money. I don't know. He should be happy, I guess." can be regarded as both Non-Malicious impoliteness and Faux Pas/Failed politeness. Carney defends himself by saying that he was paying Bieber a compliment that Bieber did not understand.

A year later, when asked about it in a Rolling Stones interview, carney explains, "I'm saying that he should be grateful that he has a f*cking career in music. And he shouldn't be f*cking telling his followers to slap me, and then also be doing anti-bullying bullshit. It's so irresponsible."

It may be argued here that Carney did indeed blatantly insult Bieber in an interview and not online, but for the sake of understanding, this quote is taken out of context and it is explained here that this is the form of impoliteness (and not trolling) that his comments would be considered had he not insulted Bieber.

- Failed (malicious) impoliteness: This is the opposite of faux pas or failed impoliteness because S's intended and deliberate impoliteness is not considered to be impolite by H at all. H either fails to identify that S is being impolite or confuses it with mock impoliteness, faux pas or failed politeness or non-malicious impoliteness.

- Thwarted/frustrated (malicious) impoliteness: In this form, the Sender is impolite towards the recipient and s/he correctly interprets this. The recipient takes no offence to it thereby thwarting the obligation to be offended. This may frustrate the Sender as the recipient reacts unexpectedly with sarcasm, condescension or amusement.

Patrick Carney's nonchalant reaction to Bieber's fans calling him immature is an example of Thwarted/frustrated impoliteness and is in fact the determining factor in calling him a troll. The very fact that he is not only unaffected but also fully aware of how he comes across to his and Bieber's fans, and that he acknowledges their disapproval and continues to parody Bieber, shows us that he is a troll. He appears to not only ignore the persistent pleas but also seeks enjoyment out of the negative attention.

- Genuine, malicious, strategic impoliteness or instrumental rudeness: The distinct characteristic of this form is that the Sender not only intends the impoliteness but ensures that his intent is conveyed to the recipient.

Again, it is important to remember, that although we have laid down a clear distinction between impoliteness and trolling, we are still using this instances of Carney trolling Bieber as examples because this impoliteness is implicit in trolling. This does not mean that it is not an instance of trolling. Almost all instances of trolling are forms of impoliteness but all forms of impoliteness are not instances of trolling. Having said that, What Carney does by parodying Bieber is definitely an instance of trolling.

As mentioned earlier, this case study attempts to serve as an example for these theories but does not promise to be one. Having established that, it can be argued that Carney may have held 'too strong' of an opinion about Bieber. Earlier, when asked by TMZ, Carney had commented that Bieber doesn't deserve a Grammy award since he is not capable enough. However, in his later interviews he says, "I mean, Justin Bieber is a f*cking moron, and that's the gist of what I was saying. And then he goes and says I should be slapped? Honestly, I feel bad for him. Every single person who works with him should f*cking be embarrassed that they don't... No one is doing him any favours, you know? And honestly, I don't dislike his music. I don't listen to his music, but he needs to not conduct himself that way. Like, really, you make millions of dollars playing music, you should feel f*cking lucky."

Carney should have chosen his words carefully because it implies that he is dissing his music without actually hearing it. By saying, "you make millions of dollars playing music, you should feel f*cking lucky," he is also implying that Bieber's success is all luck and not work hard enough. He may have said this because he and his partner Dan have toured the roads for years to get recognized, while Justin Bieber's road to fame was relatively easier in comparison. But there is also a debate that Carney may have insulted Bieber with such fervour in order to promote his new album. Why else, we may question, would he rekindle his wrath towards Bieber a whole year later?

FLAMING OR TROLLING?

The two concepts – flaming and trolling have subjective definitions and seem to share common characteristics. Juxtaposing the terms, flaming and impoliteness, with trolling can be understood as:

- Subtle and deceptive nature of trolling.
- A successful trolling situation has a high potential of turning into a flame war. Flaming is something that ensues after a troll trolls within a community and is often something that the troll anticipates. It is a *modus operandi* of trolling and may therefore be sometimes confused with trolling itself (Tkacz, 2013)

There is a natural tendency for online discussions to turn into a flame war. A flame war is defined as an escalated, heated argument that potentially steers the conversation away from the original discussion. Trolling differs from flaming in the sense that flaming is very direct in nature – there is no ambiguity about whether or not there is a disagreement or aggression. The comments are derogatory in their implication and blatantly direct towards the victim. However, as it was mentioned earlier, the patterns of these flame wars fairly resemble those of trolling and/or are usually outcomes of trolling (Angouri and Tseliga, 2010).

Such spiraling flame wars eventually leads to decay of the thematic line of the discussions and may consequently result in disruption of the online community. As it will be mentioned hereafter, this disruption is one of the four key characteristics of trolling.

TYPES OF TROLLS

One of the first attempts of defining the word troll comes from a book called 'Netlingo' in the mid 1990s. Netlingo is now a virtual dictionary where people can look up what online lingos mean (Netlingo, 1999) [Online].

Netlingo too uses the finishing analogy to describe a troll by saying that a troll is someone who baits, fishes, entices or allures. Netlingo also distinguishes trolls into the following four categories:

- Playtime Trolls: They are direct in nature as they blatantly go about their business, and are relatively easy to identify, as their identity is fairly two-dimensional.
- Tactical Trolls: They take their trolling a little more seriously than playtime trolls. They create and maintain an identity for themselves so as to gain acceptance of genuine players and when the timing is right, they create conflict in the subtlest way.
- Strategic Trolls: A whole different ballgame wherein the troll (or trolls, in this case), as their name suggests, act very strategically and this strategy or planning can take up to months or years to develop and execute. It may include people working together in order to invade a list too.
- Domination Trolls: Here is where it extends to the making and maintaining of apparently bona-fide mailing lists.

Bishop (2014) defines two distinct types of trolls namely Classical trolling that was prevalent in the 1990s and Anonymous trolling, a modern form of trolling, possibly popularized and proliferated by the hacktivist group 'Anonymous' around the year 2010.

Classical trolling was considered to be more amicable than anonymous trolling as it was supposedly done for the "betterment" of the community, in the sense that it strengthened bonds and relationships and welcomed the "newbies" of a community by familiarizing them with the environment. It is said that this type of trolling also runs parallel to Kudos trolling, a form of trolling, in which trolls ask seemingly sincere questions as conversation starters in order to throw the community into a useless conversation. This type of trolling is distinctive because of the element of 'humour.' Kudos trollers think they are including an interesting and humorous mood to the scene. In this type of trolling, the victim gains a sort of acceptance as he transitions from a novice or beginner to an experienced group member.

Anonymous trolling on the other hand was more concerned with humiliating and demeaning the victim for personal enjoyment. This type of trolling runs parallel to flame trolling. Flaming or Anonymous trolling engages in transgressive and subversive humour that targets vulnerable people (Bishop, ibid).

Towards a Definition of Trolling

An effective way of formulating an objective definition of "trolls" is to strip off our techniques of including morally charged notions to trolling situations. The research-oriented view must not try to look into the right and the wrong of the situation or the degree of wrong conducted but it must try to look for patterns arising from similar situations and arrive at common characteristics.

The word 'troll' does not have one single, all encompassing, acceptable definition that accurately explains it. This is because all the different definitions that people use are so different from each other that they can't be put under one category. The applied definition of the word "troll" ranges from meaning someone who is simply a nuisance in the online world, to someone who completely disrupts online communities and hijacks online discussions (Merritt, 2012).

Trolls, as of what is known of them, are like parasitic vermin for online communities. They are known to feed off other people's insecurities and weaknesses for their personal satisfaction and to get a kick out of another person's distress. Hardaker (2010) states the following as the essential characteristics of trolling - Aggression, Success, Disruption, Deception (Hopkinson, 2013). It has been earlier said by Brandel (2007) that trolls tend to validate their self worth in proportion that amounts disruption they stir up.

The mass media have extensively popularized the word "troll" by using them in their headlines and news stories and used it as a blanket term for any form of harassment on the Internet. They do so with the intent of creating a sense of moral panic among the public, or for the simple reason that the word 'troll' draws more attention and adds an entertainment value to the story (McRobbie and Thornton, 1995). This is not surprising especially as we learn from Bishop's (2013) emphasis on news organizations that tend to engage in sensationalism in order to boost sales and repute.

One such example is the case of abusers posting inflammatory content on Facebook memorial pages of young deceased people who committed suicide.

When this happened, news agencies thrived off these stories and exploited them extensively. They emphasized on what the abusers (trolls) did. This included posting photo -shopped pictures of the deceased, pictures of babies in meat grinders or writing insensitive comments towards the deceased child's parents. To mainstream public, this may seem as inhumane monster. However, when asked, these so called "trolls" to justify their behaviour by saying that their intention is to disrupt online memorial Facebook pages because something as sensitive as death shouldn't be a publicized on Facebook, a commercial website that indirectly makes millions off of its users (Phillips, 2011). They want to obliterate the 'rose-tinted' glasses, which people wear when they mourn online. According to them, the online world is not an appropriate place to grieve because passers-by who don't even know the deceased show up and sympathises or "grieve" by posting heartfelt comments. Some trolls claim to find this "tacky" (Chen, 2012).

PROCESS OF TROLLING

According to Hopkinson (2013) a troll begins his/her infiltration into an online community by either pretending to be a fellow member or by feigning belongingness and genuineness or he can begin outright by posting an exaggerated, controversial and provocative comment. This process is known as a baiting. It is metaphorical bait set up, as one would for a fish. The troll will then wait for the victim to 'bite' onto his bait. In retrospect, Patrick Carney impersonating Bieber cannot be called "pretending" because even though he was pretending to be Bieber, it was obvious to everyone that he was aware of what he was doing. Yet, considering all the other factors, this situation can still be called trolling.

THE DIFFERENT DYNAMICS THAT AFFECT TROLLING

Hardaker (2010) states that trolls aim to cause disruption or exacerbate conflict *for the purposes of their own amusement*. This may serve as a problem to researchers because it is not always possible for them to identify that the intent is amusement unless it is explicitly stated or obvious. As such, it is not possible for them to be classified as trolls. Hopkinson (2013) claims intent to be a determining factor in the definition of trolls with the following quote from a troll taken from his corpus on the Daily Express, a national newspaper website:

> "I love winding them up with bits of pedantry. It makes my day go a little faster and I know they're not quite smart enough to realize that if they don't bother rising to the bait that I said, I'll just go away frustrated. But not, these morons and bigots and racists will always come out and have their say, they can't let anything lie, and there's always a simple way to make them look and feel a little more stupid."

When it comes to impoliteness, there are two sources of pleasure or thrill that one may derive from flaming: voyeuristic pleasure that the spectators derive although while not directly participating, but while happening the event unfold in front of them. This enjoyment may occur when the spectators either (a) support the troll and (b) feel vicariously embarrassed because they have identified the troll but the victim couldn't. The second source may the excitement felt while contributing directly to the ensued flame war (Culpeper, 1996).

Another very striking feature of trolls is not simply that they disagree with the in-group members, but the fact that they exaggerate or overtly express what the in-group members expect out of the out group members. Put simply, rather than disagreeing with the in-group members, they appear so guilelessly opposed that it comes off as seeming slightly absurd to them. Perhaps, this is where the element of humour comes into play. The fact that someone would actually fall prey to such seemingly obvious pretence is probably what the trolls find amusing.

Carney's trolling incident was obviously done for obtaining thrill and humour, apart from wanting to tell Justin Bieber off. He not only pretended to be Bieber, but mockingly echoed Justin Beiber's behaviour and mannerisms in a satirical way. In other words, he gave Justin Beiber's fans tweets that they would expect out of Bieber, but in a sardonic way. He used words and phrases such as "swag" or "never say never" in his tweets in an ironic way. To make his sarcasm clear, he overdid the whole façade by deliberately misspelling his words and tweeting grammatically incorrect sentences.

Exploiting the right of freedom of expression: Trolls often defend themselves by claiming their innocence through the path of freedom of expression. This is contrary to the truth, because trolls, with their intimidating threats and mockery, often scare away people who have genuine opinions and people who actually care about their online community (Nicol, 2012).

Justin Bieber @patrickcarney 6 hrs
U seem kewl. RT @biebslevine: and your looking like a obsessed idiot who's pressed that at 18 justin is more famous than you'll ever be
Expand

Justin Bieber @patrickcarney 6 hrs
U look great and young. #jealous RT @MaddiBelieber01: do you even know how stupid and immature u look doing this. arent u like fifty?
Expand

Justin Bieber @patrickcarney 6 hrs
U r my mirror RT @KSaebin: @patrickcarney you look in mirror urself u will never be justin stop lying to urself is so patetic ok, swag out
Expand

Justin Bieber @patrickcarney 6 hrs
I m justin RT @honeybiebSJD: @patrickcarney why are you copying Justin Bieber? By copying him your dream will not come true to be like him.
Expand

Justin Bieber @patrickcarney 6 hrs
Your looking good bud. RT @biebslevine: @patrickcarney do you know how fucking dumb your acting and how stupid you look lmao.
Expand

Justin Bieber @patrickcarney 6 hrs
Ur bio is beautiful and inspiring. RT @ILoveKingJustin: @patrickcarney your Life must be so sad
Expand

Justin Bieber @patrickcarney 6 hrs
A lot. u r perfect though. true swag boss. RT @DABieberBreezy: What the fuck is wrong with you @patrickcarney

Some trolls though, do it "for the lulz," a term often used in the troll world, which means causing disruptive harm to someone for personal amusement. This is a standard reply by any troll when asked why they do what they do. An indication of this is that they do not understand the gravity of their actions.

Kathy Sierra, a well-known American game developer and blogger was harassed to the point of fearfully suspending her blog and ceasing to make public appearances. It went as grotesquely far as images of her and a noose, being circulated on the Internet. Frustrated, she briefly suspended her account after receiving a series of sexual and death threats (Brandel, 2007). Thus, contrary to the popular belief of "freedom of speech" being a righteous asset for one and all, it is quite debatable whether or not the trolls can continue to oppress their victims and also, whether or not this affects the "freedom of speech" of bloggers (Nicol, 2012).

An extremely important step of gaining an understanding of trolling activities is to understand how trolls see themselves.

Kathy Sierra, in her post, "Trouble with Kool-Aid," says that when things go out of hang, trolls often justify their behaviours by claiming that the victim deserved it and "had it coming." In troll logic, it is only a matter of concern if legal authorities are involved (Sierra, 2014). Some people use trolling not to put forth their political ideologies but to mock others, stir up commotion and is, basically just a medium of pure unadulterated satire (International business, 2013).

Some trolls though, do it "for the lulz," a term often used in the troll world, which means causing disruptive harm to someone for personal amusement. This is a standard reply by any troll when asked why they do what they do. An indication of this is that they do not understand the gravity of their actions.

Sierra also explains in her post that some even do it to outdo other trolls. With inherent disregard of the victim's plight as it is, in a bid to out do other trolls, the troll may even cross a lot of lines and harm the victim severely, without even knowing.

Carney also uses the Kool aid analogy in his interview: "If you're a 34-year-old f*cking loser like me, and you go on Justin Bieber's Twitter account like a total pervert every time that he gets in trouble, you should look at his tweets the next day. It's always like, 'I love you guys so much, always believe, never stop believing.' He's feeding them the Kool-Aid more and more,"he says. "He pours it on heavy, though. It's so manipulative! And whoever taught him that that was OK, whoever's watching him and is like 'that manipulation is acceptable,' should be really ashamed of themselves."

Action against Trolling

Anti-troll.org is an anti-trolling alliance that has its own official website that are proactively working towards the recognition of trolling as a recognized criminal offence. They are working with the anticipation that soon trolling incidents will initiate responses of the same seriousness with which cyber stalking is considered. They also anticipate the inclusion of trolling in the US Federal Anti-Cyber-Stalking Law so that it becomes a punishable offence (Anti-troll.org, *undated*) [On-line].

Anti-troll.org, like other official bodies that try to understand trolling, tries to draw a connection with other forms of online abuse such as cyber stalking and cyber bulling. Although the research seems less thorough, it is worth mentioning as it is the only online organization that claims to be officially working towards turning trolling into a punishable offence.

Conclusion

Even though trolling does not have a single acceptable definition that takes into account all the different kinds of trolling, it does have some common characteristics that distinguish it from other forms of online aggression. Trolls may be driven by intents and purposes or they may be doing it for the fun of it, however, at a very basic level, trolling is just a medium of pure unadulterated satire or sarcasm that is not always necessarily done in the name of holding a political or ideological opinion (Zara, 2013).

The extent to which the abuse is being exercised and the perception of the same are relative to the person conducting abuse and the person experiencing victimization. This contributes to the subjectivity that is associated with trolling. Thus, it is quite difficult to come up with a single working definition of trolling because of its discrete and deceptive nature. Redundancy and recurring patterns in trolling and other forms of online aggression such as flaming, cyber bullying, cyber stalking, etc. all contribute towards the ambiguity associated around the definition of trolling.

In retrospect, it can be said that although CMC is a fertile land for the growth of cyber bullies and trolls alike, the need for a definition of trolls is more pressing because it is still an unknown phenomenon that has disruptive consequences.

In: Media Anthology
Editor: Theophilus Kofi Gokah
ISBN: 978-1-63484-931-9

Chapter 12

REBIRTH OF VAMPIRE IMAGERIES IN THE 21ST CENTURY: AN APPRAISAL

Suha Sabith*
School of Media and Communication,
Manipal University Dubai, United Arab Emirates

'There is a vampire for every generation'

(Nina Auberch, 1995)

ABSTRACT

The 21st century has seen an explosion of vampires in different forms of medium like literature, film, television and music. This paper focuses on the unearthed vampire and tries to find out the character modifications and changed presentation of these vicious creatures that has started a mass fan following especially after 2005. The study will be looking at famous movies like Underworld (2003-2012), Twilight (2005-2012), from Hollywood and certain other international movies such as 'Let the Right One In' (2008), to ascertain a particular transition that help shaped a hunger for the previously dead genre. Comparing the new predators with cult classics like Fright Night (1985), Dracula (1931), to analyse the modifications of a feared predator and the repercussions they have on the present generation. This paper will also be discussing about the

* Corresponding author: Suha Sabith. E-mail: sabithsuha@gmail.com.

international appeal of the vampires and the effect of Hollywood movies on them. What is in the future for these fascinating creatures in terms of visual and literary representations and popularity?

INTRODUCTION

Vampires traditionally are defined as blood sucking creatures that prey on unsuspecting humans for survival (Hudson, 2009: 125). Like Hudson, Liedtka (2011) reminds us that vampires have been roaming the earth much before the 14th century. However, their true nature was cloaked under the 'Demonic' category (ibid). Early literature on vampire and films portrayed vampires as ugly and ill-mannered beasts of nature (Bloom, 2014). Their predatory skills were magnified on the movie screens, making them the ultimate villain. *Dracula* the novel was released in 1897. The impeccably dressed villain gained international fame and everybody started noticing vampires as a different kind of a villain. The popularity of vampire books, inspired adventurous filmmakers to bring the predator onto the big screen. A good example of vampire adoption into the movies was *Nosferatu: A Symphony of Horrors (1922).* The vampire from this movie was considered cruel and repellent (Beck, 2011). This was markedly different from *Dracula*, who was portrayed as an impeccably dressed, rich owner of a mysterious castle. The Dracula novel (1897) brought a character that was refined in his ways of handling people. The adapted movie (1931) further accentuated this feature by humanizing the physical appearance of Dracula. Bela Lugosi, who was portrayed as someone who is mysterious, and in his dramatic black cape, played the well known villain, he offered a handsome, though eerie figure (Beck, 2011). Nosferatu and Dracula though different in their appearance shared one commonality - their predatory nature as well as their hunger for trouble and chaos. Their ruthlessness was evident in their predatory demeanour. Though audiences devoured Dracula-movie and the book, they however had a different reaction to its successors. These movies were not well received and in some cases did not even make it to the theatres. The rapid decline in popularity of vampire movies were attributed to them being mirror images of their predecessors (Leeder, 2009).

Modern discourse has however altered drastically imageries of vampires to fit into the modern world. They are no longer the feared villains and in most cases are identified as the heroes. This paper will focus on the different aspects of vampire movies and books to determine what makes them popular and what the factors that lead to the revamped vampire were.

CONTEXT

Vampire movies during its period of decline were mostly used for parody purposes without any regard for the character's inbuilt nature for horror. Vampires were given a backseat till the movie 'The Hunger' was released in 1985. It showed the vampires in a new light even though the word vampire was not mentioned even once in the whole of the movie. Night (1985) changed this scenario by bringing back the love for vampire by adhering to the basics. Though the vampire 'Dandridge' from the movie *Fright Night* is a traditional one, it however had a few new modern tweaks. No longer was the vampire confined to its manor or area but was a wondering one that explored the city's crowded area (Leeder, 2009). After these however, vampire still posed as the lead character in literary works. Annie Rice's *The Vampire Chronicles* for example, arrived in the 1970's. Similarly, *Interview with a Vampire* was published in 1976, with nine subsequent books released between 1985 and 2003. Some books in the series were also produced in movies like *The Vampire Lestat* (1985), The *Queen of the Damned* (1988) and *Interview with the Vampire* (1994).

HEROES, HYBRID GENRES, EXCEPTIONS

Present day vampires are very different from their predecessors. In Charlaine Harris's *Sookie Stackhouse series* (2001), the existence of vampires is very much known to humans and both are considered equal (Mutch, 2011). The vampires also in some cases underwent massive change of feeding from human arteries to animal blood, seen in series like *The Vampire Diaries* (1991-1992) and *Twilight* (2005). The portrayal of vampires as noble creatures that suppress their dark side and work towards the good of humanity is what is considered as the attraction in these creatures. In movies like *Underworld and Blade* where vampires are a mix of good and evil, the good is always shown to triumph over evil (Clapp, 2010). Some academic researchers e.g., Tenga and Zimmerman (2013) claim that vampires are no longer seen, as the 'parasitic monster' that has no feelings but instead they are perceived as sympathetic creatures that want to blend in. It is this reversal of vampire roles as monsters with a conscience that pulls the crowd. Williamson (2005) adds to the debate by arguing that the main reason for the change of audience attitude towards vampires is, due to the inclusion of melodrama in their stories and that the use of melodrama was what makes these predatory beasts seem appealing to audiences.

Further insight by Rochelle Wright relate factors that counts for the success of the Swedish vampire film - *Let the Right One In (2008) as* emerging from several genres which creates a hybrid form that appeals widely to divergent audiences (Wright, 2010). The movie drifts from conventional methods of vampire story telling and embarks on true visual experience. The movie is neither aimed at teenagers nor at avid horror genre fans. This is another significance of the movie's divergence from recent trends (ibid, 2000).

Vampires have taken the role of heroes in many works and this adds to the creature's appeal. Internal struggle is the key word to be noted while talking about these transformed heroes (Hillman, 2004). Rather than fighting the 'bad' guys, these vampires struggle to keep themselves humane or try and stop other vampires from killing. This internal struggle makes the audience sympathize with the vampire character. As the main character, the plights and sufferings of vampires are highlighted for the audience to experience the same (Austin, 2014). Romance also appears to be an integral part of heroism. In other words, the race of the vampire to save the damsel in distress does seem to appeal (especially to teenage girls) everywhere (Pierce, 2012).

Representational Rights and Wrongs

Popular culture has used vampire to voice the 'fear of change' and 'fear of the other' (Heidenreich, 2012). Vampires have been exceptional characters in the sense that they have been used from time to time to portray political and gender issues. This may explain why some authors, for example Ames (2010) believe that representation of vampires in literary works or in a movie are a product of their time, a view that can sometimes generate intense debate. Notwithstanding, Bella from the *Twilight series* is represented as a delicate, weak teenager who requires super powerful men around to carry her in order to avoid her falling down (Siebert and Steinhoff, 2011) [Online]. In a research conducted by Mercer (2011), she asked teenage girls what they thought about *Twilight*'s lead character, Edward, who becomes aggressive to the heroine-Bella. She concluded from their responses that, like in many romance novels,

Twilight showcases male anger, threatening and dangerous rather than love and devotion (Mercer, 2011). These sorts of misrepresentations can affect future generation as they mistake violence for love.

CONSUMERISM

Since the exposition in *Twilight* on the big screen, there has been a well-made market of merchandizing that is tailor-made to target young audiences. *Vampire Diaries,* a television show, for example, is an adaptation of the 1990 novel series of the same name written by L.J. Smith. The books have sold a lot after the television show started. The truth is that, both the novel and television series are different from each other. They maintain the pretext of being closely linked to tap into the fan-base of the book for the television series and vice versa. New books in the series have since been released which are not written by Smith but marketed under her name to ensure the fan-base doesn't dwindle (Bridgeman, 2013). A large marketing plan is thus set, with these young adults in mind as the target audience to promote the vampire world. This will account for the changing character of vampires in different genre. It is not surprising that the vampire has changed from aristocratic invader (*Dracula*) to addict (*The Addiction*), anti-hero (Rice's *Lestat*), wayward child (*Lost Boys*), to female liberationist (Nancy Collin's *Sonja Blue*) (Nahrung, 2007).

METHODOLOGY AND STUDY DESIGN

To properly appraise the re-birth of vampires in the media, a qualitative approach was adopted. In-depth conversation with experts on vampire genre shed light on existentialist views of vampire culture and their future. Three (3) focus groups with vampire movie fans and non- members of the vampire fandom was undertaken to solicit views on the subject under discussion i.e., re-birth of vampires in movies and what attracts them to these movies.

When asked about vampire characterization in the present day movies about vampires, It was untypical for respondents to believe that vampires have indeed been "humanized" to be more appealing especially to younger audiences. An example is this respondent:

> They are romantic heroes now rather than monsters. They all tend to be quite young, targeting a youth market. Misunderstood, often day

> walking, always gorgeous, the film vampires also seem to prefer black leather. I think they lack the menace, mystery, and melancholy of early films (*Victoria,* respondent)

Not everyone however shares the above views. An example is this film critic:

> I think the keyword here is "diversification." Like so many other iconic figures or stories, the depiction of vampires has taken on a horizontal (not just linear) progression. In the same era of time we get classic vampire types (Dracula Untold); new age "humanized," "romantic" or even "heroic" vampires (Twilight, Vampire Diaries, Underworld); or even vampires as disease or biological infection (The Strain). In short: with time, there are more diverse interpretations of what vampirism means as a literary or cinematic metaphor (*Kofi,* Film Critic).

From the different narratives, there seems to be a pattern where audience members are in fact, leaning towards the 'heroism' of vampires. Though most of them are against the idea of the vampires falling into the romantic genre, they however want the protagonist to remain "humane." The youth audience wants the vampires to uphold a system of beliefs as a justification for their actions- whether it is wrong or right. They are not interested in the strictly horror genre vampire movies like *30 Days of Night* which is considered to be gruesome and from the audience perspective, disliked.

The shifting nature of vampire stories begs the question of whether vampire movies would ever return to horror genre. This can sometimes elicit different views even among experts:

> Despite all of the bloodletting and CGI out there, the vampire film has become more of a traditionally melodramatic battle between good vamps and bad others. The horror, the fear, and the threat—that's gone. So is the eroticism, the forbidden elements of the Gothic embodied in earlier films (*Amador*, Expert on Vampire genre).

Amador is quick to also add that:

> Probably in independent films, vampires might go back to the horror genre, but not in Hollywood cinema. This can be taken true in while analysing the success of the Swedish movie - 'Let the Right One In.' The

movie was also made by Hollywood in English. The Hollywood version however failed to reach the success of its Swedish counterpart.

Others shared similar views; for instance Melissa says:

> The horror factor has dissipated, as vampire narratives has became part of hybrid genres. However, they still share some affinity with the horror genre – which usually exists to help us work through our cultural fears in some allegorical way or to represent the dark side of humanity but very few vampire films and books would be housed on such shelves at the local video or book store.

This is proven true especially when talking about the popular Hollywood movie *Underworld: Rise of the Lycans*, in which vampires are shown as tyrant rulers with an exception of few. The dark side of humanity- power driven and greed is attributed to the 'evil' vampires. Film Critic, Kofi, disagrees on this latter point that vampires have left the horror genre:

> Vampires are more than just horror now; they are romantic heartthrobs and/or action heroes. They never left the horror genre; they just transcended that one genre to be mixed in with others. There will always be vampire stories that are exclusively horror, though. A small group of audience are in favour of the vicious vampires but they insist that there must be sufficient reason as to why the vampires are vicious. Although most of the audience members prefer the heroic vampire, they still want *Dracula* to be the traditional vampire. Not a hero but the villain.

Set designing had played an important part in the vampire movies of yester years. 'Nosferatu: A Symphony of Horrors' had a set that consisted of large archways, etc. that contributed to the overall characterization of the protagonist. Subplots consisted of supporting characters that contributed to the overall narrative. When asked whether these qualities still hold for modern vampire movies, Melissa, a respondent said that 'she feels the subplot and set designs in these movies are still able to carry out social commentary to some degree'; while Amador, another respondent was of the opinion that they have not yet accomplished the task of applying technological innovations to improve the set design:

> The interiors of Coppola's Dracula were gorgeous, of course, but now, despite the huge budgets, the set designs are simply grand rather

than eerie or ancient... As to the subplots, most vampire films now offer a silly comic character in a subplot, so there's no real interest or fear or concern for those characters or that story line.

Some respondents however felt that there is sufficient evidence that present day vampire movies do in fact give importance to set designs.

It's hard to look at a film like Dracula Untold and not appreciate the level of detail and work that went into the set design ... The members of audience are concerned more with the graphic details of the creatures involved than the set designs. They are only concerned with the set design when it comes to *Dracula* related movies, where they expect to see large castles and mystery (*Kofi*)

This respondent holds strong opinions about subplots and believes they are an entire discussion in themselves. He attributes the lack of subplots to the modern conventions of cinematic story telling. He takes the example of the movie 'Dracula: Untold' - "Dracula Untold had many subplots in its original script that were filmed during production and ultimately cut to make the theatrical film a simpler (and shorter) action/horror origin story. That change was made for business reasons (marketing the movie to audiences), not creative ones." This stands true in case of *Twilight*, wherein the original scripts had subplots but were removed to give more focus on the central characters. Since the audience are attracted to the central couple. Audiences are shifting away from comic characters in subplots due to emergence of strong and dramatic characters in television serials.

The cravings of teens are met with the likes of *Twilight,* and *Vampire Diaries* that breed the same sort of vampires. Hollywood, for example, believes that this stylization of vampire works due to the attention of teens all over the world. At least, all three experts agree audience hold a great power in deciding the parameters of a vampire movie or any movie for that matter:

Movie audiences had, have, and will continue to have the same indisputable power they always have: the power of their wallets," says Outlaw... What they pay to see determines what Hollywood does. When people aren't seeing a particular type of movie, Hollywood moves to another type, people had to stop paying to see a *Twilight movie*, which is not very likely since there's an obvious audience for that series (*Kofi*, Film Critic).

Amador agrees and adds that the audiences that have the most influence on the said genre are teens, at least from Hollywood's perspective. This answers the question as to why *Twilight*, a romantic movie in essence ranks above a purely horror flick like *30 Days of Night*. Movies like *Twilight* helped restart the melodramatic vampire with mix of romance. "Those of us who prefer a more traditional or terrifying vampire are out of luck," says Amador.

Seeing the amount of vampire movies released every year, a person could conclude easily that the genre is overused but Amador does not believe so. She points out that vampires have existed in folklore for around 1000 years and in movies for around 100 years, a fact annotated in Harrison (1999). She firmly believes that vampires do have potential to develop and grow. This belief does not hold for Ames, who says that "vampires like many genres rises with popularity at times in which it is useful; that is, the vampire narrative is a particularly useful space to critique issues surrounding gender and sexuality and so it only arises at certain time periods."

From the foregone discussion, the vampire genre is eclipsed by narratives, which are able to critique other cultural concerns. This can be seen through the success of zombie-based series such as *The Walking Dead*, 'iZombie.' The mixing of vampire and zombie also generates disinterest from them. We heard from Kofi, a film critic's views that vampire genre will continue to exist, maybe with a different approach so long as there is a diverse selection of quality stories. Should this happen it will be a situation arguably comparable to the superhero movie *boom*. The belief that vampires will stay for even longer is accentuated by the positive response of the focus groups to whether they would watch future vampire movies. Audiences want the vampires to not lose their humane quality. Only till then will they stay as loyal viewers.

Conclusion

The vampire movies have utility and seem likely to stay. So long as there is a large fan base that stays loyal to their hero. A common agreement can be seen among experts that the changes vampires have gone through over the years have helped them survive public scrutiny till today. The *romantic hero*; *the rebel*, are examples of movies that have contributed to vampire popularity. Anything other than these narratives has not faced success as much as their romantic counterparts. Though the changes seem to stay, independent filmmakers are breaking the *status quo* with creative narratives. A character that is seen alike through all eyes is *Dracula*. Experts and Audience members want to see the same kind of *Dracula* - traditional, eerie and tragic. From the responses acquired, the audience seems to love *Dracula* movies in which the character is the villain or at the least an anti-hero; the opposite is true where movies with romanticized Dracula have failed.

In: Media Anthology
Editor: Theophilus Kofi Gokah
ISBN: 978-1-63484-931-9

Chapter 13

GRATIFICATION OF THE SELF: REASONS BEHIND THE PHENOMENON OF 'RETWEETING'

Sabir Haque[1,*] and Seena Biju[2,1]
[1]Department of Media and Communication,
Manipal University Dubai, United Arab Emirates
[2]Department of Management Studies,
Manipal University Dubai, United Arab Emirates

ABSTRACT

One of the important characteristics of Twitter when it comes to diffusion of ideas, information and opinion is the multiplier effect of Retweeting. Retweeting is a fundamental part of the Twitter experience: we reciprocate and in return yearn to be retweeted as well. Retweet offers the user to quickly share information while attributing the original source. A closer look at retweets reveals that any retweeted tweet is to reach an average of 1,000 users no matter what the number of followers is of the original tweet. Once retweeted, the 1st hop of tweet is almost instant, signifying fast diffusion of information. Like researchers before us, we argue that among the factors driving this diffusion are status attainment

* Sabir Haque is with Department of Media and Communication, Manipal University Dubai, e-mail: sabir@manipaldubai.com; twitter/google+: \ideaminefield.
[1] Seena Biju is with Department of Management Studies, Manipal University Dubai, e-mail: seena@manipaldubai.com.

and information seeking. This study explores the various factors, which drives this inherent behaviour on tweeple. A mixed approach was used and the results compared with a dataset of retweets, which were captured from a real time interval over designated period using a Twitter API. The validation process looked into the available theories such as Uses and Gratification theory and Social Exchange theory to validate if the tweeple responses can be mapped into a working model. The findings reveal that a list of significant determiners to this behaviour has implications for directions towards further study.

INTRODUCTION

Twitter lets people post a quick 140 characters updates or 'tweets' to a network of Twitter users. A short answer to 'What's happening?" creates a continuous flow of updates from people, news agencies, government agencies, celebrities, corporations, news ogranisation ranging from mundane to breaking news, shared links, thoughts on life and the like. By encouraging shorter posts, the user's requirement of time and reflections is greatly shortened and content generation pace increases (Java, et al., 2007). The power of its democratizing effect gives us what Goffman (1959) refers to as an access to the 'Backstage' which constitutes 'places where the camera is not focused at the moment.'

The information flow that is prevalent on Twitter is not always direct from its original source, but often via retweets. No matter how many followers a user has, the tweet is likely to reach a certain number of audience, once the user's tweet starts spreading via retweets (Kwak, 2010). Retweet has immense capability to spread information widely. The fog of war has become the downpour of texts and tweets (Goodman, 2009). Twitter tracks phrases, words and hash tags and keeps an updated 'Trending Topics,' which reflects according to geographical locations, where the bulk of discussion among its users are transpiring. The role of Twitter as a media for breaking news is in a manner close to an omnipresent CCTV collective intelligence (Kwak, 2010).

Interactions between Twitter users used to be traditionally available through two methods: retweet and replies. While replies were always a part of Twitter, Retweets were not natively supported until November 2009 (Meeder, et al., 2010). The convention of retweeted required the user to add a 'RT @ username' at the beginning of the tweet to indicate, that it's a retweet from the mentioned user. At present, Twitter offers direct/automatic retweet, or allows the user to add a comment. The dataset used in the research, allows us to separate the manual from the automatic retweets. Liu, Lilman-Silver and

Mslove (2014) found an interesting trend from their dataset. They saw a rapid adoption of reply mechanism, peaking at 35% of all tweets in 2010 while declining henceforth. Whereas on retweets, there was a small percentage of retweets due to the requirement of creating manual retweets natively until 2009. By 2013, the number of retweets has exponentially increased, and its percentage is greater than the replies. Researchers have tried to understand various aspects of user's behaviour in using twitter, be it motivation behind Retweeting (Macskassy and Michelson, 2011) or statements of support (Recuero, Araujo and Zago, 2011).

This brings us to the discussion on Reciprocity. Reciprocity refers to exchange between two or more actors, generally (though not always) for mutual benefit. In social life, positive forms of reciprocity, such as kindness in response to previous kindness, are considered the very "starting mechanism" through which personal relations are established (Gouldner, 1960). We understand from Kwak et al. (2010) that the top users of Twitter with the highest number of followers are Celebrities. The median number of followers of the top 10 users according to Kwak et al. is 114. So for users of Twitter, it is rather a source of information than mere social networking sites. The median number of followers of the top 0 users is 114 (Kwak, Lee, Park, and Moon, 2010). So, Twitter shows low levels of reciprocity.

Twitter is also seen more as a source of information than mere social networking sites. And for journalist, an increasing dependency on twitter as a source for instantaneous information is cited by various studies (Hermida, 2010; Blasingame, 2011; Burns, Highfield and Link, 2010).

During Natural and manmade calamities, when the impact is significant and proximity is low, people engage and seek instant sharing of information (Burns, 2003). Twitter provides that functionality. These characteristics are described as 'gatejumping' (Brogan and Smith, 2010). For example, if radio is a gatekeeper industry, podcast is a 'gatejumper.' It facilitates a better way of reaching out when every other media form is too busy to notice. Twitter has the capability to 'jump' the traditional workflow of a news item in reaching the audience. We can conceive social media as mainly a 'medium' which 'ordinary' people in an ordinary fashion, strikingly different from professional news gatherers, create 'news.' The 'social' part of this social media refers to its distinction from 'traditional' media (Murthy, 2011).

The retweet function enables a user to spread the word foreword; the popularity of the user with higher number of followers enables the multiplier-effect of a message. 'Influencer' is a term attributed to someone on Twitter who amasses the most number of followers and with their regularity of tweets pertaining to news or trends, the opinion of such an 'influencer' facilitates multicasting (broadcasting of many to many). Specifically, if an unknown person sends a fabulously interesting tweet, it is most likely destined never to be read. Of course, this is true of any communication in that reception (Murthy, ibid). When someone retweets, the original newscaster's name is referred in the tweet itself (through an @ reference, i.e., @7DaysUAE). But, as the string develops and the tweets get more multi-casted, the original newscaster may get consciously or unconsciously ignored.

Kwak (2010) notes that once a tweet is retweeted (regardless of the number of followers the original Twitter user has), it reaches an audience (mean) size of 1000. Thus, any ordinary individual has a chance of being heard equally in the Twitter sphere. Bridging the geographical and temporal frame, this equity of utterance is what makes twitter a force in 'Social Media' channels.

A study was conducted by Jae-Hwa and Cameron (2003) on South Korean and American journalists and found that, although journalists depend on the web for background information and story ideas, 'the majority of journalists remain sceptical about most websites' as sources. In the UAE, Twitter often acts as a space where twitter feed triggers news stories. Journalists often collaborate with Twitterati's, and after going through the process of validation, their news is posted (Haque and Biju, 2013).

THEORETICAL FRAMEWORK

A Theoretical framework is required to understand Twitter and the phenomenon of Retweeting. Uses and gratifications approach has previously been used to study audiences' motives for media use for over 60 years (Rubin, 2002) and is useful for studying competition between the Internet and traditional media use. Collectively, past research suggests that motivational factors drive users to share information including information seeking, socializing, entertainment and status seeking (Lee and Ma, 2012). To remind readers, the objective of this study is to investigate this list of factors further evaluating it with other theoretical framework and weigh them across different accepted models and map their relative importance using a dataset of public captured re-tweets.

Social Media – A Build Up of Community

Social Networks sites can provide rich sources of naturalistic behavioural data. Nowel, et al. (2005) studied what motivates people to join particular communities. The formation of like-minded members and the genesis of community growth and its evolution have also been studied in detail by Backstrom, et al. (2006). Profile and linkage data from Social Networking Sites (SNS) can be gathered either through the use of automated collection techniques or through datasets provided directly from companies, enabling network analysis researchers to explore large-scale patterns of friending, usage, and other visible indicators. As defined by Boyd and Ellison (2007), social network allows users to maintain a 'public or semi-public' profile within a bounded system, while social media allows interaction among strangers and bridges gap between the ordinary and extraordinary.

Huyssen (2000) points to a 'society of experience,' where everyday conversation becomes event-driven. Twitter and other social media create a society unbounded by temporal and geographical barriers, where immediate publicity is driven mainly by user-generated updates. In a sense, Twitter markets us through our tweets and, as such, shifts us more towards 'an age of advertisement,' where we are not necessarily advertising products, but rather ourselves (and our self-commodification) (Murthy, 2012).

Boon and Sinclair (2009) eulogises status updating as a meaningful part of social media user's identities. With the regularity of such acts makes one a serious player in a micro blogging space; this is paramount as it acts to maintain their identity (Gackenbach, 2011). Specifically, Twitter seems to provide ways for individuals to assert and construct the self, which are contingent on a larger dialogic community (Bakhtin, 1981).

Garcia, et al. (2014) in their longitudinal study identifies the following types of users based on their tweeting behaviour over time:

1. Endogenous: users in this group use Twitter like any social media. The dominant types of tweets are self-contained tweets created by the user.
2. Conversationalist: Users in this group are more like Endogenous, but they place emphases on interacting with other users more than sharing self-contained ideas
3. Generalists: This category uses the retweet function with links and more inclined to obtaining external information

4. Echoers: Users in this category retweet, but without any links. People who post quotes, jokes and positive thinking, etc., they also indulge in chats and replies.
5. Link Feeders: Media producers like journalist, SEO specialist and expected audience of their tweets are the general public. Most of the tweets have no mention of an external user.

Echoers are the users who remain active throughout the year while over the years the number of conversationalist has gone down as they have migrated into other messaging services.

As Chris Anderson announced, online data deluge will make theories obsolete (Anderson, 2008). Perhaps, Dellarocas (2003) may have foreseen this situation occurring and suggested new ways of capturing, analysing, interpreting and managing social media content from the tyranny of large-scale, anonymous, and ephemeral nature of the Internet. Providing advices to other users finds its root in word of mouth/Psychological Ownership Theory. According to Pierce, et al. (2003), the desire by the consumer to control through such communications may result in feelings of efficacy, intrinsic pleasure, and extrinsic satisfaction in providing such advice to others.

Looking for acceptance among peers online can be understood in Social Exchange Theory (Liang, Liu and Wu, 2008). This behaviour to communicate or exchange with each other is contingent on reciprocal actions from the other communicating party (Emerson, 1976). The mutual reinforcement of retweet is a social reward such as opportunity, prestige, conformity, or acceptance. Social Exchange theory posits the following reasons: (1) expected gain in reputation or influence on others (2) anticipated reciprocity.

TrensStream Limited (2010) tracks online consumers and suggests that users of social media are divided into: (a) Watchers (b) Sharers (c) Commenters (d) Producers (Li, 2010). Here, it is important to note that Garcia et al.'s study (as earlier reported) may not necessarily be a contradiction of Li's. If anything, the differences in information can be attributed to 'perspectives' or 'semantics' used by the different authors. Notwithstanding, the tendencies of sharers find commonality in Twitter, as these online users retweet. Arguably, one of the more attractive characteristics of social media is its support for user-generated content, transforming individuals from passive consumers of content to active producers.

Uses and Gratification Theory attempts to explain what social and psychological needs motivate audiences to select particular media channels and content choices (Rubin and Perse, 1987; Ruggiero, 2000). Contributing to that debate, Morgan and Naaman (2007) argues that in social media motivational factors include status attainment and information seeking. Similarly, Hsu and Lin (2008) adds establishing social relationship and building reputations for sharing content in the blog space. In Dunne, et al.'s (2010) contribution, they also added several gratification such as entertainment, information search, peer acceptance and relationship maintenance. Lee and Ma (2012) prefer to 'raise the bar' by arguing that that U and G Theory is not enough to explain users' motivations because it assumes that users are constantly active participating in media selection and use whereas in reality, such participation may simply be borne out of prior experience, even though, Armstrong and McAdams (2009) had previously pontificated that media audiences are goal-directed and purposefully attempting to achieve those goals by using specific media channels and content. Notwithstanding the argument between these authors, there is no doubt that the diversity of information has exploded and that Internet users have a plethora of lessons to learn through such interactions (Ames and Naaman, 2007).

Users satisfaction and their desires influence the success of SNS significantly. The influential factors can be studied using Unified theory of acceptance of the new technology and Tiger pleasure framework (Azjen and Fishbein, 1975). The performance expectancy, which refers to the degree to which the individual believes that the system will help to attain gains in job performance, is similar to the following constructs: Perceived usefulness (TAM, C-TAM-TPB); Extrinsic motivation (MM), job-fit (MPCU); Relative advantage (IDT) and Outcome expectation (SCT).

Perceived Usefulness (PU) indicates that the use of a new technology will enhance his/her job performance. The Model of PC utilization (MPCU) is another theory that its core constructs consists of factors such as job-fit, complexity, long-term consequences, effect towards use (feeling of joy, pleasure, depression, disgust, etc.), social factors, and facilitating conditions (objective factors in the environment that observers agree make and act easy to accomplish).

Several influential factors on Twitter's usage are based on the socio-pleasure, for instance - socio-pleasure: online-offline relationship, constant contact, instant messaging and status updates in SNSs, openness, mobile platform; psycho-pleasure: playfulness (enjoyment), expression; ideo-pleasure: privacy issue; and pycho-pleasure and ideo-pleasure categories of Tiger's pleasure framework.

RESEARCH DESIGN

The 1st Phase of the research where Twitter stream (Tweets) was captured and studied is quantitative while the 2nd Phase where the Twitter User's responses is analysed is qualitative. As described by Denzin (1970), methodological triangulation will help overcome measurement bias from Phase I while Phase II will explain the dimension of the phenomenon of Retweeting.

Research on Twitter is usually carried out over datasets captured during a specific period. These public streams or crawl dataset can be captured using a Twitter API. API, an abbreviation of Application Program Interface, is a set of routines, protocols, and tools for building software applications. The API specifies how software components should interact and APIs are used when programming graphical user interface (GUI) components. The limitation of using an API to capture tweets is that the captured tweets are mostly of active users only. Second, Twitter does not inform us when users leave the network. To address these limitations, a convenient sampling (Phase II) of 200 twitter users was taken. More than 1000 request were sent out at random, and 200 twitter users responded. The user-sample here represented a random sample of users instead of tweet.

The demography of respondents who took part in this survey were found to be from a wide spectrum of workgroup that included, students, academicians, radio Jockeys, Journalists, reporters, News readers, Media Producers, Designers (Fashion, Interior, Game) Photographers, Media Consultants, Entrepreneurs, Advertising professionals, Event Managers, Film Critics, Financial Consultants, Travel Administrators, Communication Specialists, Editors, Bloggers, Business Analysts and Physicians. The responses broadly classified into five categories are as in Figure 1.

News and matters of information were quoted as high prominence and reasons for Retweeting. As Diana Khambatta, Student comments:

> If anything is news worthy, like a breaking news, your first instinct is to be one of the first to share the news, although inexplicable

Most users insisted, retweeting, doesn't imply endorsement. As Multimedia Journalist, Deepti Unnikrishnan notes:

> If I retweet statements made by individuals, then my act don't imply I endorse the individual's opinion. I share, so that I can get feedback on

what other's think about is being opined and sometimes that adds to my own opinion as well.

Twitter, when compared to other Social Networks display lower levels of reciprocity. 67.6% of users are not followed by any of their followings in Twitter (Kwak, Lee, Park and Moon, 2010). We conjecture that for these users Twitter is rather a source of information than a social networking site. As McCombs and Reynols (2009) notes, how news content has much more impact on civic agenda, seen in light of accuracy and objectivity, respondents Retweeting mostly well known, recognized Tweeter Accounts of Mainstream Media in particular broadcast media.

Majority of the respondents foreworded quotes (both humorous and otherwise), and believed that to be retweeted often. The respondents were supportive of their favourite celebrities while Retweeting, alternatively giving themselves an element of self-popularity of mutually re-tweeting each other, as one of the respondents stated: "I RT U – U RT ME"!

Macskassy and Michelson (2011) in their study of behavioural models for Retweets, conclude that users in the majority of cases do not retweet information on topics that they themselves Tweet about as or from people who are "like them" (hence anti-homophily).

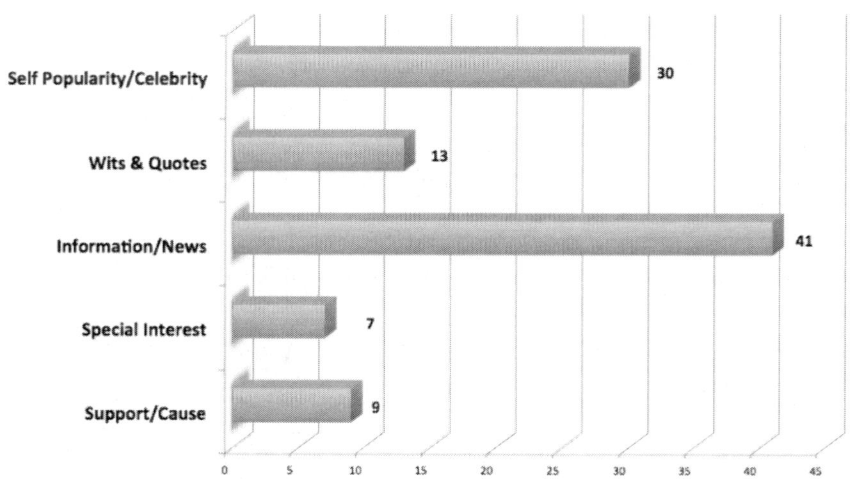

Figure 1. The demography of respondents classified into five categories.

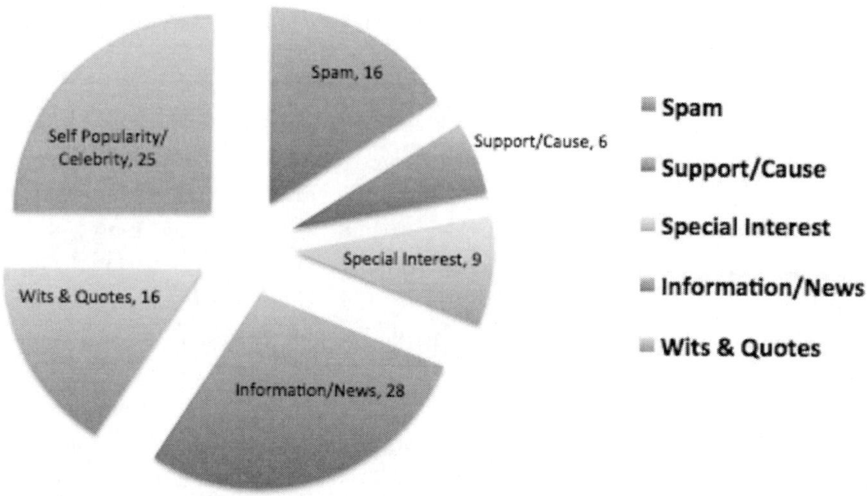

Figure 2. Justifications of Retweeting classified into five categories.

In Phase II, about 500+ re-tweets were captured over five time intervals. The numbers of re-tweets were then mapped on to the five categories. The objective here was to justify the underlying reasons of Retweeting with the live snapshot from Global Twitter sphere. Over 16% of the tweets were regarded as spam. As expected News and Information related retweets were among the highest captures as seen in Figure 2.

This study's mapping threw interesting connections to Influencers as well, Tweets on Celebrities even though the contents were mere banal to insignificant had a great number of retweets. Although, the data collected also revealed the frequency of retweets, this was beyond the scope of this study and can possibly be a part of future studies.

Figure 3 is a comprehensive mapped model, based on the interaction of our results from the global dataset and the data collected from active users. This map combines and collates information between tweets independently captured and twitters users. According to global dataset – the leading retweets were self-popularity/celebrity retweets 66%, while Twitter users opined Information/news to be their leading source of retweets. The results don't correspond with each other. The mismatch is likely caused due to the snowball sampling method of collecting reasons of Retweeting from Twitter Users. However, the top reasons in general do have a positive relationship with the global dataset. Researchers have since been gaining a better understanding of how users socialize with others in the network: those conversations typically mention another user (Macskassy 2012), and the top trending topics generated using hash tag (Huang, Thornton, and Efthimiadis 2010; Yang et al. 2012).

Conclusion

A two-pronged approach in the Methodology helped to bridge the gap between active users who were approached personally and the global snapshot from the millions of twitter streams updated regularly.

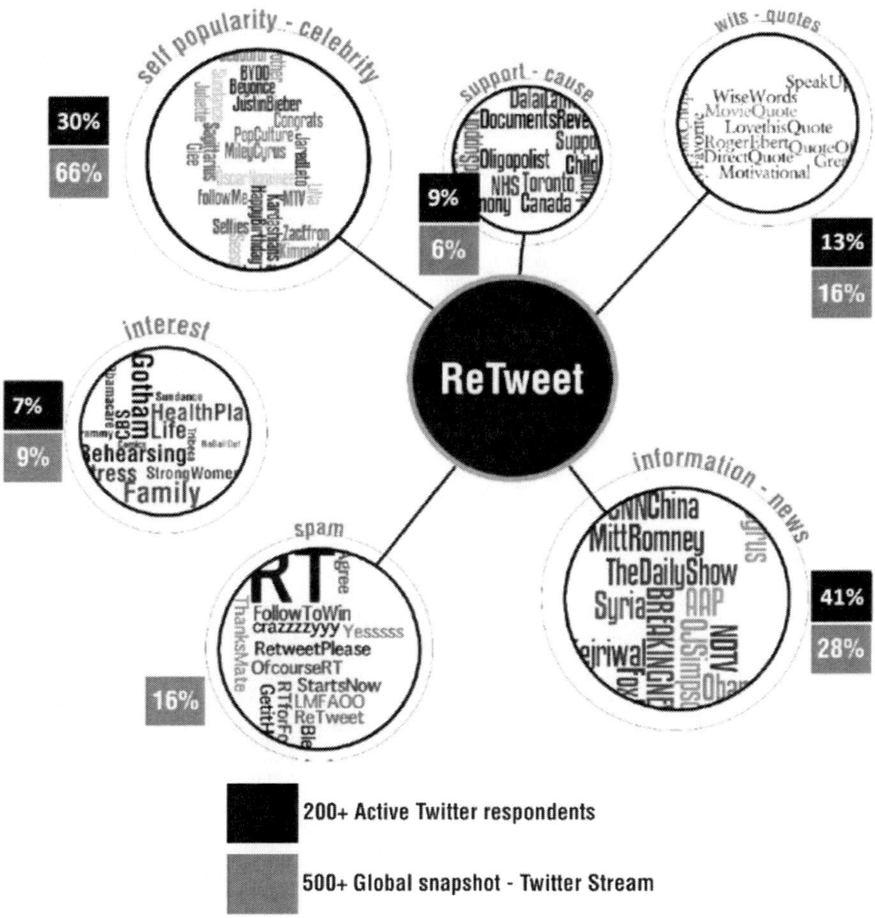

Figure 3. A comprehensive mapped model, based on the interaction of our results from the global dataset and the data collected from active users.

Twitter rate-limits 20,000 requests per hour per whitelisted IP. A Twitter API was used to track down tweets, which were using manual Retweeting methods using RT in the subject matter. Various Twitter API were available for analytics and data collection purposes. Specific for this study, Topsy was used, which avails the user's analytics options as well.

The conclusion drawn from this comparison helped to uphold the various criteria, which satisfied previous studies (i.e., Purcell, et al., 2010; Lee, et al., 2010; Dunne, et al., 2010 and Goode, 2009) undertaken to understand the nature of user's interaction in social media networks, including Twitter.

Twitter is abuzz as more users join in, it has changed self-production, self-gratification, the way people use language and various products created in the Market of Tweets. There is value, therefore, in suggesting further studies into understanding the significance of multiplier-effect in Retweet Trees drawing on User Interconnectedness within Social Network Theory.

In: Media Anthology
Editor: Theophilus Kofi Gokah
ISBN: 978-1-63484-931-9

Chapter 14

ETHICAL THEORY AND SOCIAL MEDIA

Abderrahmane Azzi*
Professor, College of Communication,
University of Sharjah, Sharjah, UAE

ABSTRACT

The paper examines ways by which ethical theory can inform the use of social media in modern society. Drawing on Kant's "Categorical Imperative"[1] and Draz's "Positive Obligation,"[2] Prof. Azzi develops the concept of "Ethical Duty" as both an imperative and a command that "ought to" guide communication in social media and modern communication technology. The "Ethical Duty," as an individual conscience inspired by value systems (rational and spiritual), requires a responsive and responsible approach to pertinent ethical decisions involved in social media communication.

---

* Corresponding author: Abderrahmane Azzi, Prof. E-mail: aazi@Sharjah.ac.ae.

[1] His major works: The Foundations of the Metaphysics of the Moral, 1785. The Critique of Pure Reason, 1788.

[2] Mohamad Draz, The Ethical Constitution of the Quran, Ph.D. Dissertation, University of Sorbone, Paris France, 1943. Soft Copy.

CONTEXT

Ethical theory can well inform communication in social media in the sense that every communication act (posting a message, uploading an image or video and interacting with others) is in essence an ethical act whether in terms of principles (deontology) or consequences (consequentialism). Ethical theory in communication raises the question of what is right and what is wrong (what is ethical and what is not ethical) in the decision making processes that involves communicating using modern technology.

Both Kant's and Draz's ethical formulations are deontological ethics. That is, ethics are objective moral values; they are right in themselves regardless of consequences. Kant's theory focuses on the "*universalisability*" criteria to determine whether any value can be labeled as such. The "*universalisability*" factor presupposes (a) that every action, to be regarded as ethical, must be formulated into a law, and (b) that actions are not measured by their consequences but by their ability to be transformed into a general law application to all under every circumstances. In Kant's terms, "I should never act in such a way that I could not also will, that, my maxim should be a universal one."[3] In short, "what is right for one is right for all."[4] Kant argues that even though individual freedom in a condition of an ethical system, they have a responsibility to act on moral principles.[5] While Kant's moral philosophy focuses on the question of "how," Draz's reading of the *Quranic Ethical Framework* (QEF) focuses on substance. That is, Kant's theory set criteria for how we can "know" what is ethical while Draz's QEF maintains that values are known (revealed), but not acted on usually, and need to be renewed across time and space.

THEORY

Kant's theory centers on the notion of "duty." The term can be roughly defined as the internal urge to do what one "*ought to do*." That is, "*the ought-to-do drive*" or the "*ought-ness question*." This is also often legitimized by the argument of "doing what is right." But then, the question can be raised as to

[3] Louis Alvin Day, Ethics in Mass Communication: Cases and controversies, 5th Edition, Thomson and Wadsworth, New York, 2006, p. 58.

[4] Clifford G. Christians, Mark Fackler, Kim B. Rotzoll and Kathy Brittain Mckee, Media Ethics: Cases and Moral Reasoning, Addison Wesley Longman, Inc. New York, 2001, p. 15.

[5] Ibid, p. 58.

"*what is right*," and how one determines that what is right is necessarily "*ethical*." Kant argues that what is good without qualification is a good will, which is good "in and of itself." The individual with good will often attains good deeds, but even if such an individual's effort fall short and cause harm; the good will that accounts for the efforts is still good.[6] Kant proposes the concept of "*the morality within*." That is, one just knows what is ethical – in reference to human nature; a person who commits wrong doings (hurting someone else) knows that what he has committed is wrong even though he/she can provide seemingly rational justifications for his/her unethical action. Still, Kant asserts that it is not always easy to determine whether a person is acting out of duty or out of self-interest; a dealer who does not overcharge an inexperienced customer is a case in question. It is not quite obvious whether the dealer performed his duty or acted to preserve his business or just to perform his/her duty. Individuals may "preserve their lives as duty requires, no doubt, and not because duty requires." Kant links duty with doing what is good and identifies two types of duty: (a) the fundamental duty which consists of what one "*ought not do*" so that the person won't undermine the dignity of the other; and (b) the incomplete duties, that is, the ones which seek to perfect oneself and bring happiness to others. The notion of happiness is presented not in the sense of utility, "but to make the other worthy of happiness."

Draz's concept of "positive obligation" is similar to Kant's duty, but more flexible and does not subscribe to a rigid process of "*universalisibilty*." In Draz's QEF, the sense of morality is the second dimension of human nature. That is, one knows what is ethical by being in touch with his/her internal nature as "*given*." In line with Kant's assertion on rational justification of unethical action, Draz makes similar claims. In the *Quranic* verse, "*then is one to whom the evil of his deed has been made attractive so he considered it good (like one rightfully guided?) For indeed, God sends astray whom He wills – and guides who He will*." Draz's also maintains that the principle of "ought not do" is the highest level of ethics in religions. There is an extensive narrative in *the Quran* on "*ought not do*" principles in every aspect of life and the moral pertinence of the narrative is to "*do no harm to others*." The same notion is found in Christianity where seven out of the Ten Commandments are in the nature of "shall not principles." This is also very much in line with Clifford's theory of global proto-norms based on "*the sacredness of human life*." If everyone refrains from causing harm to others, the outcome is an ethical and ideal society or what Kant would call "The kingdom of ends." As Kant puts it,

[6] Michael J. Quinn, Ethics in the Information Age, Addison and Wesley, New York, 2009, p. 69.

"every rational being must act as if by his maxims he were at all times a legislative member of the universal kingdom of ends."[7]

In Kant, the core of morality also involves the respect of humanity in the other as we respect it in "ourselves" as humanity is an end itself. That is, the other is viewed as an independent rational being who is endowed with dignity and thus entails respect. People should always be treated as "ends unto themselves, never as means to an end."[8]

The humanity principle is the core most religions as the message is aimed at to all beings and not to any local setting. For Draz, the essence of religion is to address humanity. In the Quranic verse, "*And We have not sent you [O Muhammad], except as a mercy to the worlds.*"[9] Individuals are not to be judged on the basis of their background differences but on their ethical stance. In another verse, *we read*, "Indeed, the most noble of you in the sight of Allah is the most righteous of you."[10] In modern terms, it is imperative that other is also respected for being different as diversity is a sign of richness and as a condition for one's humanness.

The notion of ends is central in Kant's theory. That is, the action is performed out of duty and the actor does not derive personal benefits out of such an action. The other human being is treated as "an end" unto himself/herself. The practical example is that "if someone provides service to you, you need to thank him/her in return. Otherwise, it may be said that the person is being used…"

In both Kant's and Draz' analysis, "ethical duty" or "positive obligations" is a conscious act based on an individual decision. This implies that personal ethical awareness is a perquisite for communication action. Ethical awareness may not be accessible without personal effort and engagement at the level of consciousness and human spirit. As Merrill states, "if media people do not care whether what they do is good or bad, then they will have little or no interest in, or consideration of, ethics." He adds that "a sense of right conduct does not come naturally; it must be developed, thought about, reasoned through, cared deeply about. In short, it must be nurtured."[11]

---

[7] Lee Anne Peck, "Immanuel Kant: Importance of Duty," in Clifford G. Christians and John C. Merrill, Ethical Communication: Moral Stances in Human Dialogue, University of Missouri Press, Columbia, 2009, p. 147.

[8] Ibid, p. 62.

[9] Surat "Al Anbya," Verse 107.

[10] Surat "Al Houjourat," Verse 13.

[11] A. David Gordon and John Michael Kittross, Controversies in Media Ethics, Longman, New York, 1999, p. 2.

The duty conscious is distinct from both inclinations and traditional collective mind. Ethical decision are not the result of self-desire; if one follows his/her desire (as money and power) he/she and without restraint and ethical discipline will resort to providing seemingly rational justifications for un-ethical action. The list of such strategies, twisted judgments and ethical fallacies is wide open and includes arguments like: "everyone is doing this." In the Quranic verse, we read," Have you seen he who has taken as his god his [own] desire, and Allah has sent him astray due to knowledge and has set a seal upon his hearing and his heart and put over his vision a veil? So who will guide him after Allah? Then will you not be reminded?"[12]

The second distinction is related to taken-for-granted traditions and the behavior of followers with a group-mind thinking. The fact that everyone is doing something is not an ethical justification as much as a social legitimization. To live ethically, one has to take ethical decision at his/her individual conscious level regardless of whether such decision is inspired by "transcendental reason" (Kant) or by reason and spirit (Draz). In the Quranic verse, "And when it is said to them, "Follow what Allah has revealed," they say, "Rather, we will follow that which we found our fathers doing." Even though their fathers understood nothing, nor were they guided?"[13]

Based on Kant's and Draz' formulations, I derived a new micro theory applicable to media practices and communication in social media. The theory is called "*the ethical duty in Media Practices*" (EDMP)[14]. The theory is based on a set of principles that lead to a number of pertinent question every communicator need to raise before any ethical decision is made in communication action. The principles are other-directed and are always about other (s) as discussed as follows:

Do No Harm

This principle is regarded as the highest level of ethics; not causing harm is the essence of any ethical theory. This requires conscious ethical discipline that pervades every aspect of communication act as in writing, photo and video shooting, texting, tweeting, etc. There are many areas of do not principles in the Quranic narrative: A) Do not disbelieve in God, "And believe

[12] Al Jathiyah. 23.
[13] Al Baqara, 170.
[14] Abderrahmane Azzi, Theory of Ethical Duty in Media Practices, Mediterranean Publishing House, Tunis, 2015 (In Arabic).

in what I have sent down confirming that which is [already] with you, and be not the first to disbelieve in it. And do not exchange My signs for a small price, and fear [only] Me."[15] B) Do not kill, "And do not kill yourselves [or one another]. Indeed, Allah is to you ever Merciful."[16] C) Do not cause corruption, "And cause not corruption upon the earth after its reformation. And invoke Him in fear and aspiration. Indeed, the mercy of Allah is near to the doers of good."[17] D) Do no wrong, "you do no wrong, nor are you wronged,"[18] "and do not transgress. Indeed, He is seeing of what you do."[19] E) Do not lie, "And do not say about what your tongues assert of untruth, "This is lawful and this is unlawful," to invent falsehood about Allah. Indeed, those who invent falsehood about Allah will not succeed."[20] "And do not pursue that of which you have no knowledge. Indeed, the hearing, the sight and the heart - about all those [one] will be questioned."[21] F) Do not destruct, "do not throw [yourselves] with your [own] hands into destruction [by refraining]. And do good; indeed, Allah loves the doers of good."[22] G) Do not follow inclinations, "So judge between them by what Allah has revealed and do not follow their inclinations away from what has come to you of the truth."[23] H) Do not commit excess, "Eat of [each of] its fruit when it yields and give its due [zakah] on the day of its harvest. And be not excessive. Indeed, He does not like those who commit excess."[24] I) Do not repeal parents, "and to parents, good treatment. Whether one or both of them reach old age [while] with you, say not to them [so much as], "uff," and do not repel them but speak to them a noble word."[25] J) Do not divide, "do not become divided."[26] K) Do not weaken, "So do not weaken and do not grieve, and you will be superior if you are [true] believers."[27] L) Do not forget graciousness, "And do not forget graciousness between you. Indeed Allah, of whatever you do, is seeing."[28] M) Do not take the money that is not yours, "And do not forget graciousness

---

[15] Al Baqara, 41.
[16] An-Nisa, 29.
[17] Al-Araf, 56.
[18] Al Baqara, 279.
[19] Hud, 112.
[20] An-Nahl, 116.
[21] Isra, 36.
[22] Al Baqara, 195.
[23] Al-Maidah, 48.
[24] Al-Anam, 141.
[25] Al Isra, 23.
[26] Al Imran, 103.
[27] Al Imran, 139.
[28] Al Baqara, 237

between you. Indeed Allah, of whatever you do, is seeing,"[29]etc. The principle of "do no harm" is paramount in what is known in Christianity as the Ten Commandments such as "You shall have no other gods before Me, You shall not murder, You shall not commit adultery, You shall not steal, You shall not bear false witness against your neighbor, You shall not covet your neighbor's house," etc.[30]

The do no harm principle, which is the core of religions, is significantly present in the code of ethics of the Association for Professional Journalists (APF) that I have translated into Arabic.[31] The second principle in the code is based on "minimize harm" and advocates treating "sources, subjects, colleagues and members of the public as human beings deserving of respect."[32] The code delineates many details as to what should not be done in ethical journalism.[33] However, codes of ethics are mostly general guidance, as Vivian asserts for example "Kant does encourage the kind of standardized approach to ethics represented by professional ethics. His emphasis, rather, is on hard thinking."[34]

The do not harm principles touches most ethical issues in communication as defamation (publication of false information that hurts the reputation of individuals or institutions), privacy (intrusion, publication of personal information, false light and appropriation), intellectual property and cyber crimes (cyber-staking, cyber-bullying, cyber-harassment, etc.).

Add Value

The purpose of communication is not only self-expression or entertainment and diversion. For communication to be meaningful, it needs to address the concerns of others. As such, it can be asserted that ethical communication is always about others. Individuals engaged in communication need to come out of the communication experience enriched and valued. In the

[29] Al Baqara, 188.

[30] The Ten Commandments at: http://www.the-ten-commandments.org/the-ten-commandments.html.

[31] Abderrahmane Azzi, "Theory, ..."

[32] Society of Professional Journalists, SPJ Code of Ethics at http://www.spj.org/ethicscode.asp.

[33] These include "Show compassion for those who may be affected by news coverage. Use heightened sensitivity when dealing with juveniles, victims of sex crimes, and sources or subjects who are inexperienced or unable to give consent. Consider cultural differences in approach and treatment."

[34] John Vivian, Media of Mass Communication, Allyn and Bacan, Boston, 1999, p. 496.

words of Freire, "only through communication can human life hold meaning."[35] The ethical individual does not accept things as they are, but ask how things ought to be. Ethics promotes "not only a better individual but also a better society."[36] Communicators (journalists) go about their work writing and reporting with the intent of "serving society,"[37] providing information and materials that can lead to informed citizens and contribute to the wellbeing of society." For Moore and Murray, ethics, as a process, "assumes journalists are thinking people who carefully weigh alternatives and choose courses that are most beneficial to society or the community. It exalts the role of a journalist."[38] The contemporary theory of communitarian ethics in that sense, asserts relocation of one's center from self to the space between selves. The theory suggests a shift "from me to us, from your mind as the focus of identity and being to the relationships you have with others as the centerpiece."[39] For communitarianism, "(the) good comes through relationships, not from assertions or moral claims conceived or adopted by your own persona."[40] However, one cannot communicate what he does not have. Not only that ethics are knowledge based, they represent what Kohlberg as a post-conventional level of consciousness. Ethical thinking goes beyond the notion of rewards and punishment or conventions and questions the nature of right and wrong. Ethics involve a course of action where reality is transformed into the image of ideals.

Provide Help

Crucial to communication act is to assist the needy and the disadvantaged. Communication ought to reflect the reality of those who suffer or struggle in their human conditions.

---

[35] Clifford G. Christians, John P. Ferre and P. Mark Fackler, Good News: Social Ethics and the Press, Oxford University Press, New York, 1993, p. 107.

[36] Larry Z. Leslie, Mass Communication Ethics: Decision Making in Postmodern Culture, Houghton Mifflin, New York, p. 19.

[37] Roy L. Moore and Michael D. Murray, Media Law and Ethics, Rutledge, New Jersey, 2009, p. 120.

[38] Moore, p. 120.

[39] Clifford G. Christians, Mark Fackler and John P. Ferre, Ethics for Public Communication, Oxford University Press, Oxford, 2012, p. vii.

[40] Ibid.

Criticize Constructively

The purpose of criticism is not to tear down but to build upon. To achieve this goal, it needs; a) to be genuine from the part of the communicator, and b) well taken and rightly perceived by the receiver. If criticism is done to put other (s) in a negative light or is personalized or that the receiver feels diminished or humiliated, then such criticism cease to be ethical and cannot achieve the purpose for which it was intended.

These four principles are core values but not exhaustible. The value system is limitless both in philosophy and religion. In a study on the morality of journalism ethics,[41] I have delineated how ethical terms in Arabic are linguistically linked to God's attributes known as 99+. The spiritual dimension cannot escape ethical values where every value is a reflection of an array of God's light. The value of seeking "truth" comes from God's attribute.

These principles "ought to" guide every communication action that involves other (s) all the time under all circumstances. These principles entails that the communicator must raise the following ethical question before an ethical decision is made as to the content and the style of writing, photo or video shooting, posting on the net, and communicating with the other (s) in general.

- Is the content provided ethical?
- Does it cause any harm to the other (s)?
- Does it put other (s) in a negative light?
- Does it add value to the other (s)?
- Is it truthful?
- Does it involve manipulation or propaganda?
- Is the criticism constructive?
- Is the communicator authentic and can responsibility stand for the content in public?
- Is the communicator willing to acknowledge his/her errors and assumes the consequences?
- Is there any personal benefits derived from it?
- Is there any conflict of interest involved?
- Can it be done in the best way possible?

[41] Abderrahmane Azzi, "The Morality of Journalism Ethics: Reading in Nursi's Theory of God's Attributes," Journalism Studies, Vol. 11, 6, 2011.

The answer to such questions is an individual conscious exercise that ought to be guided by principles. The question of how one knows whether a communication decision is ethical or not is a matter of awareness as Kant asserts in his concept of "the morality within." It is, in Draz's formulation, a sense that reflects the preferred positive aspect of human nature. In listening to one's internal voice, one is also listening to the voice of his Creator, as Draz would avow.[42] Ethical awareness rest on individual conviction and does not lend itself to any form of coercion.

This "ethical mind" in Kant and Draz is distinguished from both personal inclinations and collective mind. The self-inclinations are the result of one's uncontrolled desires and instincts (i.e., money, sex and power); what one desires is not necessarily ethical as it is based on considerations of immediate gratification, domination and self-pleasure. Desires, when unconstrained, lead to excesses and other forms of extremity. Similarly, blind submissions to traditions and collectivism limit the development of ethical conscience based on choice and personal commitment. Still, the ethical mind is not a form of pure individualism as much as "feeling the other" based on genuine personal sense of duty and obligation. Moore and Murray state that "By its nature, journalism is supposed to serve the public, so any ethical dilemma in which a reporter or editor chooses personal gains ahead of societal good is not ethical journalism, even if it might be good for the career of the reporter." They add, "Journalism is not a profession practiced by bodies lacking consciences, souls, or values. A reporter's own values are put to a test time after time in ethical dilemmas… and many reporters studied to be journalists because of deep personal commitments to truth, justice, freedom and humanitarianism."[43]

Larry provides the following advice for the ethical use of the Internet: "maintain a balance… do not embrace new media unreservedly… consider it a tool."[44] He adds that such position is supported by several ethical philosophies, i.e., Aristotle's golden mean of avoiding extremes and Aquinas' virtues of prudence, justice, temperance and courage. Larry makes a flowing pertinent conclusion with regard to the ethical behavior in postmodern society. He says, "The postmodern tendency is to embrace all things new, labeling them as progress. However, just because something occurs later in time than some other event does not necessarily mean it is as good – or better – than what went before. The good, thus, does not necessarily progress in leaner fashion. Avoiding extremes and using reason and prudence to help you reach a solution

[42] Mohamad Draz, p. 16.
[43] Roy, pp. 120-121.
[44] Larry, p. 299.

to an ethical dilemma is a decidedly more modern than postmodern approach."[45]

Charles Ess also argues that "some of the new ethical challenges evoked by these technologies may be met through the emergence of both old and new ethical frameworks, including a resurgent of virtue ethics…" He adds, "these ethical frameworks are especially promising for a global digital media ethics, one that enjoys recognition and application across diverse culture and traditions… because they allow for pluralistic interpretation." Ess concludes that "one can be cautiously optimistic that we will learn how to use these technologies effectively and in ethically responsible ways, both as members of our own tribes, and, perhaps, as genuine cosmopolitans."[46]

About the Author

Prof. Abderrahmane Azzi holds B.A in Journalism from the University of Algiers, Algeria, (1977), M.A. in Journalism (1980) and Ph.D. in Sociology of Mass Communication (1985) from NTSU (US). Before that, Dr. Abderrahmane worked as a reporter for *El Chaab* daily newspaper in Algiers for 3 years. Dr. Abderrahmane's experience in teaching and research extends to more than 30 years. He has taught in many universities, NTSU (US), University of Algiers (Algeria), IIUM (Malaysia), King Saud University (Saudi Arabia), UAEU (United Arab Emirates) and University of Sharjah (UAE). Dr. Abderrahmane held many academic positions as Chair of the Scientific Council at the Department of Mass Communication, University of Algiers, Vice-Chancellor for Post-Graduate Studies and Scientific Research at the University of Algiers, Chair of the Department of Mass Communication at IIUM University, Malaysia, and Chair of the Department of Mass Communication, UAEU, United Arab Emirates. Dr. Abderrahmane taught a variety of communication courses (at both undergraduate and graduate levels in Arabic and English). These include theoretical courses as Introduction to Communication, Communication Theories, Media Ethics, Sociology of Mass Communication and practical courses as Printing Technology, Newspaper Layout and Design and Computer-Assisted Reporting. He has published and co-authored numerous books (28 books) as "Modern Social Thought and Communication," "Toward a Distinctive Theory of Communication," and

[45] Ibid, p. 300.

[46] Charles Ess, "Ethical Dimensions of New Technology/Media," in George Cheney, Steve May and Debashish Munshi, The Handbook of Communication Ethics, Rutledge, New York, 2011, pp. 216-217.

"Media Ethics and Social Media: Readings in Ethical Theory" (in Arabic) and Ethical Competence in the Information Age (in English). Dr. Abderrahmane also published more than 50 articles and studies in many academic journals such as *Journalism Studies* (UK), *El Fikr El Arabi* and *El Mustaqbal El Arabi* (Lebanon), *El Bahith El Arabi* (UK), *Dirasat Ilamia* (Egypt), *Etajdid* and *Discourse* (Malaysia), *Revue Tunisienne de Communication* (Tunisia), *Revue Algerienne de Communication* (Algeria), *Annals de l'Universtity d'Alger* (Algeria), *Al Manhal* (Saudi Arabia), *Journal of Human Sciences* (UAE), *Islamic Studies*, *Journal of Global Communication (India)*, etc. His research interests include values and communication, media ethics, global media ethics, media effects and technology. Dr. Abderrahmane is most know for his theory called VDT (Value Determinism Theory of Media), a theory which is praised and commented by eminent media scholars as Prof. Christians G. Clifford, Prof. Max Macomb, author of Agenda-Setting Theory, and Prof. Em Griffin. In 2012, Dr. Abderrahmane received Ben Badis Prestigious Award for his contribution to ethical communication by the University of Mostaganem. He has supervised numerous research projects and Master theses - and participated in many local and international conferences on a variety of communication issues.

REFERENCES

Agarwal, D. P., Kumar, M. M & Kumar, M. P. (2013). 'Impact of Celebrity Endorsement in Advertisement on Customer Buying Patterns. *International Journal of Research in Management, Economics and Commerce* 2 (1): 17 - 31.

Agger, B (2015). *Oversharing: Presentations of the Self in the Internet Age.* New York: Rutledge.

Agger, B (2015). 'Between Self and Selfie'. *International News Gallery*. 28 Nov 2013. Web. 7 May 2015.

Aidman, A & Reese D. (1996). 'Pocahontas: Problematizing the Pro-Social'. Paper presented at the 46th *Annual Meeting of the International Communications Association*. Chicago, IL. May 23 – 27.

Alvarado, A (2014). *World*. Retrieved from CNN: http://edition.cnn.com/2014/12/18/world/how-did-edm-get-so-popular/] [Accessed: December 18].

Angouri, J & Tseliga, T (2010). 'You Have No Idea What You are Talking About: From e-disagreement to e-impoliteness in two online fora. *Journal of Politeness Research, Language, Behaviour & Culture 6*: 57 – 82.

Anonymous (2015). "Between Self and Selfie." International New Media Gallery. [Available: http://www.inmg.org/cc/selfie/] [Accessed: Web. 7 May, 2014].

Anti-troll.org (Undated). Campaigning to make 'trolling' a recognised criminal offence [Available: http://www.anti-troll.org] [Retrieved: November 7, 2015].

Anzaldúa, G (1987). *Borderlands/La Frontera*. San Francisco: Aunt Lute Books.

Apejoye, A (2013). 'Influence of Celebrity Endorsement of Advertisement on Student's Purchase Intention'. *Journal of Mass Communication 3* (3): 152. Doi: 10.4172/2165-7912.1000152.

Azuma, K (1979). *Sesa no syakai shinri gaku (Social psychology of gender).* Tokyo: Dainippon Tosyo.

Bailey, J (2012). 'Informal screen casting: results of a customer-satisfaction survey with a convenience sample'. *New Library World* 113 (1/2): 7 – 26.

Balakrishnan, M. S (2008). 'Dubai – a star in the east: A case study in strategic destination branding'. *Journal of Place Management and Development* 1 (1): 62 – 91.

Bandura, A (2009). 'Social cognitive theory of mass communication'. In: J. Bryant & D. Zillman (Eds.). *Media effects: Advances in theory and Research.* [Pp. 121 – 153]. Hillsdale, NJ: Lawrence Erlbaum.

Bates, A (1999). 'The Newsworthiness of Crime'. *The British Journal of Forensic Practice* 1 (2): 22 – 27.

Batran, S (2013). *Watching the wheels of steel with the UAE's aspiring DJs.* [Retrieved from http://www.thenational.ae/arts-culture/watching-the-wheels-of-steel-with-the-uaes-aspiring-djs] [Accessed: November 17].

Baum, P. B. (2008). 'The Relationship Between Mass Media, Public Opinion and Foreign Policy: Toward a Theoretical Synthesis'. *Annual Review of Political Science* 11: 39 – 65.

Beckett, R (2003). 'Communication Ethics: principles and practice'. *Journal of Communication Management* 8 (1): 41 – 52.

Belkhyr, S (2013). 'Defining the 'self' and the 'other' in Disney song lyrics'. *International Journal of Human Sciences* 10 (1): 1366 - 78.

Berman, S (2004). 'Media and entertainment 2010 scenario: the open media company of the future'. *Strategy & Leadership* 32 (4): 34 – 44.

Bhabha, H (1994). *The Location of Culture.* London: Rutledge.

Bishop, J (2014). Representations of 'trolls' in mass media communication: a review of media-texts and moral panics relating to 'internet trolling'. *International Journal of Web Based Communities* 10: 7 – 24.

Borthaiser, N (2008). 'A Whole New World? - Rereading Disney Animations of the Early 1990'. *Americana: E-Journal of American Studies In Hungary* 4 (1): 5.

Bose, D (2006). *Brand Bollywood: A New Global Entertainment Order.* New Delhi: Sage Publications India.

Brandel, M (2007). 'Blog trolls and cyberstalkers: How to beat them. [Available: http://www.computerworld.com/article/2552596/ networking /blog-trolls-and-cyberstalkers--how-to-beat-them.html] [Retrieved: November 7, 2014].

Brief, A. P & Barsky, A (2000). 'Establishing a climate for diversity: The inhibition of prejudiced reactions in the workplace'. In: Arthur P. Brief &

Adam Barsky (Ed.). *Research in Personnel and Human Resources Management (Research in Personnel and Human Resources Management* [Volume 19, pp.91 – 129]. London: Emerald Group Publishing Limited.

Brosekhan, A. A & Velayutham, C. M (2008). 'Consumer Buying Behaviour – A Literature Review'. *IOSR Journal of Business and Management*: 08-16.

Brownmiller, S (1985). 'Prologue' *Femininity*. United States: Ballanttine. Print. Xv-xix.

Brown, D. (2012). 'Consuming Television Crime Drama: A Uses and Gratifications Approach'. *American Communication Journal* 14 (1): 47 – 60.

Brown, J. K (1970). 'A note on the division of labour by sex'. *American Anthropologist* 72 (5): 1073 – 78.

Brown, L. M & Gilligan, G (1992). *Meeting at the crossroads: women's psychology and girl's development*. Cambridge, MA: Harvard University Press.

Bruce, C., Somerville, M. M., Stoodley, I and Partridge, H (2014). 'Diversifying Information Literacy Research: An Informed Learning Perspective' In: Christine Bruce, Kate Davis, Hilary Hughes, Helen Partridge and Ian Stoodley (Eds.). *Information Experience: Approaches to Theory and Practice. Library and Information Science* 9: 169 – 86. London: Emerald Group Publishing Limited.

Buckley, R and Caple, J (2007). *The Theory and Practice of Training* [5th ed.] London: Kogan-Page.

Byrne, A., Whitehead, M & Breen, S (2003). 'The naked truth of celebrity endorsement'. *British Food Journal* 105 (4/5): 288 – 96.

Cavender, G & Deutsche, S. K (2007). 'CSI and Moral Authority: Police and Science'. *Crime Media Culture* 3 (1): 67 – 81.

Cecil, D. K (2010), Televised images of jail: Lessons in controlling the unruly, in Mathieu Deflem (ed.). *Popular Culture, Crime and Social Control (Sociology of Crime, Law and Deviance*. [Volume 14, Pp. 67 – 88]. London: Emerald Group Publishing Limited.

Chan, Angela, K. P & Chan, Vanessa M. S (2012). 'Public Perception of Crime and Attitudes toward Police: Examning the Effects of Media News'. *Discovery - SS Student E-Journal* 1: 215 – 37.

Chau, T (2014). *EDM Artists*. [Retrieved from: http://popcrush.com/edm-artists-to-watch-2014/] [Accessed: 10th August]

Chen, A (2012). 'Why People Troll Dead Kids on Facebook'. [Available: http://gawker.com/5868503/why-people-troll-dead-kids-on-facebook] [Retrieved April 1, 2015].

Chermak, S (1995). 'Image control: how police affect the presentation of crime news'. *American Journal of Police* 14 (2): 21 - 43.

Cho, S. E & Shin, D. H (2014). 'Media discourse in a hyper connected society: a comparison between media frame and Twitter discourse during media strike'. *Information* 16 (2): 67 – 79.

Chrissy. 'Self(ie) (2015). 'Representation, Feminism and Motherhood'. 29 January. Web. 6 May.

Cocks, S & Simpson, S (2015). 'Anthropocentric and Ecocentric: An Application of Environmental Philosophy to Outdoor Recreation and Environmental Education'. *Journal of Experiential Education* 39 (3) doi: 10.1177/1053825915571750. September.

Cole, S. A (2009). 'Investigating the CSI Effect : Media and Litigation Crisis in Criminal Law'. *Stanford Law Review* 61 (6): 1335 – 74.

Coontz, S (1992). *The Way We Never Were*. New York: Basic Books.

Cuddy, C (2006). 'The Internet: A Historical Encyclopaedia'. *Library Journal* 131 (6): 120 – 50.

Culpeper, J (1996). 'Towards an anatomy of impoliteness'. *Journal of pragmatics* 25: 349 – 67.

Curtis, A. (2011). 'The brief history of social media'. [Available: http://www.uncp.edu/ home/acurtis/ NewMedia/ SocialMedia/ SocialMediaHistory.html] [Accessed: 9th November 2015].

Dasgupta, D. A & Alvi, A (2001). 'Socially Expressive Commercially Impressive'. *IOSR Journal of Business and Management* 3: 6 – 8.

Davis, Joseph E. (2003). 'The Commodification of Self'. *Hedgehog Review*: 41-49. Summer.

Day, R & Mackey. W (1986). 'Role image of the American Father: An examination of a Media myth'. *Journal of Comparative Family Studies* 17 (3): 371 – 88. Autumn.

De Vries, R (2010). *Dear Mr. Miyazaki: your girl characters aren't real at all and seem strange to me… MA-scriptie Film- en Televisiewetenschappen.* Rick Dolphijn: Universiteit Utrecht.

DeFeo, D. J (2013). 'Toward a model of purposeful participant inclusion: examining deselection as a participant risk'. *Qualitative Research Journal* 13 (3): 253 – 64.

Dengra, M (2014). Impact of Celebrity Endorsement on Customer's Buying Behaviour with Reference to Indore City. *Altius Shodh Journal of Management & Commerce*. Retrieved September 25, 2014, from http://www.altius.ac.in/pdf/30.pdf.

Desai, M. K. (2013). 'Globalization of Bollywood: Gain of Markets or Loss of Audiences' ? *Media Watch* 4: (1) 52 – 66.

Dirani, K. M (2012). 'Professional training as a strategy for staff development'. *European Journal of Training and Development* 36 (2/3): 158 – 78.

Dong-Hee, S (2006). 'Convergence of telecommunications, media and information technology, and implications for regulation'. *Info* 8 (1): 42 – 56.

Dowler, K (2003). 'Media Consumption and Public Attitudes toward Crime and Justice: The Relationship between Fear of Crime, Punitive Attitudes, and Perceived Police Effectiveness'. *Journal of Criminal Justice and Popular Culture* 10 (2): 109 – 126.

Droitcour, Brian. Qtd in 'Selfie without the self' by Rob Horning in the New Enquiry 23 Nov 2014. Web. 10 May 2015.

Dudrah, R (2012). *Bollywood Travels: Culture, disapora and border crossings in popular Hindi cinema.* New York: Routledge.

Duff, Alistair S. (1999). 'Ink into Bits: A Web of Converging Media'. *Library Review* 48 (4): 330 – 31.

Dundes, L (2001). 'Disney's modern heroine Pocahontas: revealing age-old gender stereotypes and role discontinuity under a facade of liberation'. *Social Science Journal* 38 (3): 353 – 13.

Dzisah, W. E & Ocloo, C. E (2013). 'Celebrity Endorsement and Consumer Buying Behaviour; Enhancing the Promotion Function of Marketing in the Central Business Area of Accra, Ghana'. *European Journal of Business and Management* 5 (25): 197 – 209.

Edgerton, G & Jackson, K. M (1996). 'Redesigning Pocahontas'. *Journal of Popular Film & Television* 24 (2): 90 – 98

EDM Junkies (2015). *EDM History*. [Retrieved from: http://edmmusicjunkies .com/ ?page_id=31] [Accessed: 10th August].

Eppler, M. J & Pfister, R. A (2014). 'Best of both worlds: hybrid knowledge visualization in police crime fighting and military operations'. *Journal of Knowledge Management* 18 (4): 824 - 40.

Escalas, J. E & Bettman, J. R (2015). 'Managing Brand Meaning through Celebrity Endorsement'. In: Deborah J., Macinnis, C & Whan, Park (ed.) *Brand Meaning Management* [*Review of Marketing Research 12*] [Pp. 29 – 52]. London: Emerald Group Publishing Limited.

Eschholz, S (2003). 'Crime on Television—Issues in Criminal Justice'. *Journal of the Instituted of Justice and International Studies* 2: 9 –18.

Eschholz, S., Mallard, M and Flynn. S (2004). 'Images of Prime Time Justice: A Content Analysis of 'NYPD Blue' and 'Law and Order.'' *Journal of Criminal Justice and Popular Culture* 10:161 – 80.

Ficarra, F. V. C., Vivas, E & Romo, J (2009). 'Credibility On-Line: Quality Metrics for Evaluation'. *HCI* (12): 172 – 81.

FL BEAT Tutorials (2015). *Layout of an EDM Track.* [Retrieved from: http://flbeattutorials.com/layout-edm-track-edm-tutorial/] [Accessed: 10th August].

Freiberg, F (2006). 'Miyazaki's heroines. Senses of Cinema, 40'. Retrieved from http://archive.sensesofcinema.com/contents/06/40/miyazaki-heroines .html.

Friedman, H. H. (1979). 'Endorser effectiveness by product type'. *Journal of Advertising Research* 19 (5): 63 – 71.

Gabriel, M (1995). *She runs, she jumps, she renounces love*. New York Times, section 2, p.25.

Galloway, C (2005). 'Hot bullets, cool media: The Middle East's high stakes media war'. *Journal of Communication Management* 9 (3): 233 – 45.

Garikaparthi, M (2008). 'Case Study: Marketing of the Brand Bollywood'. *Journal of Management & Research* 2 (4): 1 – 12.

Garrat, R (2013). 'Musi Festivals'. *Timeout Dubai* . October 13.

Garrat, R (2014). 'A guide to Electronic Dance Music (EDM) ahead of Abu Dhabi's F1'. *The National*. October 29.

Geoffrey, J., Arora, N., Mishra S and Lefort, A (2014). 'Can Bollywood Go Global'? *Harvard Business School Case* 806-040. July.

Gerbner, G (1998). 'Cultivation analysis: An overview'. *Mass Communication & Society* 1 (3/4): 175 – 94.

Gerbner, G., Gross, L., Morgan, M & Signorielli, N (1986). 'Living with Television: The Dynamics of the Cultivation Process'. *Journal of communication* 26 (2): 172 – 94.

Gerth, M.A and Siegert, G. (2012). 'Patterns of consistence and constriction: how news media frame the coverage of direct democratic campaigns'. *American Behavioural Scientist* 56 (3): 279 – 99.

Gessner, G. C., Chandler, A & Wilcox, W. S (2015). 'Are you reaching your audience? The intersection between LibGuide authors and LibGuide users'. *Reference Services Review* 43 (3): 491 – 508.

Ghani, U & Kakkahel, T (2011). 'The Impact of Celebrity Endorsement on the Youth of Pakistan'. *IPEDR* 16: 79 – 83.

Giroux, H. A (1995). 'Animating youth: the Disneyfication of children's culture'. *Socialist Review* 24: 23 – 55.

Gitlin, T. (1980). *The Whole World is Watching: Mass Media and the Making and Unmaking of the New Left*. Berkeley, CA.: University of California Press.

Gokah, T (2006). 'The Naïve Researcher: doing social research in Africa'. *International Journal of Social Research Methodology* 9 (1): 61 – 73.

Gokah, T (2009). 'Bridging Contested Spaces in IE&C Theory and practice'. In: T. Gokah [Ed.]. *Contemporary Discourses on IE&C Theory and Practice*. [Pp 3 – 7]. New York: NOVA Science Publishers.

Gokah, T (2009). 'Interlocking Media for Community Training & Education.' In: T. Gokah [Ed.]. *IE&C Practice for Social Change*. [Pp. 267 – 82]. New York: Nova Science Publishers.

Govil, N (2007). 'Bollywood and the frictions of global mobility. In: D. K. Thussu, *Media on the Move* (pp. 76-88). New York: Routledge.

Gram, S. (2014) "The Young-Girl and the Selfie." *Textual Relations*. BlogSpot, 15 Jan. 2013. Web. [http://text-relations.blogspot.in/] [Accessed: 7 May, 2014].

Gregory, N (2005). 'Offender profiling: a review of the literature.' *The British Journal of Forensic Practice* 7 (3): 29 – 34.

Griffith, C. J., Mathias, K. A & Price, P. E (1994). 'The Mass Media and Food Hygiene Education'. *British Food Journal* 96 (9): 16 – 21.

Guha, R (1989). 'Radical American environmentalism and wilderness preservation: A Third World critique'. *Environmental Ethics* 11: 71 – 83.

Hardaker, C (2010). 'Trolling in asynchronous computer-mediated communication: From user discussions to academic definitions'. *Journal of Politeness* 6 (2): 215 – 42.

Harris, D (2011). 'Celebrity Deaths'. *Antioch Review* 69: 884 – 92.

Harris, P. B & Long, S. O (1999). 'Husbands and sons in the United States and Japan: Cultural expectations and caregiving experiences'. *Journal of Aging Studies* 13 (3): 241 – 67. Fall.

Heath, L (1987). *Television Viewing and Fear of Crime : Where is the Mean World.* London: Lawrence Erlbaum Associates, Inc.

Heinrick, J (2006). 'Everyone's an Expert: The CSI Effect's Negative Impact on Juries'. [Retrieved from: www.archive.cspo.org/ documents/ csieffectheinrick.pdf] [Accessed: April., 2014].

Henke, J. B., Zimmerman, D & Smith, N. J (1996). 'Construction of the female self: feminist readings of the Disney heroine'. *Women's Studies in Communication* 19: 229 – 49.

Hewat, J (1997). 'Whither media training? New developments in media management'. *Journal of Communication Management* 2 (1): 92 – 97.

Hirotani, M (2013). 'Synchronous Versus Asynchronous CMC and Transfer to Japanese Oral Performance'. *CALICO Journal* 26 (2): 413 – 38.

Hobbs, R (1998). 'Teaching with and about film and television'. *Journal of Management Development* 17 (4): 259 – 72.

Holbert, R. L (2004). 'Fear, Authority and Justice: Crime Related TV Viewing and Endoresements of Capital Punishment and Gun Ownership'. [Retrieved from: journalism.wisc.edu: journalism.wisc.edu/~dshah/JMCQ2004b.pdf] [Accessed Sept. 2014].

Hopkinson, C (2013). 'Trolling in online discussions: from provocation to community-building'. *Brno Studies In English* 39: 5 – 25.

Hughes, T (2007). 'The Perceived Impact of Crime Scene Investigation Shows on the Administration of Justice'. *Journal of Criminal Justice and Popular Culture* 14 (3): 260 – 76.

Ito, Y (1978). 'Seiyakuwari no hyouka ni kansuru kenkyuu (Evaluation of sex-roles as a function of sex and role expectation)'. *Japanese Journal of Educational Psychology* 26 (1): 1 – 11.

James, C (1995). 'Belle and Ariel never choose duty over love'. New York Times, section 2, p.13.

Jean, S (2011). 'Brand parody: a communication strategy to attack a competitor'. *Journal of Consumer Marketing* 28 (1): 19 – 26.

Johson, T.J. and Fahmy, S. (2010). 'When 'good' conflicts go bad: testing a frame-building model on embeds' attitudes toward government news management in the Iraq War'. *The International Communication Gazette* 72 (6): 521 – 44.

Jungwoo, S & Sohn, S. Y (2015). 'Analyzing technological convergence trends in a business ecosystem'. *Industrial Management & Data Systems* 115 (4): 718 – 39.

Justis, G. G & Chermak, S (2010). 'Framing the scene: presentations of forensics programming in the news'. In: Mathieu Deflem (Ed.). *Popular Culture, Crime and Social Control (Sociology of Crime, Law and Deviance, Volume* 14; pp. 219 - 241). London: Emerald Group Publishing Limited.

Kalland, A (1995). *Culture in Japanese nature. Asian Perceptions of Nature: A Critical Approach*. Richmond, UK: Curzon Press.

Kalland, A (2002). 'Holism and Sustainability: Lessons from Japan'. *Worldviews: Global Religions, Culture & Ecology* 6 (2): 145 - 58.

Kalland, A & Asquith, P (1997). *Japanese perceptions of nature: Ideals and illusions, Japanese Images of Nature. Cultural Perspectives*. London: Curzon Press.

Kara Chan, K., Ng, Y. L & Luk, E. K (2013). 'Impact of celebrity endorsement in advertising on brand image among Chinese adolescents'. *Young Consumers* 14 (2): 167 – 79.

Kasana, J & Chaudhary, N (2014). 'Impact of celebrity endorsement on consumer buying behaviour: A descriptive study'. *International Research Journal of Commerce Arts and Science* 5 (2): 319 – 47.

Kashiwagi, K (1972). 'Seinenki ni okeru seyiakuwari no ninchi II (A factor analytic study of the cognitive development of sex role in adolescence II)'. *Japanese Journal of Educational Psychology* 20: 48 – 59.

Kaur, B (2014). 'Product Placement in Movies: The Bollywood Experience'. *Global Journal of Finance and Management* 6 (1): 53 – 58.

Keep, E. (1989). 'Corporate training: the vital component'. *Human Resource Management* 6 (2): 5 – 21.

Koh, T.T.B (1994). 'Asians, too, want good environment'. *The New York Times*. February 1. [Available: http://www.nytimes.com/ 1994/02/01/ opinion/ 01iht-edkoh.html] [Accessed: April 2014].

Kraemer, C. H (2004). 'Between the Worlds: Liminality and Self-Sacrifice in Princess Mononoke', Journal of Religion and Film 8 (1): [Available: <http://avalon.unomaha.edu/jrf/Vol8No1/BetweenWorlds.htm] [Accessed: April 2014].

Kwak, A (2004). 'Asian Americans in the television media: creating incentive for change'. *Third World Law Journal* 24 (2): 395 – 420.

Lane, S. R & Fisher, S. M (2015). 'The influence of celebrity chefs on a student population'. *British Food Journal* 117 (2): 614 – 28.

Lorenzen, M & Taeube, M. L (2007). 'Breakout from Bollywood? Internationalization of the Indian Film Industry'. Danish Research Unit for Industrial Dynamics, DRUID, *Working Paper* No. 07-06. Pp. 1 - 41.

Lutfy, M. A. (2013). 'Media Effects and the Criminal Profiling Illusion: How Fictional Representations Influence the Perception of Police Efficiency'. *Thesis*. Carleton, Canada: Carleton University.

Madureira, R (2005). 'The role of personal contacts of foreign subsidiary managers in the coordination of industrial multinationals'. In: Arch G. Woodside (ed.) *Managing Product Innovation (Advances in Business Marketing and Purchasing* [Volume 13, Pp. 337 – 521]. London: Emerald Group Publishing Limited.

Manjusha, T. V & Segar, D. V (2013). 'A study on impact of celebrity endorsements and overall brand which influence consumers' purchase intention - with a special reference to Chennai City'. *International journal of marketing, financial services & management research 2* (9): 78 – 85.

Marginal Utility Annex. 'Selfies are not self-expression'. *Marginal Utility Blog*. Wordpress, 26 April 2013. Web. 7 May. 2012.

Martens, Y (2011). 'Creative workplace: instrumental and symbolic support for creativity'. *Facilities* 29 (1/2): 63 – 79.

Mateas, M (2005). 'Procedural literacy: educating the new media practitioner'. *On the Horizon* 13 (2): 101 – 11.

McCracken, G. (1989). 'Who Is the Celebrity Endorser? Cultural Foundations of the Endorsement Process'. *Journal of Consumer Research 16*: 310 – 21.

McHugh, S (2010). 'Being Out of Time: Animal Gods in Contemporary Extinction Fictions'. *Australian Literary Studies* 25 (2): 1 – 16.

McNeely, C. L (1995). 'Perceptions of the Criminal Justice System: Television Imagery and Public Knowledge in the United States'. *Journal of Criminal Justice and Popular Culture* 3 (1): 1 – 20.

McRobbie, A & Thornton, S. L (1995). Rethinking 'moral panic' for multi-mediated social worlds. *British Journal of Sociology* 46 (4): 559 - 74.

Menon, S (2005). 'The role of diverse institutional agendas in the importation of convergence policy into the Indian communications sector'. *Info* 7 (4): 30 – 46.

Merritt, E (2012). An Analysis of the Discourse of Internet Trolling: A Case Study of Reddit.com. Ph.D. thesis [Available: https://ida.mtholyoke.edu/ xmlui/bitstream/ handle/ 10166/1058/ EmilyMerrittThesisUpload. pdf?sequence=1] [Accessed: 16 November 2015].

Merton, R. K (1968). *Social theory and social structure*. Glencoe, Illinois: The Free Press.

Morady, F (2010). 'Iran: Islamic republic or God's kingdom? The election, protest, and prospects for change'. In: Paul Zarembka (Ed.). *The National Question and the Question of Crisis. Research in Political Economy.* [Volume 26 pp.69 – 97]. London: Emerald Group Publishing Limited.

Mukherjee-Das, M (2013). 'Innovation in Public Relation Strategies in Film Promotion - A Study'. *Global Journal of Management and Business Studies* 3 (6): 619 – 24.

Music Trades (2013). 'Just How Big is EDM'. *Music Trades*: pp. 68 - 74. November.

Naess, A (1989). *Ecology, Community and Lifestyle (translated and edited by D. Rothenberg)*. Cambridge: Cambridge University Press.

Napier, S. J (2001). 'Confronting master narratives: History as vision in Miyazaki Hayao's cinema of de-assurance. *Positions* 9 (2): 467 – 93.

Napier, S. J (2005). *Anime from Akira to Howl's Moving Castle. Experiencing Contemporary Japanese Animation*. London: Palgrave Macmillan.

Nardo, M (2004). 'Mapping the trails of financial crime.' *Journal of Financial Crime* 12 (2): 139 – 43.

Netlingo (1999). 'The Internet Dictionary'. [Available: http:// www.netlingo. com/] [Retrieved November 4, 2015].

Nicol, S (2012). 'Special feature / Cyber-bullying and trolling'. *Youth Studies Australia* 31: 3 – 4.

Noe, R.A., Hollenbeck, J.R., Gerhart, B and Wright, P. M (2006). *Human Resource Management: Gaining a Competitive Advantage* [6th ed.]. Boston, MA: McGraw-Hill Irwin.

O'Malley, Z (2015). 'Avicii And The Ever-Changing Definition of EDM'. *Forbes*: 8-8. January 3.

Oliver, P (2006). *Purposive Sampling*. London: Sage Publication.

Papademas, D (2011). 'Human Rights and Media'. In: Diana Papademas (ed.) *Human Rights and Media (Studies in Communications.* [*Volume* 6, Pp. vii - xiv). London: Emerald Group Publishing Limited.

Parkman, I. D., Holloway, S. S & Sebastiao, H (2012). 'Creative industries: aligning entrepreneurial orientation and innovation capacity'. *Journal of Research in Marketing and Entrepreneurship* 14 (1): 95 – 114.

Phillips, W (2011). LOLing at tragedy: Facebook trolls, memorial pages and resistance to grief online. *First Monday 16* (12). doi:10.5210/fm.v16i12. 3168.

Pina, C. (2013) 'A Greener Disney'. *Undergraduate Review* 9: 177-181.

Poturak, M & Kadric, N (2013). 'Students perception about celebrity endorsements'. *European Researcher* 59 (9): 2331 – 41.

PR Newswire (2014). 'SiriusXM and YouTube Announce New Electronic Dance Music Show: The YouTube EDM 15'. *Newswire* . November 11.

Pradiptarini, C (2011). 'Social Media Marketing: Measuring Its Effectiveness and Identifying the Target Market'. *UW-L Journal of Undergraduate Research* 14: 1 – 11.

Prais, S. J. (1995). *Productivity, Education and Training: An International Perspective*. Cambridge: Cambridge University Press.

Preve, F (2014). 'Ten Essential Dance Sounds'. *Emusician* 68 – 71. May.

Prosise, T. O (2004). 'Law Enforcement and Crime on 'Cops' and 'World's Wildest Police Videos'. *Western Journal of Communication* 68 (1): 72 – 91.

Rajadhyaksha, A (2007). The 'Bollywoodization' of the Indian Cinema: Cultural Nationalism in the Global Arena. In: K.-H. C. Huat, *The Inter Asia Cultural Studies Reader* (pp. 449-466). New York: Routledge.

Rashid, M. Z., Nallamuthu, J & Sidin, S. M (2002). 'Perceptions of Advertising and Celebrity Endorsement in Malaysia'. *Asia Pacific Management Review* 7 (4): 535 – 54.

Riemenschneider, C (1995). 'Pocahontas fans prefer happy endings'. Los Angeles Times, p. F5.

Roll, M (2014). *Branding and Celebrity Endorsements.* [Retrieved from: http://www.martinroll.com/resources/articles/marketing/branding-and-celebrity-endorsements/] [Accessed: February 24, 2014].

Rolling Stone, R (2013). *Patrick Carney vs. the Bieber: The 12 Funniest Tweets*. [Available from http://www.rollingstone.com/music/news/patrick-carney-vs-the-beliebers-the-12-funniest-tweets-20130214] [Retrieved 3 June 2015].

Ruddell, R and Jones, N (2013). 'Social media and policing: matching the message to the audience'. *Safer Communities* 12 (2): 64 – 70.

Saltzis, K and Dickinson, R (2008). 'Inside the changing newsroom: journalists' responses to media convergence'. Aslib Proceedings 60 (3): 216 – 28.

Seong, Eun, C & Dong-Hee, S (2014). 'Media discourse in a hyper connected society: a comparison between media frame and Twitter discourse during media strike'. I*nfo* 16 (2): 67 – 79.

Shah, N. (2015). 'The Selfie and the Slut: Bodies, Technology and Public Shame'. *Economic and Political Weekly* 1 (86): 86 – 93. April 25.

Shrestha, S (2008). 'Global Bollywood: Travels of Hindi Song and Dance'. *International Journal of Communication* 4: 1- 5.

Sierra, K (2014). 'Why the Trolls Will Always Win | WIRED'. [Available: from http://www.wired.com/2014/10/trolls-will-always-win/] [Retrieved January 8, 2015].

Silvera, D. H & Austad, B (2004). 'Factors predicting the effectiveness of celebrity endorsement advertisements'. *European Journal of Marketing* 38 (11/12): 1509 – 26.

Smith, M. J & Parsons E (2012). 'Animating child activism: Environmentalism and class politics in Ghibli's Princess Mononoke (1997) and Fox's Fern Gully (1992)'. *Journal of Media & Cultural Studies* 26 (1): 25 – 37.

Smith, N. S (2002). 'Abolitionism and social theory: Slavery, "wage-slavery," and the visibility of oppression'. In: Jennifer M. Lehmann (ed.) *Bringing*

Capitalism Back for Critique by Social Theory (Current Perspectives in Social Theory. Volume 21, Pp.143 - 181. London: Emerald Group Publishing Limited.

Solber, R. T (2014). 'Waiting for the Bass to Drop'. *Dancecult: Journal of Electronic Dance Music Culture:* 61 – 82.

Soo-Guan, C., Armineh, K., Jin-Cheon N. N (2012). 'Sentiment analysis of online news text: a case study of appraisal theory'. *Online Information Review* 36 (6): 858 – 78.

Stone, R (2014). *Black Keys' Patrick Carney Unleashes Fresh Batch of Justin Bieber Hate*. [Available from http://www.rollingstone.com/music/news /black-keys-patrick-carney-unleashes-fresh-batch-of-justin-bieber-hate-20140509] [Retrieved 3 June 2015].

Strong, P (1996). 'Animated Indians: Critique and Contradiction in Commodified Children's Culture'. *Cultural Anthropology* 11 (3): 405 – 24. August.

Sturges, P (2004). 'Information in the national liberation struggle: developing a model'. *Journal of Documentation* 60 (4): 428 – 48.

Sugihara, Y & Katsurada, E (2000). 'Gender-role personality traits in Japanese culture'. *Psychology of Women Quarterly* 24 (4): 309 – 18. December.

Swan, M. (2014). 'Young People Influenced by Celebrity Endorsement'. *The National, UAE* [May 3 Edition]. Retrieved from: http://www.thenational.ae/uae/education/young-people-in-the-uae-not-influenced-by-celebrity-endorsements] [Accessed: February, 2014].

Swatman, P. M. C., Krueger, C & van der Beek, K (2006). 'The changing digital content landscape'. *Internet Research* 16 (1): 53 – 80.

Tala, M (2014). *EDM: Dance Music Genres Characteristics Defined*. [Retrieved from: http://www.djmastercourse.com/edm-dance-music-genres-characteristics-defined/] [Accessed: July 17].

Tasker, Y and Negra, D [Eds.]. (2007). *Interrogating Postfeminism: Gender and the Politics of Popular Culture*. NC: Duke UP, 2007.

Tehran Bureau. (2014). 'Selfie Culture a New Battleground for the Iranian Regime'. *The Guardian.* Retrieved from Available: http://www. theguardian.com/world/iran-blog/2014/jun/13/selfie-culture-a-new-battleground-for-the-iranian-regime] [Accessed: August 2014].

Thussu, D. K (2012). 'Cultural Practices and Media Production: The Case of Bollywood'. In: E. S. Isabelle Rigoni, *Mediating Cultural Diversity in a Globalised Public Space.* London: Palgrave Macmillan.

Tkacz, N (2013). FCJ-154 Trolls, Peers and the Diagram of Collaboration. *The Fibreculture Journal 22*: 15 – 35.

Tucker, J. A (2003). *Anime and Historical Inversion in Miyazaki's Hayao's Princess Mononoke*, East Carolina: East Carolina University Press.

Tyler, T (2006). 'Viewing CSI and the Threshold of Guilt: Managing Truth and Justice in Reality and in Fiction'. *The Yale Law Journal* 115 (1): 1050 – 85.

U.S. Bureau of Census (1997). *Statistical Abstract of the United States* 117th ed. Washington, D.C: U.S. Government Printing Office.

Upadhyay, N. T. (2010). 'Tangibilising the intangibles of entertainment services: a success of 3 idiots movie'. *Spectrum*: 135 – 55.

Urde, M (1994). 'Brand Orientation - A Strategy for Survival'. *Journal of Consumer Marketing* 11 (3): 18 – 32.

Van-Heesvelde, E (2000). 'Convergence between fixed and mobile communications'. *Info* 2 (3): 271 – 75.

Warschauer, M (2001). 'Online communication'. In: R. Carter & D. Nunan (Eds.). *The Cambridge guide to teaching English to speakers of other languages*. Cambridge: Cambridge University Press.

Waterman, D & Han, S (2010). 'Broadcasters *vs.* MVPDs: economic effects of digital transition on television program supply'. *Info* 12 (4): 15 – 24.

Watt, N (Ed.). (2012). Celebrities and Cyberstalkers: The Dark Side of Fame in the Internet Age. [Available: http://abcnews.go.com/ Technology/ celebrities-cyberstalkers-dark-side-fame-internet-age/story?id= 16741230] [Retrieved October 26, 2014].

WhatsOn. (2015). *Clubbing In Dubai*. Retrieved from WhatsOn: [http://whatson.ae/ dubai/knowledge/19874/clubbing-in-dubai-analog-room-profile/#gallery-3] [Accessed: October 5].

Whitley, D (2012). *The Idea of Nature in Disney Animation: From Snow White to WALL-E*. Farnham: Ashgate Publishing Ltd.

Whittle, D (2014). 'The Rise and Rise of Electronic Music'. *Music Week:* 12-12.

Williams, J. E & Best, D. L (1990). *Measuring sex stereotypes: A thirty-nation study*. Newbury Park, CA: Sage.

Williams, P. (2000). 'Worry About Victimization: An Alternative And Reliable Measure for Fear of Crime'. *Western Criminology Review* 2 (2): 1 – 26.

Wilson, J. M (2014) Revising national/diasporic imaginaries: Bollywood & diasporic Indian cinema and globalization. Invited Keynote presented to: International Conference on Diasporic Indian Cinemas and Bollywood on the Diaspora: Re-Imagings and Re-Possessions, University of Osmania, Hyderabad, India, 22-24 January.

Winseck, D (1999). 'The quest for information highways and media convergence in Canada'. *Info* 1 (6): 539 – 61.

Yoshida, K (2011). 'Self and Other Representation in Pocahontas and Princess Mononoke'. *Electronic Journal of Contemporary Japanese Studies*. Article 5. September [Available: http:// www.japanesestudies.org.uk/articles/ 2011/Yoshida.html] [Accessed: April 2014].

Yoshizumi, K (1995). *Marriage and Family: Past and Present. Japanese Women*. New York: The Feminist Press at the City College of New York.

Zach (2014). *How to Produce and Write Dance Music*. Retrieved from: http://www.wikihow.com/Produce-and-Write-Dance-Music] [Accessed: October 5].

Zara, C (2013). *Don't Like Where Online Journalism Is Going? Blame Trolls. International Business Times*. [Available: http://www.ibtimes.com/dont-where-online-journalism-going-blame-trolls-1101148] [Retrieved 2 June 2015].

Zhou, Y. and Moy, P. (2007). 'Parsing framing processes: the interplay between online public opinion and media coverage'. *Journal of Communication* 57 (1): 79 – 98.

About the Editor

Theophilus Kofi Gokah
Interdisciplinary and Research Professor
Manipal University Dubai [MUD]
School of Media & Communication
International Academic City
P. O Box 345050
Dubai, UAE

Professor Gokah has an interdisciplinary background in general research methodology, media, sociology, education management & leadership and law. He also has interest in public health communication. Professor Gokah has had a distinguished career as an outstanding educator in Higher Education in the United Kingdom and the United Arab Emirates. He has authored and co-authored many academic articles and books on interdisciplinary themes.

INDEX

D

E

F

G

N

O

P

Q

R

S

Z